and the Fate of Black Schools in the South

Along Freedom Road

David S. Cecelski

© 1994 The University of North Carolina Press
All rights reserved

Manufactured in the United States of America

The paper in this book meets the guidelines for
permanence and durability of the Committee on
Production Guidelines for Book Longevity of the
Council on Library Resources.

Historian David S. Cecelski is a research fellow at
the Institute for Southern Studies in Durham,
North Carolina.

Library of Congress Cataloging-in-Publication Data
Cecelski, David S.
    Along freedom road : Hyde County, North
Carolina, and the fate of Black schools in the
South / by David S. Cecelski.
        p.   cm.
    Includes bibliographical references (p.   ) and
index.
    ISBN 0-8078-2126-8 (alk. paper). —
ISBN 0-8078-4437-3 (pbk.: alk. paper)
    1. Segregation in education—North
Carolina—Hyde County—Case studies.
    2. School closings—North Carolina—Hyde
County—Case studies.   3. Afro-Americans—
Education—North Carolina—Hyde County—
Case studies.   I. Title.
    LC212.522.N8C43   1994
    370.19'344'09756184—dc20   93-32687
                                           CIP

04   03   02   01   7 6 5 4

Hyde County, North Carolina

The University of

North Carolina Press

Chapel Hill & London

To Laura

Maps

Photographs

I have many friends and colleagues to thank for making this a better book. During my student days at Harvard, Sara Lawrence Lightfoot, Courtney Cazden, and Michael Fultz reviewed my first drafts and offered crucial encouragement and criticism. Later, on my return to North Carolina, George Noblit, Cynthia Brown, Christina Greene, and Greg Field contributed thoughtful, informed readings. At every stage, Maruja García Padilla provided sharp insights into Hyde County events and my relationship to them.

Beyond my gratitude for their rigorous remarks on the manuscript, I owe an added debt to Emilie V. Siddle Walker at Emory University and Tim Tyson at Duke University. Professor Siddle Walker generously shared with me the early fruits of her pioneering research on African American schools in the segregated South. Likewise, Tim Tyson improved the book immeasurably by sharing his extensive knowledge of civil rights history in North Carolina.

I thank Alex Charns, Wilma Dunaway, Jacquelyn Dowd Hall, Jim Lee, Gerald Wilson, George Esser, Page McCullough, and Leslie McClemore for helping me clear difficult research hurdles. My editor at the University of North Carolina Press, David Perry, and the outside readers of my manuscript gave both strong encouragement and useful substantive advice, for which I am very grateful. I would also like to acknowledge the Ford Foundation, the Lyndhurst Foundation, and the Aspen Institute for Humanistic Studies for their financial support.

In eastern North Carolina, I would like to thank several individuals whose hospitality, friendship, and insights have been indispensable to writing this book. Ida Murray, Henry Johnson, Jr., Thomas Whitaker, Julia Bick, and Greg Zeph made me feel at home in Hyde County and taught me a great deal about local politics and history. Don Richardson, who has opened his doors to so many wayfaring strangers, also welcomed me during my frequent visits. R. S. Spencer, Jr., and Phillip Greene, Jr., introduced me to invaluable local records. Willie Dawson,

Viola Davis, Mayor Edward Credle, Carol Grolnick, Susan Perry, Mamie Flowers, Roy and Elaine Schaal, the Reverend Jud Mayfield, Steve Ambrose, Willis Williams, Cindy Arnold, the late Beulah Sharpe, Sister Bettie Bullen, Debby Warren, and Rosetta Meadows also supported my work in vital ways. They educated me and frequently fed me as well. In addition, I have been privileged to work closely with Jim Grant and Frank Adams, two legendary human rights activists who know eastern North Carolina's backroads as well as anybody. Nothing could have prepared me better for writing this book.

Finally, my family has not only tolerated my abiding passion for recovering the lost and seldom-heard voices of my native coastal North Carolina but has also been my strongest support and constant inspiration. I am deeply appreciative of my siblings, great-aunts and -uncles, and cousins all, but here I most want to thank my mother and father, Vera, and of course my most devoted enthusiast and editor—my wife, Laura.

One hundred years before Chief Justice Warren
declared that racial segregation in public schools "is
a denial of the equal protection of the law," another
chief justice declared that Negroes had no rights
which a white man must respect. Thus in a century
this nation has taken mighty steps along Freedom
Road and raised the hopes of mankind, black, yellow,
and white. . . . But we must go further and insist that
great as is this victory, many and long steps along
Freedom Road lie ahead.

—W. E. B. Du Bois, May 31, 1954

National Guardian

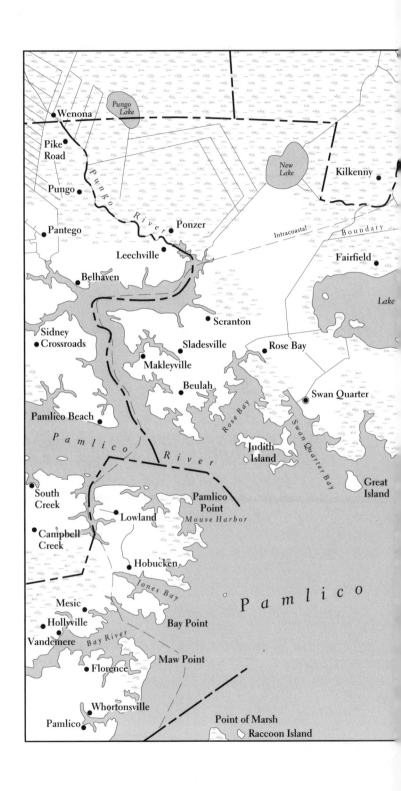

Wenona

Pungo
Lake

Pike
Road

Pungo

New
Lake

Kilkenny

Pantego

P u n g o   R i v e r

Ponzer

Leechville

Intracoastal

B o u n d a r y

Fairfield

Belhaven

Lake

Scranton

Sidney
Crossroads

Sladesville

Rose Bay

Makleyville

Beulah

Swan Quarter

Pamlico Beach

P a m l i c o

R o s e   B a y

Judith
Island

S w a n   Q u a r t e r   B a y

R i v e r

Great
Island

South
Creek

Pamlico
Point

Lowland

M o u s e   H a r b o r

Campbell
Creek

Hobucken

J o n e s   B a y

P a m l i c o

Mesic

Hollyville

Bay Point

Vandemere

B a y   R i v e r

Maw Point

Florence

Whortonsville

Pamlico

Point of Marsh
Raccoon Island

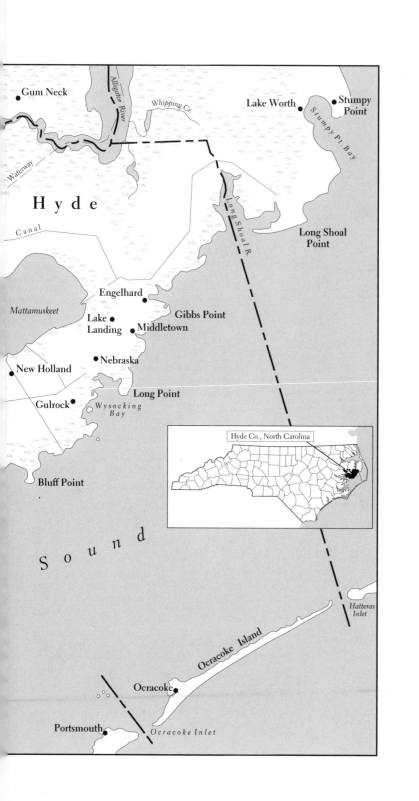

Gum Neck

Alligator River

Whipping Cr.

Lake Worth

Stumpy Point

Stumpy Pt. Bay

Waterway

H y d e

Canal

Long Shoal R.

Long Shoal Point

Engelhard

Mattamuskeet

Lake Landing

Middletown

Gibbs Point

New Holland

Nebraska

Long Point

Gulrock

Wysocking Bay

Hyde Co., North Carolina

Bluff Point

S o u n d

Hatteras Inlet

Ocracoke Island

Ocracoke

Portsmouth

Ocracoke Inlet

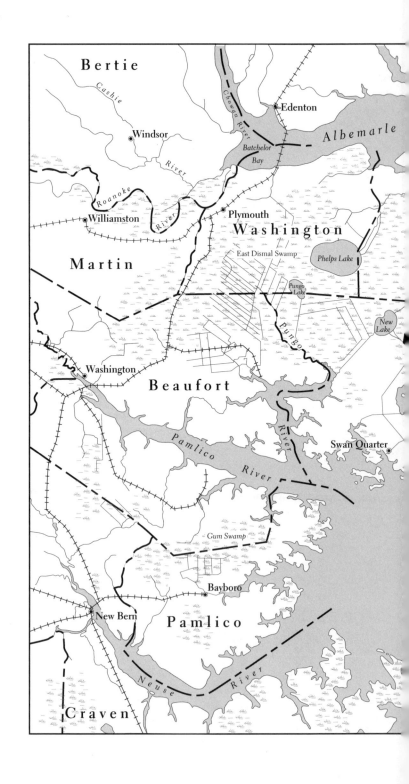

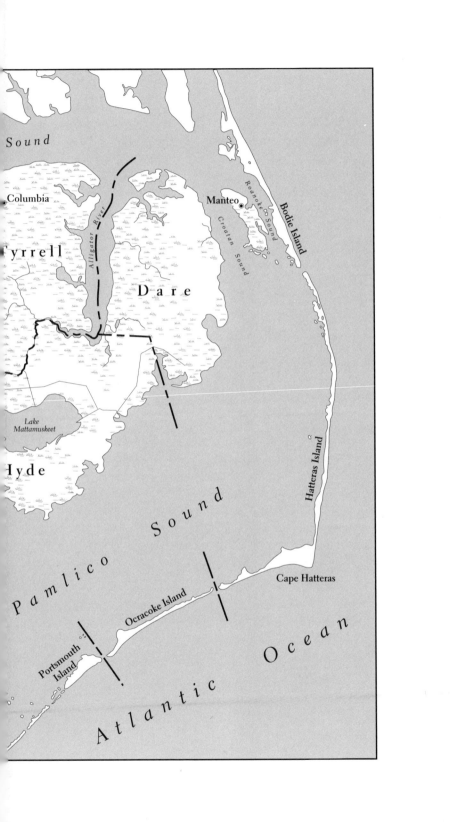

Sound

Columbia

Manteo

Roanoke Sound

Bodie Island

Tyrrell

Alligator River

Croatan Sound

D a r e

Lake
Mattamuskeet

Hatteras Island

Hyde

P a m l i c o   S o u n d

Ocracoke Island

Cape Hatteras

Portsmouth
Island

A t l a n t i c   O c e a n

Introduction

Like chimneys standing in the cold ashes of a tragic fire, the old school buildings endure in towns and rural communities across the southeastern United States. A few have been reincarnated as textbook warehouses, old-age homes, or cut-and-sew factories. More commonly, though, they sit vacant and deteriorating in older black neighborhoods. People called them the "Negro schools" in the era of racial segregation, when millions of black children enlivened their classrooms. As school desegregation swept through the region in the 1960s and 1970s, white southern school leaders routinely shut down these black institutions, no matter how new or well located, and transferred their students to former white schools.[1] No commemorative markers reveal what the black schools used to be, who once studied and taught in them, or why so many closed their doors a generation ago. Behind their weathered facades and boarded-up windows lies an important, hidden chapter in American history.

This is the story of an extraordinary struggle to prevent two historically black schools from closing. It is also necessarily about the fate of black schools throughout the South. From this history comes a new perspective on how black southerners survived in the age of segregation and how black schooling contributed to, collided with, and adapted to racial integration. Ultimately, it is a book about equality, community, and autonomy.

The mass closing of black schools was only part of a broader pattern of racism that marred school desegregation throughout the South. In its 1954 decision in *Brown v. Board of Education*, the U.S. Supreme Court had ruled that racially segregated public schools were unconstitutional, but the court left local school boards with the power to implement its ruling. Instead of reconciling black and white schools on equal terms, white leaders made school desegregation a one-way street. Black communities repeatedly had to sacrifice their leadership traditions, school cultures, and educational heritage for the other benefits of desegregation. While historians have justifiably focused on the struggles for racial integration, they have neglected to explore the black school closings or their far-reaching consequences.[2]

School desegregation devastated black educational leadership. In North Carolina, typical of the southern states in this regard, school closings and mergers eliminated an entire generation of black principals.[3] From 1963 to 1970, the number of black principals in the state's elementary schools plunged from 620 to only 170. Even more striking, 209 black principals headed secondary schools in 1963, but less than 10 still held that crucial job in 1970. By 1973, only three had survived this wholesale displacement.[4] Other educational leadership positions proved no more accessible to black men and women. By decade's end, when black children represented 30 percent of the state's 1.2 million public school students, not one of the 145 school districts had a black superintendent, and 60 percent of those districts did not employ any black administrators.[5]

The effect of school desegregation on black teachers was less severe but profoundly important. North Carolina was second only to Texas in the number of jobs lost by black teachers: by 1972, an estimated 3,051 blacks in North Carolina had lost teaching jobs after the merger of black and white schools. This number represented 21 percent of the expected black teacher population.[6] Several studies confirmed this trend. In 1970, for example, the U.S. Civil Rights Commission surveyed twenty North Carolina school districts and found 145 fewer black teachers in 1970 than in 1968, though there had been an increase of 22 teaching positions in those districts.[7] White school leaders also shunted black educators into lower-prestige assignments and away from the high-profile jobs of guidance counselor and sports team coach.[8]

These patterns were similar to those in other southern states, where an estimated 31,504 black teachers were displaced by 1970.[9] In a five-state survey, the U.S. Department of Health, Education, and Welfare (HEW) confirmed that between 1968 and 1971 alone, at least 1,000 black educators lost jobs while 5,000 white teachers were hired.[10] Teachers' unions, a U.S. congressional committee, and several scholars documented widespread displacement of black educators across the South.[11] Holding less than 2 percent of local school board positions in the region, black citizens did not have the political power to stem this tide.[12] The phenomenon was so widespread that in 1966, when New York City faced a severe teacher shortage, it developed Operation Reclaim specifically to recruit black teachers who had been fired below the Mason-Dixon line.[13]

Blacks lost important symbols of their educational heritage in this process. When black schools closed, their names, mascots, mottos, holidays, and traditions were sacrificed with them, while the students were transferred to historically white schools that retained those markers of cultural and racial identity.[14] When former black high schools did not shut down, they were invariably converted into integrated junior high or elementary schools. White officials would frequently change the names given the school buildings by the black community and would remove plaques or monuments that honored black cultural, political, or educational leaders. They hid from public view trophy cases featuring black sports teams and academic honorees and replaced the names of black sports teams with those used by the white schools. The depth of white resistance to sending their children to historically black schools was also reflected in the flames of the dozens of these schools that were put to the torch as desegregation approached.

The school and the church had long been the most important institutions in rural black communities. White dominance during desegregation, however, undermined the school's traditional place in black society. For many black parents, the desegregated schools too closely resembled the former white schools in values, traditions, political sensibilities, and cultural orientation.[15] In losing black educational leaders, they also felt deprived of an effective voice in their children's education. This educational climate and the loss of community control alienated some black citizens so thoroughly that they found it difficult to support the new schools. Many parents also observed a decline in student motivation, self-esteem, and academic performance. Racist treatment of black students within biracial schools only worsened an already difficult situation. Black students repeatedly encountered hostile attitudes, racial bias in student disciplining, segregated busing routes, unfair tracking into remedial and other lower-level classes, low academic expectations, and estrangement from extracurricular activities.[16]

Naturally, strong undercurrents of ambivalence toward school desegregation emerged among southern blacks in the late 1960s and early

1970s. Most blacks had supported the courageous struggles of the National Association for the Advancement of Colored People (NAACP) against both school inequality and school segregation. The demise of their schools and the inequitable burdens of school desegregation, however, raised new doubts. There emerged a notable continuity between older, more conservative African American voices, which had given the building of strong black schools priority over desegregation, and the newer "militant" expressions of black separatism and community control. Simultaneously, a white backlash against school desegregation meant that its support dwindled from both sides, for very different reasons.

School desegregation was a far more complex matter than a demand by blacks to attend school with reluctant or hostile whites. By 1966 and 1967, few black communities failed to raise objections to school closings and teacher displacement. Black North Carolinians had organized several formal protests, and pressure on civil rights and political leaders for racial equality in school desegregation began to surge. Between 1968 and 1973, school boycotts, student walkouts, lawsuits, and other black protests challenging desegregation plans grew common at the southern grass roots.[17] One of the strongest and most successful protests, the first to draw national attention to the problem, occurred in one of the South's most remote and least populated counties.

The school boycott in Hyde County, North Carolina, in 1968 and 1969 signaled that black southerners, in the words of an HEW official, "were tired of bearing the burdens of school desegregation."[18] For an entire year, Hyde County's black students refused to attend school. They did so to protest an HEW-approved desegregation plan that required closing the two historically black schools in this poor, rural community surrounded by swamps and coastal marshlands. Black citizens held nonviolent demonstrations almost daily for five months, marched twice on the state capitol in Raleigh, organized alternative schools in their churches, and drove the Ku Klux Klan out of the county in a massive gunfight. In the year after the assassination of Martin Luther King, Jr., the school boycott became one of the most sustained and successful civil rights protests in North Carolina, and in the South as a whole.

Though the size and resolve of black dissent there was clearly exceptional, from 1954 to the outbreak of the school boycott in the autumn of

1968 Hyde County was basically a microcosm of school desegregation throughout the South—especially the rural South. Even the school boycott was not unusual at heart; it only crystallized social and political forces that were present but less focused during school desegregation in every community. Understanding Hyde County history, then, should help to answer key questions about the era. How did the experience of school desegregation in the South differ from black to white communities? Why were black schools shut down? Who had power and influence over the local process of school desegregation, and how was it used? How did black activists balance the competing desires for racial integration and community control? How did educators, administrators, students, and alumni of the historically black schools respond to the school closings? How did black attitudes toward school desegregation evolve during the civil rights movement, and how did white citizens respond to those changes? Finally, what role did state governments, the federal courts and such agencies as HEW and the U.S. Department of Justice play in determining the fate of the black schools?

Few scholars have explored those questions. Historians and journalists have described massive white resistance to school desegregation, as in Little Rock, New Orleans, and Prince Edward County, Virginia.[19] Sociologists have evaluated the impact of desegregation on student life and school quality.[20] Scholars from many disciplines have analyzed how the federal judiciary and national politics shaped school desegregation.[21] Other historians and civil rights leaders have chronicled the role of major civil rights groups, though rarely, in the words of historian William Chafe, "from the point of view of people in local communities, where the struggle for civil rights was a continuing reality, year in and year out."[22]

Though they offer other crucial insights, these works have not explored the dismantling of black education during school desegregation, its meaning within communities, or the struggles against it.[23] This lack exists in part because historians have seldom studied school desegregation in the South after 1968. Yet in the southern states, the large majority of black and white children—in North Carolina, two-thirds— first attended classes together after 1968. With a few important exceptions, local case studies have focused on the dramatic racial conflicts in the early stages of school desegregation, especially in the Deep South and Virginia prior to 1965 and in the urban north and west after 1971, before the full implications for black schooling were clear.[24] Similarly, patterns of racism in the process of integration were more pronounced in rural areas, where blacks usually held less political power, yet historians have emphasized the more visible school conflicts in southern cities.[25] One consequence has been to silence the voices of poorer, rural blacks in favor of more educated, middle-class black activists in the urban South. Finally, prevailing assumptions about the poor quality of the black schools has given credence to the idea that their closing was inevitable and has tempered interest in this aspect of desegregation. By looking at what happened in Hyde County, North Carolina, from the U.S. Supreme Court's *Brown* ruling in 1954 through the school boycott in 1968–69, this book begins to fill these gaps in the history of school desegregation.

This story also encourages reassessment of two widely held assumptions about education in this era. First, a grassroots movement to increase local control over schools, popularly called the community school movement, has been defined as a separate phenomenon occurring largely in the Northeast. During the 1960s and 1970s, large numbers of parents and students attempted to decentralize control over schools and make them more responsive to local needs and cultural backgrounds. The school boycott in the Ocean Hill and Brownsville sections of Brooklyn, New York, has been the most widely remembered community school protest. But community control over education was a vital issue in school desegregation conflicts throughout the South. Both black and white citizens felt strong tensions between community control and school desegregation—tensions that complicated the essential issues of racial justice and educational equality.

The second reassessment concerns the social and cultural role of the black schools in the segregated South. The literature on their inferiority and negative effect on black students is voluminous and was critical to the Supreme Court's ruling in *Brown*. More recent scholarship has emphasized the historic role of those schools in socializing black children to accept their second-class status in southern society.[26] Those viewpoints undoubtedly hold a great deal of truth. They may seem like the whole story from a regional perspective, from aggregate data using standard definitions of "quality" schooling, or from a structural view of power relations over education. But the Hyde County boycott and other examples of black activism emerging from and supporting a vibrant and distinctive African American educational tradition raise important questions about how local black citizens viewed their schools, and what real sustenance their communities derived from them. They also point to the true quality that black educators, parents, and students managed to foster in those educational institutions despite vastly unequal funding, poorer physical plants, and white school leaders determined to mold black children into second-class citizens.

This book is primarily the chronicle of an important untold moment in civil rights history. The NAACP's long crusade toward *Brown*, the Montgomery bus boycott, the Greensboro sit-ins, and a handful of other civil rights events have gotten rightful recognition. However, they provide only crowded snapshots of a mass movement that extended into every corner of the South. While writers have recently begun to flesh out a broader history of the civil rights era, there remains much to learn.[27] In eastern North Carolina, survivors of the civil rights movement tell a story that indicates what has been missed elsewhere. Their agricultural coastal plain encompasses approximately a third of the state. It has historically been North Carolina's Black Belt, with every county having at least a sizable and sometimes a majority black population.[28] Yet its civil rights history has been almost entirely unexplored; there have been no books written and no journal articles published, and literature on the civil rights movement contains hardly a passing reference to the most widespread and significant mass movement in the state's history.[29] This dearth of scholarship has led even the most astute observers of southern politics to conclude mistakenly that eastern North Carolina was, in Jack Bass and Walter DeVries' words, "bypassed by the civil rights movement."[30]

When—or if—historians and other writers turn their attentions to the Williamston Freedom Movement, the Wilmington 10, the Halifax County Voters Movement, or the great strike at Rose Hill Poultry, they will discover stories no less powerful or poignant than the famous protests in Montgomery and Selma. This saga of the Hyde County school boycott is only a first small step toward retrieving a rich civil rights legacy in eastern North Carolina; many similar stories lie waiting, recorded only in the memories of participants. The same could be said for rural areas all over the southern states.

If those struggles for racial justice are only dimly recalled today, it is not yet for lack of source materials. In writing this kind of book, there is a sense of urgency: civil rights activists age and pass away, and government agencies store and dispose of invaluable records. Presently, though, a wealth of eyewitness accounts and documentary records still awaits those who wish to seek them. This book draws extensively on both interviews and documentary sources. The oral testimony has been indispensable, and interviewees have included students and parents who participated in the school boycott; black and white educators; other Hyde County residents; civil rights leaders; and local, state, and federal officials. Documentary sources consisted of many newspapers, government agency files, public meeting minutes, court records, civil rights archives, and local school materials. HEW and U.S. Department of Justice files proved especially useful for examining school desegregation and racial incidents in Hyde County, as they included internal memoranda, minutes of meetings with local officials, reports of civil rights investigations, and transcripts of interviews with black students and parents.

Two unusual sources merit special mention. First, the State Highway Patrol (SHP) headquarters in Raleigh and its regional office in Greenville made available several hundred documents on school desegregation in Hyde County, including day-by-day reports obtained from firsthand observations and local informants. This is apparently the first instance in which a researcher has been granted access to North Carolina's SHP files, which also include State Bureau of Investigation (SBI) field and investigatory reports that are otherwise exempt from public access laws.

Second, the National Education Association (NEA) provided access to its extensive internal files on an investigation into the origins of the school boycott. In the winter of 1969, at the request of black teachers, a team of NEA investigators tape-recorded testimony by dozens of school boycott activists and Hyde County educational leaders. Though few of those records were used in the resulting NEA report, the transcripts and the field staff's notes and correspondence are a marvelous source for understanding the school boycott. Together, these sources have been richly informative.

A final word should be offered concerning the meaning of the school boycott for contemporary society. For several decades, school integration was central to the struggle for racial equality in the South. Until the Black Power movement in the late 1960s, W. E. B. Du Bois's cautious dissent in a 1935 edition of the *Journal of Negro Education* was one of the last serious voices of opposition to school integration as a key to black advancement.[31] Enduring doubts about the loss of black control over education were muted in those years by the desire for equal schools and the need to establish a united front against white resistance to equal education for blacks.

In the 1990s, two and three decades removed from those battles for the right to an equal education, a reassessment of school desegregation and a redefining of "just schools" is beginning to occur in public discussions. A small but growing number of prominent black scholars have begun to emphasize more what their communities lost than what they gained during school desegregation.[32] Other scholars, while supporting racial integration, have started to rediscover the good qualities of African American schooling in their search for new and better ways to teach children today.[33] A national magazine deeply committed to racial justice recently published an entire issue addressing the question "What's Wrong with Integration?"[34] And in many southern school districts that have drifted back to de facto segregation, black parents and educators are fighting against any school mergers, redrawing of districts, or busing that would dilute black community control by reintegrating the local schools. In these ways, the complex issues that colored school desegregation a generation ago—issues of political power and cultural survival, ethnic traditions and community control—are again entering public discussion. The school boycott in Hyde County offers valuable insights on these challenges encountered in the attempt to create better schools and communities for all children.

Prologue, 1954–1964

Swamp and salt marsh had begun taking back Hyde County when the United States Supreme Court ruled on *Brown v. Board of Education of Topeka, Kansas* on May 17, 1954. The population had never been large. Though for two centuries slaves and convict laborers had dug drainage canals, the East Dismal and Great Alligator swamps had not yielded more than a foothold to civilization. The county had experienced rapid growth and some prosperity during a timber boom from 1870 to 1920, but the northern timber companies abandoned the region as they cut the last old-growth cypress, juniper, and oak. A succession of visionary plans to develop the swamplands had subsequently failed. Only a labyrinth of deserted streets marked a typical scheme to build a city in the swamps near Alligator Lake. Likewise, the tiny village of New Holland was the only remnant of several prodigious efforts to drain and develop Lake Mattamuskeet. The great lake, roughly fifteen miles long and five miles across, had gradually taken back every acre of its bottom.[1]

Local residents who had lived through the hurricanes of 1899, 1933, or 1944 realized only too well how fragile their hold on this land was. None of the county rises more than a few feet above sea level, and even in clear weather the many tidal and blackwater creeks seem on the brink of inundating the countryside.[2] The largest hurricanes can engulf Hyde County overnight.

By the time of *Brown*, Hyde County's population had been declining steadily for half a century. Producing enormous harvests of corn, soybeans, and truck vegetables, the county remained primarily agricultural. But tobacco, the crop that most eased the general rural decline elsewhere in eastern North Carolina, did not grow in Hyde County's humus soils.[3] Also, the county had remained untouched by the rapid industrial growth, paced by the textile industry, that was occurring in the Carolina Piedmont.[4] Massive federal investments in highways, defense

Downtown Fairfield, 1918. Even during the timber boom, Hyde County towns experienced limited growth and prosperity. (Selby et al., Hyde County History)

industries, and military bases during World War II had lifted nearby sections of the coast out of the Great Depression and laid a strong foundation for economic development after the war. The military's capital and infrastructure, however, had not extended to Hyde County. Fading with the timber boomtowns, the county lost at least 10 percent of its population every decade after 1900, and the total had fallen under 7,000 by the 1950s.

Wilderness had by then reclaimed several villages that had been prosperous in the nineteenth century. Even lumber mill towns that boasted a post office, motels, boarding houses, bars, railroad lines, and regular boat traffic in 1900 had vanished by 1954.[5] Only the elderly

could recognize Makleyville, Piney Woods, Hydeland, or Wapoppin in clusters of old brick cisterns and forsaken outbuildings. Mere shadows of their pasts, Scranton, Middletown, and New Land were rapidly dwindling away. No community, in fact, had been spared by the decline. In downtown Swan Quarter, the county seat, most of the commercial buildings had been left vacant and dilapidated. Fairfield, an important farming and logging center on Lake Mattamuskcet, had lost half its population since 1900; it no longer had a mayor, a town hall, or a jail. The county had only published a newspaper sporadically since 1941, and to this day it has not had a single stoplight.[6]

Surrounded by sea and swamp, Hyde County seemed almost a world

Draining Lake Mattamuskeet. In the early twentieth century, wealthy investors financed several attempts to drain and farm the lake bottom. (Selby et al., Hyde County History)

unto itself. The broad, shallow waters of the Pamlico Sound lay to its south, separating the county from the Outer Banks by 35 miles.[7] To the east, a lone two-lane road skirted uncharted pocosins and other wetlands for 50 miles. The route north was almost as desolate. Highway 94 passed for 25 miles through the Hollow Ground Swamp into Columbia, itself only a small, hardscrabble logging town. To the west, Highway 264 ran between salt marsh and the East Dismal Swamp for 30 miles before reaching Belhaven, a fishing village in Beaufort County. Belhaven at least had a modest hospital, but Hyde County residents had to travel 30 miles farther west to Washington or northwest to Plymouth to find many other town amenities. The closest cities, Norfolk and Raleigh, each lay more than 150 miles away. Not served by an airport, railroad, major highway, or bus line, Hyde County had few visitors other than the sports fishermen and hunters who relished its abundant wildlife and austere beauty.

By the 1950s, a small number of absentee owners had held dominion over this isolated land for more than two centuries. The federal government and a few timber corporations and agribusinesses held deeds to almost 90 percent of Hyde County. Local residents received few benefits from that land; neither the government's wildlife reserves nor the companies employed many people locally, and they paid little in property taxes. Several farmers and seafood cannery owners had grown fairly wealthy, and a couple hundred farming, fishing, and merchant families would have been called middle-class by the standards of the South in that day. But the large majority of the population, both black and white, suffered from the great inequalities in land ownership and wealth. In 1950 the average median income of all Hyde residents was only $914, and more than 80 percent of local families earned less than $2,000 a year.[8] North Carolina was a poor state, and of its hundred counties, only two—both in Appalachia—had poverty more sweeping than Hyde County's.

Most people struggled daily to keep food on the table, wood in stoves, and children clothed. They survived by fishing, hunting, trapping, and gardening, much as they and their ancestors had for generations. Strong bonds of family, school, and church helped local communities to weather hard conditions. But while southern towns and cities blossomed in the post–World War II years, Hyde County, like many other areas of the rural South, seemed as if it might slowly fade away, eventually descending back into the drowsiness of the swamps.

Few citizens had much money or an easy life in Hyde County, but the African Americans who composed half the mainland's population lived under incomparably worse conditions than their white counterparts did. Most blacks were, as the expression went, "fatback poor." Theirs was life on the hardest edge of survival. In 1950 the United States census takers did not identify a single black family that had hot running water or a flush toilet. Approximately a third of local white families possessed both luxuries. The vast majority of black Hyde Countians still depended on community wells for their drinking, cooking, and bathing water. Very few had electric lighting or owned a refrigerator, and a significant number could not even afford iceboxes.[9] They lived in ramshackle homes crowded onto the mosquito-ridden banks of drainage canals or blackwater creeks, often exactly where their great-grandparents had once lived in slave quarters or settled in the first years after the Civil War.

Hyde County's white citizens had colluded for generations to thwart black aspirations for political and economic advancement. Black men and women could not vote or serve on juries. Local electoral laws, intimidation, and inherited custom had disenfranchised them, and no black person had been elected to public office since the "Red Shirt" terror at the end of the nineteenth century.[10] Economic improvement was also discouraged. Few white farmers would sell land, the key to power in any agrarian society, to a black family. As a matter of principle, the local bank would not extend many kinds of credit to blacks. White employers seldom hired black workers except for unskilled labor. Excluded from serving in the local sheriff's department, the State Highway Patrol, the judiciary, and even the National Guard, black residents also could not count on the law and order necessary for economic growth. They could not even join the county firemen's brigades intended to protect their homes and businesses. In addition, local political leaders carefully routed roads, utilities, and other economic infrastructure well away from their communities.

A few blacks gained an important measure of economic independence by commuting weekly or monthly to work at the government shipyards in Norfolk, the Weyerhaeuser lumber mill in Plymouth, and other out-of-county locales. Those opportunities were hard to come by, however, and most people could not afford to travel such distances on a regular basis. Employment within Hyde County was limited almost exclusively to seasonal piece work in agriculture and seafood. These jobs were grueling and dangerous. They paid little, were irregular, and provided no benefits or security. The black "middle class" included only educators and a handful of farmers and storekeepers. Not a single black physician or lawyer lived in the county. Most black citizens shucked oysters, packed crabmeat, cut fish, and did agricultural labor for a living. The unemployment rate often reached 30 percent in winter, and the average manufacturing wage fell to among the lowest in the United States—only $1,156 per year as recently as 1968.

In the 1950s Jim Crow remained at the heart of the social order, as it did throughout the South. Racial segregation stretched from the church to the graveyard, the schools to downtown businesses, social occasions to sports events. For example, black customers at Midgette's, the only restaurant in Engelhard, were forced to enter by the back door and carry their dinners out or eat them in a cubbyhole behind the kitchen.[11] The Engelhard theater seated white patrons downstairs, blacks upstairs. The local drugstore did not allow black shoppers to sit at its lunch counter, and the few county motels simply did not serve black travelers. Housing was no less segregated. Black citizens did not live in downtown Swan Quarter, but in Job's Corner or farther out in the country. White authorities did not even allow black guides or hunters on the Mattamuskeet National Wildlife Refuge.[12]

The subtle permutations of segregation and their capacity to disempower black citizens often seemed inexhaustible. A prominent landlord uniformly rented dilapidated shacks *with* indoor plumbing to white tenants and equally decrepit houses *without* indoor plumbing to black tenants.[13] The East Carolina Bank, the only banking company in Hyde County, required that a white person "stand for" the creditworthiness of black veterans and other pensioners seeking to cash their government checks.[14] A black man might have lived in Hyde County his entire life, but he could not redeem a U.S. government check without a white person vouching for his good name.

Although racial segregation was generally inviolable, there was on occasion some flexibility in the barrier between blacks and whites. The owner of a nightclub in Fairfield, for instance, divided his main room with a low wooden partition that allowed his black and white customers to talk and drink together without literally violating local customs against racial intermixing.[15] Most transgressions of Jim Crow remained very serious, however, and none posed a greater danger than unsanctioned intimacy between blacks and whites. Many black Hyde Countians still blame such dangerous liaisons for two mysterious and very violent attacks on black individuals in the 1950s.[16] In their eyes, those episodes underscored old realizations: threats of coercion and violence underlie all racial segregation, and interracial relationships pose a special danger to a society built on white superiority.

These patterns of racial control had shaped a social order where challenging the absolute power of the white majority often seemed out of the question. To survive in Hyde County, black men and women drew on a strong tradition of community self-help, organizing mutual aid societies, public health campaigns, a community-owned funeral home, and other projects. But dissent seemed futile, dangerous, or simply unimaginable. "We just didn't think about [changing the county] before the school boycott," recalled James "Little Brother" Topping, a New Holland resident who in the 1970s would be elected Hyde County's first black commissioner. "[Whites] used to say we were happy, and in a way, maybe we were . . . because we could not even imagine things being different."[17] Ida Murray, a resident of the Ridge community, shared that feeling. She remembered that "there were all kinds of problems, but nobody talked about them . . . or even thought about it."[18] After the Supreme Court's ruling in *Brown*, however, blacks and whites both wondered whether—or when—this would change.

Avoiding *Brown*: The Pearsall Plan

Life in Hyde County did not change very much during the decade after *Brown*. The Supreme Court had ruled that race could no longer be a factor in the assignment of children to public schools. Building upon precedents that spanned an entire generation, the NAACP had convinced the court that racial segregation in education amounted to inherently unequal protection under the law. The long-standing doctrine of "separate but equal" expressed six decades earlier, in *Plessy v. Ferguson*, thereby violated the Fourteenth and Fifteenth amendments to the Constitution.[19] *Brown* was a great victory not only for the NAACP's talented attorneys but also for the hundreds of local chapters that had built the NAACP into the largest civil rights organization in the nation, and the only civil rights group with a strong presence in the small towns and rural communities of North Carolina. Yet in Hyde County, as throughout the South, little movement toward school integration occurred between *Brown* and the Civil Rights Act of 1964.

Black citizens of Hyde County did organize a local NAACP chapter in the mid-1950s. Led by ministers and lay activists at Old Richmond, a Baptist church founded by ex-slaves only six years after the Civil War, this courageous group concentrated first on a voter registration campaign, not school integration. NAACP activists met resistance to voting, including white intimidation and illicit "citizenship tests," but they persisted and made important headway in registering black voters.[20] The first barriers to school desegregation proved more unyielding. Believing that white political leaders would never allow black children to have equal school facilities until they attended classes with white children, the local NAACP members began to push for school integration in the early 1960s. Their periodic petitions for school integration were greeted by the Hyde County Board of Education with polite tolerance and stony silence.[21]

School officials in Hyde County did not need to respond seriously to local demands for school integration because for a decade the State of North Carolina shielded them from the power of the federal courts. After some initial signs of conciliation, or at least resignation, white politicians in North Carolina opposed school integration with the same conviction as their counterparts in other southern states, and with more acumen. In the spring of 1955, the General Assembly resolved that "the mixing of the races in the public schools . . . cannot be accomplished and should not be attempted."[22] Under the leadership of Gov. Luther Hodges, the state engineered a series of legal and administrative barriers to school integration that, although very effective, did not appear openly to defy the Supreme Court.

Most important was the passage of the Pupil Assignment Act in 1955. Designed to discourage a statewide civil suit by the NAACP, the act delegated all authority for public education to local school districts. The act also established a series of vague criteria for student transfers between schools that included previous schools attended by the child and "other local conditions"; these criteria permitted school boards to deny black students admission into white schools without citing race as the reason. The act also created a complicated, multistep appeals process designed to discourage black students from challenging school assignment decisions in the first place. The effect of the Pupil Assignment Act was, first of all, to create a prohibitive number of targets (the 140-plus school districts in North Carolina in 1955) instead of one for potential civil rights lawsuits. And second, the act gave local school officials a number of workable strategies for avoiding school desegregation that were legal under state law. Yet the state attorney general's office, while avoiding legal responsibility for the evasive actions of local school districts, would until 1969 lend its legal expertise and financial resources to any school district sued for failing to permit black children to attend school with white children.

In a special legislative session called to respond to the *Brown* decision during the summer of 1956, Governor Hodges introduced even more insidious measures for dodging school integration while continuing to avoid an open confrontation with the federal courts. The Pearsall Plan, as it was later known, gave local citizens the power to close their schools by popular referendum if desegregation occurred. It also permitted state tuition aid to go to white students attending private schools in those districts.[23] The plan did not literally prohibit school integration; it simply left the decision of whether or not to desegregate schools to local citizens while giving them a powerful legal tool for defending a decision to resist desegregation. Because blacks composed a small minority of enfranchised persons even in black-majority counties, the Pearsall Plan in effect gave authority over the implementation of *Brown* to local white leaders and set up a false rubric of democratic choice to ensure racial segregation.

White politicians, policymakers, and newspapers widely endorsed the Pearsall Plan, which bec... part of the North Carolina Constitution with the passage of a 1956 reic.endum.[24] During the decade that the Pearsall Plan was state policy, the right wing of the Democratic Party often advocated more militant resistance to school desegregation. Militancy had prevailed in other southern states, where political leaders closed public schools entirely, persecuted NAACP members, and challenged federal authorities to force them to mix black and white students. But political opinion across the spectrum of North Carolina politics coalesced around a more "effective" and "moderate" path. The state's political spectrum was not, however, a wide one. No prominent white politician in North Carolina openly supported school desegregation until the 1970s. Even Gov. Terry Sanford, the most liberal postwar governor in North Carolina, opposed school desegregation and supported the Pearsall Plan during his 1960–64 term.[25]

The Pearsall Plan was praised nationally as a "moderate route" between the two "extremes" of massive resistance, on the one hand, and the NAACP's insistence on the prompt enforcement of *Brown*, on the other.[26] From 1954 to 1965, federal courts and civil rights groups concentrated their limited resources on enforcing *Brown* in southern states where resistance to school integration was more outspoken, uncompromising, or violent. No fiery demagogue posed defiantly on the schoolhouse steps in North Carolina. Yet the Pearsall Plan and the Pupil Assignment Act together allowed local school boards in North Carolina to delay school desegregation for more than a decade, longer than many school districts in the Deep South and Virginia where militant resistance to school desegregation had occurred.[27]

The Hyde County school board embraced these evasive measures and passed several new pupil assignment policies between 1955 and 1959 that corresponded to the new state laws.[28] Only a handful of black students requested transfers prior to 1964, and the school board found grounds to reject them all. Several school districts in North Carolina strategically permitted small numbers of black children to enroll in white schools in order to reduce their vulnerability to class action lawsuits, but the Hyde County Board of Education did not feel compelled to do likewise. Thus racial segregation remained the rule in Hyde County's schools for a full decade after *Brown*.

Complying with *Plessy* instead of *Brown*

Through the Pearsall Plan and the Pupil Assignment Act, the State of North Carolina had given white leaders in Hyde and other school districts the necessary tools for delaying, rebuffing, or frustrating any efforts by black citizens to integrate the public schools. Racial segregation, economic leverage, and other traditional forms of social control also deterred black demands. All the same, many school officials recognized that other steps would be necessary to lower the risk of lawsuits or other pressure toward school integration. They could not afford to underestimate the forces challenging their authority, for in their eyes biracial education posed a threat both to their power over the school system and to white rule in the county.

As in many other school districts in North Carolina, white school leaders in Hyde County sought to defuse and lower black expectations for racial integration by dramatically improving the black schools. Between 1955 and 1965, Hyde and other local school boards acted as if the Supreme Court had recently ruled on *Plessy v. Ferguson*, the court's 1896 "separate but equal" ruling, instead of *Brown*. They hoped that black children would want to remain in their own schools with their own friends and teachers if the boards finally provided the approximately equal education promised by *Plessy* sixty years earlier.[29] Consequently, those white educational leaders undertook extensive projects to upgrade black schools or to build modern schools for black children, often raising new funds and diverting large proportions of their school budgets to these schools for the first time. At bottom, they preferred the fiscal costs required to improve the black schools to racial intermixing and its political costs.

White school leaders understood that black expectations for better schools had heightened after World War II. As early as March of 1951, coastal blacks had sent a powerful signal of those new expectations to the white establishment, when the Wilmington Committee on Negro Affairs filed a federal lawsuit based on *Plessy* that soon compelled the New Hanover County Board of Education to equalize black and white school facilities. After *Brown*, black demands rose higher yet and led to widespread protests when black schools remained underfunded and in poor physical condition at the end of the 1950s.[30] In eastern North Carolina, black students demonstrated against deteriorating facilities by conducting school boycotts in Greene County in 1959, Northampton County in 1960, Warren County in 1961, and Granville and Martin counties in 1963.[31] Other kinds of protests were also common. These demonstrations often involved issues more complex than the inferior condition of a school's physical plant. In Northampton County, for example, black students protested the traditional "harvest recess" that required the black schools (and only the black schools) to open in early August so that they could close later in the summer for the students to labor in local tobacco and cotton fields.[32]

Similarly, school officials in Hyde County and other school districts were well aware that nearby NAACP chapters had filed lawsuits demanding school integration long before the Pearsall Plan and even before *Brown*. The first and most famous case arose in the remote coastal village of Oriental, located across the Pamlico Sound from Hyde County. In 1951, fifty-five NAACP members had filed a federal lawsuit against the Pamlico County Board of Education seeking school equalization or—if they were denied equality—school integration.[33] (This was only the second such lawsuit filed in the United States; NAACP attorneys had incorporated the first, originating in Clarendon County, South Carolina, into *Brown*.) Throughout the South, white leaders watched the school board in this rural, poor county refurbish black schools, build new schools, eliminate overcrowded classrooms, improve libraries, and equalize bus service rather than submit to racial integration.[34] If true equality remained elusive, the black schools still improved dramatically. NAACP chapters in Washington, Martin, and several other eastern counties soon followed the Pamlico County pioneers with similar lawsuits or petitions, and they generally had promising results.[35]

For all of these reasons, between 1953 and 1964 the Hyde County school board carried out the largest construction program in its history and dedicated unprecedented attention to the quality of the black schools. Prior to 1953, more than a dozen two- and three-room elementary schools served black youngsters in Hyde County. The quality of the buildings and educational facilities varied considerably, but most reflected decades of official neglect and underfunding. None could compare favorably to the white school facilities. Older black children could attend the Hyde County Training School, a public high school in Sladesville, but it could accommodate only a small proportion of the county's black children and required the additional and often prohibitive costs of boarding for children who did not live in the vicinity. Consequently, few black children had access to a high school education. All white children, on the other hand, could attend one of two comprehensive schools, the East Hyde School in Engelhard or the West Hyde School in Swan Quarter. Both had modern libraries, cafeterias, gymnasiums, laboratories, and full bus services.

By 1964, Hyde County's black schools had improved enormously. The small community schools had been merged into two modern buildings—the Davis School in Engelhard and the O. A. Peay School near Swan Quarter—spacious enough to serve every black child in the county for a full twelve years. The O. A. Peay School opened in Job's Corner on the outskirts of Swan Quarter in 1953.[36] Three more classrooms and a science laboratory were built in 1958, then a gymnasium and an agricultural workshop in 1964. The old Davis School, one of the larger community schools, was enlarged in 1954 into a high school with eight new classrooms, a library, and a home economics laboratory, and in 1964 the school board funded six more classrooms and a gymnasium. Both schools occupied solid, well-lit brick buildings comparable to East Hyde and West Hyde.[37]

To finance these improvements, Hyde County political leaders had to issue two expensive municipal bonds and increase taxes. Many white citizens felt that their children deserved better schools as well, if they were going to support the bond referendums necessary to fund such large improvements in the black schools. For that reason, the Hyde County Board of Education consolidated East Hyde and West Hyde into a new facility called the Mattamuskeet School, built near the lake's southern shore. However, the consolidation process led to a bitter conflict over the loss of the two schools and divided white residents into several factions. Nonetheless, all white children attended classes at

Mattamuskeet after 1963.[38] An important disparity in black and white school facilities continued to exist, but it had been reduced considerably.

Traditional patterns of racial intimidation, the Pearsall Plan, and the major improvements in black school facilities worked together to forestall local pressure for school integration from 1954 to 1964. Hyde County changed little over that decade. The living conditions for the average family had improved only marginally, and the population continued to decline as young people emigrated in search of greater opportunity.[39] Though school improvements and NAACP organizing signaled the emergence of a voice for black citizens, ultimately the power structure remained unaltered. The walls of segregation stood solid, in the school system and beyond.

Elsewhere in North Carolina, black activists had made substantial progress toward school integration in only a few counties by 1964. White defiance remained especially formidable in the rural east.[40] Yet a powerful civil rights insurgency was sweeping across eastern North Carolina. Though it had not yet prevailed against school segregation, black activism had already made an assault on other aspects of Jim Crow. Local movements had won victories as fundamental as the integration of downtown businesses, hospitals, and other public accommodations, and as symbolic as the removal of "colored" and "white" signs and the promise that whites would use courtesy titles when speaking to black elders.

Using nonviolent tactics to triumph over harsh opposition, black Carolinians extended civil rights activism into the most rural sections of the east's Tobacco Belt and Tidewater. Their struggles to end Jim Crow had shone with special radiance in New Bern, Williamston, Wilmington, Dunn, and Edenton.[41] Other black communities, most notably in the northeastern Black Belt counties, had waged bold campaigns to secure the rights to vote and serve on juries, and in several larger towns they had made important breakthroughs against job discrimination.[42] While those civil rights battles raged, Hyde County seemed as quiet as the most solitary hammock in the swamplands that surrounded it.

CHAPTER 1

White Folks' Ways

On a late summer day in 1965, Vanderbilt Johnson was at a filling station west of Engelhard when for the first time in his life he saw a school bus carrying black and white children. He could not speak for his astonishment. "I never thought I'd see the day in Hyde County," he told a friend later.[1] The black veteran of World War II recognized immediately that he had witnessed a locally historic moment and a first small step toward racial equality. He also understood at once that some of his white neighbors would lash out against the black community for encouraging children to ride that bus. Thinking of a brighter future for his children, the prospect did not intimidate him. Yet neither he nor other black citizens could predict that morning that the school bus portended a more lasting danger. They did not yet suspect that the wondrous sight of black and white children together might also signal the beginning of the end for the historically black schools and a threat to the rich and vibrant heritage of African American education that had nourished Hyde County blacks for generations.

How did the promise of school integration evolve from Vanderbilt Johnson's cautious hope in 1965 for a new era in race relations into a fervent campaign to dismantle the black schools only three years later? That question bears not only on Hyde County but on the entire South as well. Between 1965 and 1968, the closing of black schools and attempts to efface their educational legacy became a standard part of school desegregation. The closing of black schools occurred in so many southern school districts because power over the implementation of school desegregation still rested in the hands of leaders who had opposed racial equality and fought biracial schools. Those white leaders adamantly defended the interests of constituents for whom the mingling of black and white children amounted to the severest violation of Jim Crow. After waging prolonged but ultimately unsuccessful struggles to resist desegregation, they rechanneled their energies and influence toward controlling its very meaning and nature. They were determined that school desegregation—if it had to happen—was going to respect traditional patterns of privilege and power.

Neither the federal courts nor federal agencies felt obligated to intervene against local school leaders. In 1969 Lloyd Henderson, the education branch chief at HEW's Office of Civil Rights, explained to a Hyde County parent that he realized that many school districts in the South were needlessly and unfairly closing black schools. "While we do not necessarily agree with such practices," he wrote Scranton's Rosa O'Neal, "we are not authorized to [prohibit them] if they are taken to eliminate the dual school system."[2] He was right. In *Brown*, the NAACP and the Supreme Court had demanded no less and no more. Consequently, white leaders routinely excluded black citizens and their concerns from deliberations over the new unitary school systems.

The First Steps Forward and Back

The integrated school bus that had passed by Vanderbilt Johnson revealed that by the summer of 1965, the barricades to school desegregation were crumbling. Widespread protests in the South had compelled the U.S. Congress to pass a landmark civil rights bill the previous year. While the Civil Rights Act of 1964 addressed a wide range of issues, Title VI of the act banned racial discrimination in federally supported programs, including local schools that received federal funds. In effect, the act provided the executive branch with the clearer legislative authority and the greater enforcement capacity necessary to promote extensive school desegregation. It also gave HEW and the U.S. Department of Justice important new penalties to impose against school districts that did not move toward desegregation. The crucial new weapon was the ability to deny these schools federal funds, which comprised as much as 40 percent of the budget in many poor districts.[3] The act was a tremendous relief for the federal courts. They had been overwhelmed by the responsibility of enforcing *Brown* with little assistance and only vague guidelines from the White House. Consequently, school desegregation gained new momentum with passage of the Civil Rights Act.

The Hyde County Board of Education was first obligated to show compliance with *Brown* when enforcement of Title VI began in the summer of 1965. At that point, HEW required the school board to "develop a plan to abolish the dual school system" and to show some initial signs of progress immediately.[4] Following the example of most other school districts in North Carolina, school officials in Hyde County adopted a "freedom of choice" plan that gave students the choice of whether to attend the Mattamuskeet School, the Davis School, or the O. A. Peay School. But the new policy did not require the reassignment of any student. No black student had to attend the Mattamuskeet School, and no white student had to transfer to Davis or O. A. Peay. School officials assured HEW that student desegregation would occur voluntarily during the 1965–66 academic year, and the school board itself agreed to integrate its faculty on a similar schedule. On the basis of this promise, HEW approved Hyde County's school desegregation plan early in the fall of 1965.[5]

A year later, however, HEW staff discovered that few black students had enrolled at the Mattamuskeet School and the number was declining steadily. Twenty-one black children had transferred from Peay and Davis to Mattamuskeet in 1965, but only seven enrolled for the 1966–67 term. Only three would attend Mattamuskeet a year later, in the fall of 1967.[6] By then, the proportion of black students in Hyde County enrolled in biracial classes would be the lowest in North Carolina.

This backward momentum occurred despite a campaign by the local NAACP chapter to encourage black families to send their children to the white school. Three NAACP members had been the first to allow their children to attend Mattamuskeet, and they quietly recruited other families to follow in their footsteps. However, white school leaders put no support or moral authority behind those efforts. Without their leadership, "freedom of choice" was bound to fail because of white resistance to school integration and, to an important degree, the disillusionment of the first black students who transferred out of the O. A. Peay and Davis schools.

During the 1965–66 school year, there were several small but painful incidents between black and white children at the Mattamuskeet School. For example, a white boy spat on the young son of Doris Weston.[7] A few threats and fights occurred. More frequently, black students felt that their white classmates did not accept them. Several white children attempted to reach out to the new students, but they found it was not easy. "When a white student befriended them," reported A. J. Howell, an investigator from HEW who later interviewed many of the children, "other white students would put pressures on [the white child] so that [the black child] would be ignored again."[8] Naturally, the black students often had difficulties enduring this treatment. But more burdensome, they would report later, was how uncomfortable they felt at the Mattamuskeet School.

The black children felt disoriented by the culture of education at Mattamuskeet. They especially missed the black teachers and principals who had been their most important role models and counselors.[9] It did not help that a few white educators allowed racial prejudice to master their professionalism. Most white teachers did try their best to support the new students; however, they simply could not replace the educators at Peay and Davis. According to one white teacher at Mattamuskeet, the black students "felt by themselves, like there was no one that they could look up to."[10] Accustomed to studying under the most honored men and women in their community, the students longed for their former mentors' high expectations and guidance.[11] The young people also discovered that white educators neither shared nor appreciated many of their cultural vantage points. Having lived in separate worlds for so long, the black students and white school teachers often communicated poorly, misunderstood one another's expectations, and mishandled classroom instruction.

The young people also yearned for the caring environment that black educators had created at Peay and Davis.[12] In interviews, alumni and ex-teachers repeatedly emphasized the spirit of caring and mutual support that they experienced in Hyde County's black schools. Often they contrasted that educational climate to contemporary schools. As Emilie V. Siddle Walker has noted of a black high school elsewhere in North Carolina, the educators and students at Peay and Davis seemed like a family.[13] The schools nourished "their minds, their bodies, and their souls," remembered one alumnus, and the training black students received in the classroom complemented the training they received in the church, the family, and the wider black community. This familial atmosphere at Peay and Davis was born out of an African American heritage and a collective struggle for black achievement and self-improvement. The Mattamuskeet School obviously could not serve black students as meaningfully unless a more fundamental merger of white and black school traditions occurred.

By their very separateness, the O. A. Peay and Davis schools rein-forced Jim Crow and to some degree inculcated in black children a sense of inferiority. They not only formed the most pervasive symbols of racial segregation in daily life but also perpetuated segregation more broadly by affirming in every new generation of children a belief in its validity and naturalness. Yet the two black schools also provided a powerful counterweight to those tendencies. Like the best of families, they func-tioned as a daily shelter for black children to learn in—one with high expectations, strong role models, and constant reinforcement of their dignity and self-respect. Admittedly, the two schools often seemed like artificial worlds. Many times their alumni described the sense of disloca-tion that they felt if, later in life, they worked for white employers or studied under white college professors. But at Mattamuskeet, the black students could find no refuge from the prejudices and racial conflicts in Hyde County at large.

The combination of racial tensions and cultural chasms led inevitably to educational problems. Some black students performed far below their abilities; others had uncharacteristic disciplinary problems. One black teenager, an "Alexander boy" mentioned in the minutes of the Hyde County Board of Education, felt so uncomfortable at the Mattamuskeet School that he continually skipped classes, a problem that he had not had previously. Though many black parents believed that his problem required a more compassionate response, Supt. Allen Bucklew expelled him for truancy. Administrators at Peay or Davis would never have given up on a black child so quickly. A pattern of such events led black parents both to grow concerned about the commitment of white administrators to their children and to suspect that Mattamuskeet's staff disciplined their children disproportionately.

Black children who transferred to the white school also felt uprooted from the social and cultural activities that revolved around the O. A. Peay and Davis schools. Though they would attend whenever possible, they often missed the planning and atmosphere that accompanied school dances, festivals, Founder's Day, and the annual homecoming. They had also left behind the comradery of sports teams, the glee club, and other extracurricular activities. "Even in church," recalled Albert Whitaker, a farmer and storekeeper in Fairfield whose son was among the first transferees, "they'd miss being at the Peay School," because some church activities raised funds for education, and other church events, such as gospel concerts, often took place at the local school.[14] His son Thomas and the other black students found themselves isolated not only at the Mattamuskeet School but also, to some extent, within their own community. The disillusionment of these students and their parents began an important evolution in black attitudes toward desegregation of the Hyde County schools.

Desegregation was very difficult for those pioneering students, but NAACP leaders and other black parents who sent their children to the Mattamuskeet School endured more harassment and intimidation than their children. "When pressed a little," stated HEW's Dewey Dodds in an internal memorandum, children who returned to the black schools after attending Mattamuskeet "admitted they returned because their parents wanted them to do so."[15] Another HEW investigator in Hyde County concluded that there was "an active effort to discourage Negro families from sending their children to [the] formerly white school."[16]

Especially in 1965 and 1966, white citizens drew on ancestral patterns of intimidation and social control to prevent black families from sending their children to the Mattamuskeet School. NAACP activists, in particular, were threatened repeatedly with violence. When NAACP leader Johnnie Midgette sent his daughter to Mattamuskeet in the fall of 1965, he began to receive anonymous death threats. A quiet, dignified man, he quoted Biblical scripture to the callers.[17] Often the Ku Klux Klan left its literature or mark around his barbershop in Engelhard.[18] On one morning, Midgette found the letters "KKK" drawn across the front of his shop from the roof to the foundation. On another morning, he discovered the same letters dangling by streamers from telephone poles on both sides of the street.[19] Early Bryant, a farmer and NAACP leader in the rural Slocumb community, also had his life threatened when his granddaughter transferred to Mattamuskeet.[20] In addition, night riders terrorized Booker Boomer several times at his home across the Beaufort County line. A Disciples of Christ minister who served Hyde congregations, the Reverend Boomer had strongly supported the NAACP's efforts to desegregate schools.[21] Klan activists undoubtedly threatened other blacks who never dared to relate the incidents outside of their community.

Economic coercion was a more prevalent, subtle, and effective way to stymie the NAACP's efforts for school integration. "Most of us were dirt poor and worked for the white man," a black leader in Swan Quarter explained. Virtually all blacks worked for white employers. "You picked his crops, shucked his oysters, cleaned his house."[22] Caleb Gibbs, a fieldhand who resided in Fairfield, was a typical victim of this form of intimidation. A white farmer who had employed Gibbs seasonally for many years threatened not to rehire him unless he withdrew his grandchild from the Mattamuskeet School.[23] When Gibbs refused, the farmer did not employ him for "a period of months," until his harvest was so far behind schedule that he grew desperate for the black man's help.

Nobody suffered more from economic reprisals than Johnnie Midgette. His barbershop, located in a white cinderblock building in downtown Engelhard, served an exclusively white clientele. (In those days, black businessmen had to choose whether to serve whites or blacks; they could never openly serve both races.) When his daughter became the first black child to transfer to Mattamuskeet, Midgette's customers disappeared completely. Midgette sat alone in the barbershop for months, and his business did not return to normal levels for years.[24] Several white clients who at first continued to patronize his barbershop found themselves targets of Klan harassment and were forced to stop.

The full extent of this open coercion may never be known, but black workers understood the threat of economic retaliation whether it was expressed directly or not. For example, the common belief that the owner of an oyster company in Engelhard belonged to the Ku Klux Klan was a powerful implicit threat for his workers. Though the Klan was supposedly an "invisible empire," Klan membership was widely known in the black community. However, Hyde County blacks were vulnerable whether or not they had racist bosses. "Even if you had a little farm or a small store," James "Little Brother" Topping of New Holland reflected years later, "if you were black in Hyde County you were *always* vulnerable in some way." In a small rural community such as Hyde— where employers, landlords, and creditors, on the one hand, and workers, tenants, and debtors, on the other, composed two fairly tight, distinct, and interrelated sets of families—it was inevitable that every black parent was potentially vulnerable to some form of white retaliation if they sent their children to Mattamuskeet. "If you couldn't be touched, then they would get your sister or your mother or your cousin," recalled Topping. "You might not even know they did get you, but you would always wonder why you didn't get that loan, or why your brother was sent to Vietnam."[25]

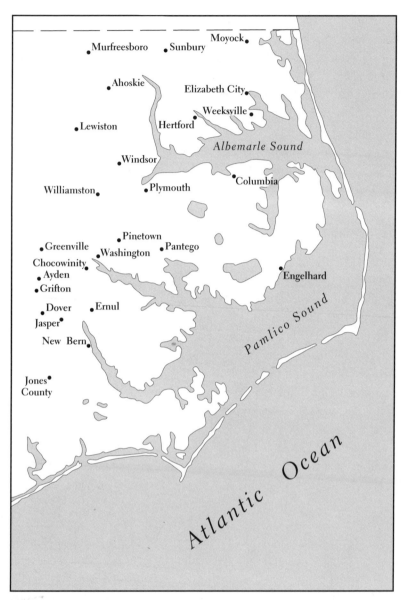

Map 3. Principal Sites of Ku Klux Klan Activism, First Congressional District, Summer of 1966

The local resurgence of the Ku Klux Klan was an important development. Since 1964, in fact, the KKK had had a great awakening in North
Carolina. The Klan had long lived in the shadows, but between 1964
and 1967 it rose out of its obscurity and walked in broad daylight.[26]
Barnstorming across the Carolina countryside like an old-fashioned
revival, Klan activists held a public rally almost every night in a different
town or hamlet (see map 3). More than six thousand joined the state
KKK, and tens of thousands attended their rallies. Within the First
Congressional District alone—the Klan's "Province 1" (of eleven),
which included Hyde County—the KKK had organized two dozen
"Klaverns" by 1965.[27] Huge crowds attended the public rallies. State
Bureau of Investigation agents and State Highway Patrol troopers regularly observed 400 to 800 people at local proceedings that culminated
with the fiery cross.[28] Their numbers also soared far higher. In 1965,
6,000 spectators crowded a Sampson County rally, and 5,000 attended a
Klan wedding in a cornfield near Farmville.[29]

   According to internal SHP and SBI documents, the Hyde County
group was fairly typical of North Carolina Klaverns. Organized by
mid-1965, the Klavern contained only a few dozen individuals. Its
influence, however, stretched far beyond the local membership. The
group owned a meeting house in Middletown, a farming crossroads near
Engelhard, and in the mid-1960s held several public, open-air rallies
that regularly attracted several hundred onlookers. On occasion, as
many as five hundred people, or 15 percent of the county's white
population, attended those events.

   The Hyde County Klavern drew support among the most prominent
white citizens, including a seafood cannery owner and several prosperous farmers. Generally speaking, local Klansmen were men of property and good standing.[30] If they did not often include "the pillars of the
community," to quote a newspaper reporter who interviewed Klansmen
in nearby Martin County, they consisted of "at least good foundation
stones."[31] Klan orators harshly berated poor whites, calling them "white
trash" and other terms that they otherwise reserved for blacks, Jews,
Communists, and Lyndon Johnson. SBI and SHP sources do not suggest that any law enforcement or judicial leaders belonged to the Hyde
County Klavern, but these agencies did tolerate Klan activities and did
not pursue local Klansmen for minor acts of terrorism such as the
defilement of Johnnie Midgette's barbershop.

The Ku Klux Klan found its most widespread appeal in a vocal opposition to school desegregation. At an April 25, 1966 rally and cross burning in Middletown, for example, Klan leaders repeatedly discussed the "anti-Christian" and "Communistic" evils of interracial schooling. A crowd of two hundred people applauded while the state Grand Dragon, Bob Jones, explained that "white students would have to lower their standards to that of the Negro" if black teachers taught at Mattamuskeet. [32] At a larger rally on the outskirts of Swan Quarter later that year, Klan leaders evoked images of miscegenation, black domination, and federal usurpation of "your rights as a citizen" in long sermons and speeches against school integration. [33]

With those very public spectacles the Ku Klux Klan sought not only to intimidate the black population but also to deter Hyde County's whites from supporting or cooperating with school desegregation. Moreover, the rallies were not their only means of coercing white citizens. Klan activists included only a small percentage of white residents, and the local Klavern often threatened whites who disagreed with their message or tactics. Klansmen left threatening leaflets and other warnings at the homes of the young women who taught in Mattamuskeet's first integrated summer programs, at the homes of Johnnie Midgette's customers, and at farms that continued to employ NAACP activists. Likewise, the first white teacher who accepted a job at the Davis School was allegedly unable to rent a house in Engelhard after the Ku Klux Klan intervened with her landlord. [34] Anybody who had anything to do with school integration was a victim. Klansmen even left threatening literature and a black baby doll at the home of school board member Walker Lee Gibbs, apparently blaming him for allowing black children to transfer to Mattamuskeet. [35] Weary of this harassment, at least one group of white residents spent a few nights lying in wait for the Klansmen. They evidently gave several young men compelling reasons not to pay them further visits.

Not all black citizens backed down under the pressure of white opposition to school desegregation. Visiting families across Hyde County, NAACP leaders continued to encourage black parents to send their children to the Mattamuskeet School. They also withstood the death threats, the vandalism, and the night riders. At times, in fact, the younger black activists could barely contain their rage at the Klan's shamelessness and immorality. After one vandalism incident at Johnnie

Midgette's barbershop, for example, an NAACP activist hurriedly gathered up the KKK leaflets that had been strewn about the storefront, stormed into downtown Engelhard, and found the known head of the local Klan sitting in his pickup truck. Angrily confronting the man, the young mother threw the leaflets through his truck window and told him, "Next time you want to send us something, use the mail."[36] Her defiance was not an isolated act. Her brashness and the imperturbable patience displayed by Midgette, who would finally outlast his customers' boycott, were two sides of a smoldering insurgency.

Yet the Klan revival still fostered a powerful atmosphere of racial intimidation that discouraged black parents from sending their children to Mattamuskeet. Naturally they feared for the safety of their children. But it was not outright coercion, real as that was, that most worried the parents. The Klan revival had begun to influence their attitude toward school desegregation itself. Many black citizens were growing disillusioned by the shape of school desegregation that was emerging in Hyde County. They wondered if their children could possibly receive a good education given present conditions at Mattamuskeet and in the community. In addition, the failure of any white parents to send their children to the O. A. Peay or Davis schools increasingly disturbed the black community. While black leaders understood that the fear of Klan reprisals might also influence whites' school choice, it still seemed to bode ill for a successful merger of the two educational heritages that had existed separately for so many years. For all of those reasons, a mere handful of black students enrolled at the Mattamuskeet School for the 1966–67 school year.

Shaping School Desegregation's Parameters

During the summer of 1966, HEW's Office of Education surveyed school integration efforts in Hyde County. William Cochran, the chairman of the school board, reported that the school district had made substantial progress and was basically complying with the Civil Rights Act. In addition to giving all students an opportunity to choose their school assignment, school administrators had conducted several biracial faculty meetings. At least one faculty in-service training program was described as "completely integrated." Two summer programs held at the Mattamuskeet School, Head Start and ESEA,[37] had included white and black children. The school board had also made some progress toward faculty integration: a black teacher had been employed at the Matta-muskeet School and a white teacher at the Davis School, and the school board was recruiting a white teacher for the O. A. Peay School.[38] In several telephone conversations, however, HEW officials insisted that the school board move more quickly. The decline in the number of black students at Mattamuskeet was of special concern to them. The local school leaders strongly disagreed with this evaluation; but they agreed to an informal visit from HEW staff to clarify their situation, and a meeting was arranged for August 19, 1966, at the Hyde County Courthouse in Swan Quarter.[39]

This meeting was noteworthy in several respects. The HEW staff came to Hyde County, in the words of team leader Dewey Dodds, "to assist you [the school board] to comply with the law" on a "voluntary basis." HEW had not yet threatened the school board with penalties or legal action for failing to make progress toward school desegregation, so the ambience of the session lacked the tension and rancor that would characterize later meetings.[40] The conversation was generally open, genial, and frank; it was without a doubt the most searching and reflective discussion that would occur between local officials and HEW's staff. The meeting revealed a great deal about the attitudes toward school desegregation, the visions of education's role in southern society, and the views of black schooling that would underlie both the school board's and HEW's actions over the next several years. Through the vital issue of who was or was not invited to join it, the conversation also reflected the relatively narrow parameters in which the struggle over school desegregation in Hyde County would occur: the HEW team leaders sent assistants to interview local black leaders during the session but did not have them attend the meetings on August 19 or later.

Local officials did not try to conceal their resentment about federal intervention in their school district. "I do not blame you [personally] at all," school board attorney George Davis told the two men from HEW, "but I do not like the attitude of any department that tries to run things that they do not know anything about." He pointedly asked Dewey Dodds, "Are you trying to tell us what we have to do?" Dodds responded coolly that his team was in Hyde County to help the school board comply voluntarily with the Civil Rights Act. But he warned them that the U.S. Department of Justice would compel them to integrate their schools if necessary. He explained that the school board basically had a contract with the federal government to comply with the school desegregation plan submitted the previous year. As a result, the participation of local black plaintiffs was not even necessary for a civil rights lawsuit to be filed against the school board.[41]

Dodds and his partner at the meeting, Louis Echols, asked little of the Hyde County school board. They seemed satisfied, for example, with the minimal level of faculty integration that had occurred in the school district, and they encouraged the school board's efforts to employ a white teacher at the O. A. Peay School. Their central concern was reversing Hyde County's steady decrease in student desegregation, but again they had relatively modest goals in mind. The HEW staff felt uncertain of the congressional support for fuller integration and did not yet have confidence in the will of the federal courts to enforce it. Consequently, Dodds was hoping to negotiate a settlement that would assure almost any forward progress toward school integration. With that goal in mind, Dodds suggested that the school board reopen student registration for three weeks and give black students another opportunity to transfer into the Mattamuskeet School. He believed that more students would transfer if they were given this chance and if the school board would encourage school desegregation through better public relations and community education.

The school board members, however, were more interested in avoiding school desegregation. They still doubted HEW's will to enforce integration, and several lower court rulings in the Deep South had recently raised their hopes that the final interpretation of Brown and the Civil Rights Act of 1964 would not require fundamental reforms. Board chairman William Cochran told Dodds and Echols that HEW did not appreciate the school board's accomplishments during the 1965–66 school year. Moreover, he argued, the Mattamuskeet School had no classroom space for additional black students. If more black children attended Mattamuskeet, "we would have to put them in tents." Cochran explained that Mattamuskeet was overcrowded already and that makeshift classrooms had been built in the gymnasium. "No matter how much we want to have more integration," Cochran told the HEW staff, "we do not have the facilities."[42]

Cochran's argument exposed a fundamental and deeply felt assumption of local school leaders: they would not send white children to the

O. A. Peay or Davis schools. Overcrowding at Mattamuskeet only prohibited school desegregation if the transfer of children occurred in one direction, from the black schools to Mattamuskeet. The limited space at Mattamuskeet would not pose a problem if white children transferred in equal numbers to the O. A. Peay and Davis schools. When the school board did not raise that option, Dewey Dodds eventually suggested the idea himself. His comment hit a very raw nerve, and it was the end of school desegregation planning for that afternoon. Superintendent Bucklew immediately argued that white children, not black children, were the troubled minority in Hyde County, because blacks represented 60 percent of students in the school district. Attorney Davis quickly agreed with him. "Those folk [blacks] are happy," he asserted. "They are more than content."[43] While HEW's staff never got the discussion back on track, the chatty and uninhibited banter that followed revealed a great deal about the school board's attitudes toward black students, the color line, and the social function of the black schools.

The local school leaders focused first on the alleged inferiority of black education. Ray Spencer, a Sladesville farmer and school board member, explained to Dodds and Echols that black students and teachers were "backwards" because they had studied in second-class institutions for so many generations. Black students simply could not be prepared to attend school with white children. If black and white children attended classes together, added Davis, the quality of education would have to suffer. "Either the white children are going to have to wait for the colored to catch up," he stated, "or the colored are going to have to drop back and let the white go on."[44]

The school leaders also expressed serious doubts about the behavior of black children. Spencer believed black teenagers would lower general expectations by not attending school regularly. Attorney Davis anticipated that black students would act disorderly in class, and he speculated that their conduct would be a drawback to the white children. He blamed the predicted bad behavior on a lack of home discipline. He and the school officials believed, in fact, that most black children did not value education as much as white children did. Contrasting Hyde County's blacks with A. J. Howell, a black member of the HEW team that was visiting the schools, Spencer observed that local blacks did not have the backgrounds that instilled a desire to learn. "I do not know how you are going to create [desire]," he told the group. "You are going to have to change the whole personality and attitude of the Negro people."[45]

The Hyde County officials argued further that black children would benefit most if they remained at Peay and Davis. Bucklew predicted that their dropout and expulsion rates would climb steeply after school desegregation. He had already expelled two black students at Mattamuskeet the previous year. The school board members agreed that segregated institutions best suited black children. In reality, however, they had only vague ideas about the real school life at Peay and Davis. They knew that on average the school district's black students scored significantly lower on standardized tests than white students, and black teachers typically had somewhat less formal training than their white counterparts. But their overarching image of the two schools had been shaped primarily by a faith in white superiority and the inherent inequality of black institutions. Their impression of Peay and Davis could not have contrasted more with the black community's view. Where Hyde County blacks perceived high expectations, rigid discipline, and challenging standards, white school leaders saw low expectations, poor discipline, and minimal standards. With racial attitudes and complex cultural values shaping both viewpoints, it was as if blacks and whites were not looking at the same schools.

Despite their poor assessment of educational quality at Peay and Davis, the school board and its staff still believed that the two schools were appropriate for black youngsters. At Davis or Peay, elaborated Ray Spencer, black students had the opportunity to get a high school diploma "whether or not they have gotten the education." At least then, he continued, when "a trucking outfit asks them if they have a high school diploma, they can show something." Similarly, Bucklew contended that the students would be ill-prepared for their life after graduation if they attended schools with white children. He clearly believed that the black school experience helped students to accept and understand a segregated society. While the school officials acknowledged exceptions, including the O. A. Peay graduate who had been admitted to the University of North Carolina at Chapel Hill the previous year, they envisioned the black schools as preparing the large majority of students for the limited opportunities and segregated society that Hyde County afforded them.

This notion that public schools ought to educate black children to accept their traditional second-class status had a long history in the white South. A generation earlier, even North Carolina school leaders who supported significant state funding for black schools had articulated this intention quite explicitly.[46] In the 1920s, for instance, the state's superintendent of public instruction, Eugene Brooks, had insisted that the General Assembly help to finance public schools for black children. "Otherwise," he warned, "they will be trained elsewhere and by other people who may not understand what is essential to the harmony and well-being of the two races."[47] At the time, this was a liberal idea; many rural whites still opposed all funding for black schools, no matter what the motivation. In the political discourse of the 1920s, racial harmony meant segregation, black disenfranchisement, and white superiority. The Hyde County school board had few other intentions in 1966; its members believed that segregation in education would support the "harmony and well-being" that remained the foundation of their bi-racial society. Bucklew swore that black parents also understood the need to prepare their children for segregation. "The colored people are not happy when they are in school with the white children," he told HEW's staff, "because they don't associate in everyday life."[48]

Indeed, the school officials argued that Hyde County's black citizens shared their commitment to racial harmony and did not want school desegregation. Suddenly changing his appraisal of the black schools' quality, George Davis explained to Dodds and Echols that local blacks had good schools with deep roots in their communities that they operated to suit their own needs. "They don't like the white folks' ways," he asserted, "and they do not want the white folks interfering with their system . . . [just as] they do not want to go to our churches." A school board member claimed that more blacks would have already transferred to the Mattamuskeet School if they really wanted school desegregation.[49] Since they had not been invited to the meeting, local blacks could not separate out the complex elements of deception and truth in this line of thinking. This argument, however, was a powerful double-edged sword that the school board would often wield. While using it as a ploy against federal intervention in local school affairs, the school board paradoxically touched on genuine concerns about school desegregation within the black community. Neither HEW nor the Hyde County Board of Education would fully realize the irony of this fatuous excuse not to desegregate until three years later, when the failure of whites to respect their educational heritage led blacks to mobilize in the school boycott.

Dewey Dodds struggled awkwardly to explain the role of school integration in what he called the "social revolution that is going on within this society," and he discussed in equally cumbersome fashion the nature of disempowerment and quiescence. But the Hyde County group had concluded that the schools could not—and should not—reform race relations so quickly.[50] In their eyes, Dodds was groping to rationalize school desegregation. They believed separate schools remained vital to the local social order and to the "race line" at its foundation, and they did not believe children should be forced to participate in what they called "social experiments." Dodds and Echols, on the other hand, viewed school desegregation as a necessary step toward racial equality.

At the end of the meeting, Dodds was prepared to stand on the law alone if moral persuasion proved inadequate. "Freedom of choice," he told them, "if it is accomplishing the purpose of Title VI of the Civil Rights Act, has to be *effective* as well as *fair*." But Bucklew concluded that he would rather go to federal court than, in his words, "assign a student to a school that they do not want to go to."[51] The school board agreed with him. The HEW team returned disappointed to Washington that evening, and the school leaders went home to prepare for the harvest season.

The Political Fight, 1966–1968

African American voice → silence

The relationship between HEW and the Hyde County Board of Education grew steadily more confrontational over the next two years. The school board moved as slowly as possible, constantly trying to avoid school desegregation or to determine the weakest reforms that the federal government would accept. The tensions displayed at the August 19 meeting in Swan Quarter tangled into a web of negotiations, threats, and legal actions. Black children by and large withdrew from the Mattamuskeet School back into the O. A. Peay and Davis schools, and their parents continued to be excluded from the conflict between local and federal officials.

Two other HEW officials, Anne Lassiter and W. Kenneth Haddock, talked with Bucklew by telephone on September 16, 1966. They discussed the fall registration and optimistically encouraged him to use his authority to accelerate school desegregation.[52] Bucklew had in fact already opened a new registration period for three weeks at the beginning of the school year. The results had not been promising: one black student at Mattamuskeet took the opportunity to return to a black school, and no black children had transferred to the white school. Haddock and Lassiter tried to persuade Bucklew to act unilaterally, either to transfer a number of black students to Mattamuskeet or to employ geographic zoning that bused children to the closest school. But Bucklew was unwilling to consider a school desegregation plan that required involuntary student assignment. Nonetheless, he wanted to avoid an impasse, so he told the HEW staff that another visit to Hyde County might be helpful.[53]

This meeting occurred in Swan Quarter two weeks later, on October 3. The school board and HEW's Dewey Dodds and Anne Lassiter had all grown considerably more frustrated and confrontational since the meeting in August. Citing recent lower court rulings, school board members immediately challenged HEW's authority over local school districts. Some also questioned the personal integrity of the HEW staff, and one asked Dodds about the possibility that he belonged to the Communist party.[54] Though the meeting progressed in a more civil tone, the two groups never negotiated seriously. The local officials revealed a stubborn rigidity, while Lassiter and Dodds spoke to them with an air of resignation and condescension.

During the meeting, the HEW delegation glibly described a model process for school desegregation while the local school officials said few words. Dodds and Lassiter discussed the value of community participation in school desegregation and outlined an elaborate program that included a series of community meetings, workshops, and a biracial planning committee.[55] They especially recommended that the school board bring together school personnel, students, and community representatives to plan the process. This proposal resembled the "good neighbor councils" established by many other school districts in North Carolina to ease community tensions and to assure greater citizen participation during school desegregation. The two visitors also encouraged the school board to send white students to Peay and Davis as well as black students to Mattamuskeet.

The school board members would not consider this last option and hardly discussed the plans laid out by the HEW staff. Utilizing Peay and Davis symbolized for them an authentic consolidation of white and black schooling that remained more inconceivable in their eyes than desegregation itself. They did not want to expose white children to black leadership, school governance, or educational traditions, and they feared that if they did, such a breakdown in white control could not be contained within the schools. Nonetheless, they instructed Bucklew to meet the next day with the three principals to plan a program for fuller desegregation. Nobody believed that this step amounted to more than an attempt to mollify HEW. Bucklew promised to report a new program to the federal officials by the next week, but Dodds and Lassiter did not expect much from him. On their return to Washington they recommended that their superiors begin the process to deny federal funds to the Hyde County school district if the new program did not show significantly more commitment to school desegregation. [56]

Three days later Bucklew met with the principals from the Peay, Davis, and Mattamuskeet schools. The situation was awkward for the two black principals. Though Fred Simons and Charles Boone privately supported school desegregation, they could not advocate effectively for it at this meeting. [57] Their security and influence was only as solid as their relationship with the school board and Bucklew. As in the past, they had to advance the concerns of the black community with caution, and they could not argue with Bucklew over how to handle an issue as volatile as school desegregation without risking their jobs. Moreover, Simons and Boone could stand on few local precedents for their involvement in educational matters that affected more than the black schools.

Consequently, Bucklew established the boundaries of discussion within the meeting. The agenda did not include community participation, geographic zoning, or student reassignment. Bucklew instead solicited from the three principals several less ambitious ideas that would increase to a small degree the level of interracial activity within the school district. The next day he wrote HEW's Dewey Dodds a letter describing several of those proposals. His new program would have integrated college extension classes for teachers, meetings of subject area teachers, and exhibitions of agriculture and shop class projects. Bucklew made clear that he was not considering more aggressive approaches. "It is our opinion," he concluded his letter to HEW, "that . . . these additional steps are the extent of our endeavors for this year."[58]

Not surprisingly, HEW was far from satisfied. Dodds was convinced that further negotiations with Hyde County officials would be fruitless.[59] John Hope, his director at HEW, subsequently wrote Superintendent Bucklew to inform him that his "program for preparation for desegregation . . . could hardly be expected to reverse the trend of student re-segregation which has begun in Hyde County."[60] Two days later, on October 27, Commissioner of Education Harold Howe informed the school board that HEW had abandoned its efforts to secure voluntary compliance. HEW immediately deferred new federal funds away from the school district and had its Office of General Counsel begin administrative actions to force compliance with the Civil Rights Act of 1964.[61]

The legal fight between HEW and the Hyde County Board of Education staggered slowly forward over the next two years, much like others in the South. Local school districts had several levels of appeal available to them within HEW before their cases could be sent to the Department of Justice's Office of Civil Rights for prosecution and enforcement—and they often used those opportunities to delay school desegregation indefinitely. The "court-ordered" desegregation plans that later drew so much ire and resentment were often the end result of those legal battles, but the large majority of school districts decided to settle with HEW rather than go to federal court. Whether or not desegregation conflicts ended in federal court, the process plodded, and negotiations could reopen at any stage and further delay a resolution.

When HEW declared its intention to cut Hyde County's federal funding, county officials claimed astonishment. In a letter to Secretary of HEW John Gardner, Bucklew complained that his school district had done everything required by HEW "except arbitrarily assign students of both races to schools they have not indicated a choice to attend."[62] The school leaders appealed HEW's decision and over the winter prepared for a hearing in Washington in April 1967. At a special session in March, school board members, their legal counsel, and Bucklew considered whether to proceed with the appeals or develop a new desegregation plan. Ultimately they decided to abide with their current plan as long as the state board of education supported them.[63] The North Carolina Department of Public Instruction had become a voluntary codefendant, providing the Hyde County school board with legal counsel from the Washington law firm of Southerland, Asbill and Brennan to represent the school board before HEW's administrative law judges. This firm represented several other school districts in North Carolina in similar proceedings with HEW.

The HEW examiners denied appeals by the Hyde County Board of Education in April and June 1967, declaring that the school board "operated the schools in a way to deprive the Negro school age children of their constitutional rights to a desegregated education."[64] Before the case could move to the Justice Department, J. D. Williams, the school board's attorney at the Southerland law firm, attempted to negotiate a new desegregation plan with the Office of General Counsel at HEW. Peter Goldschmidt, who was handling the case for HEW, had apparently told Williams that a settlement might be reached if the local officials held a new "freedom of choice" period prior to the fall semester, accompanied by a good public relations campaign encouraging black families to send their children to the Mattamuskeet School. Goldschmidt believed those steps would lead to a "substantial amount of student desegregation," according to a July 4 letter from Williams to local attorney George Davis.[65]

What HEW considered a "substantial amount of school desegregation" remained very little. Because of understaffing, the complexity of enforcement, and the lack of political support from the White House and Congress, HEW had failed to enforce a high standard for school desegregation after passage of the Civil Rights Act. Between 1965 and 1967, school desegregation plans that achieved the most modest success were often accepted by HEW.[66] The situation in Hyde County was typical in this respect. Based on his discussions with Goldschmidt, Williams advised the Hyde County Board of Education that HEW would agree to a settlement if 6 percent of all black students transferred to the Mattamuskeet School.[67] This goal would have been met if, of the approximately 850 black students enrolled at O. A. Peay and Davis, only fifty-one—instead of the current three—attended Mattamuskeet. Nothing was said about encouraging or requiring white students to transfer to black schools.

If HEW would truly accept a desegregation plan that required only a few dozen black students to attend Mattamuskeet and no white children to relocate to Peay or Davis, the local officials were gladly willing to enact a new "freedom of choice" period. Evidently anticipating its success, they encouraged Goldschmidt to visit Hyde County to discuss a settlement.[68] The school board saw the proposed plan as a very containable threat, and a couple of members had long held that school desegregation might be acceptable if only the "talented tenth" of black students transferred to the white school. But a goal of 6 percent black enrollment was still a long way from the current 0.3 percent at Mattamuskeet. In fact, the die had already been cast. White resistance to school desegregation was still strong, black distrust still deep, and school leadership still unprepared to overcome those tensions. The school board allowed students to select new schools from August 16 to 29 but failed to enroll a single black student at Mattamuskeet. When the new school year began, the conflict was still headed for the federal courts.

New winds were blowing that would soon force the Hyde County Board of Education to reconsider school desegregation. In the fall of 1967, HEW began to display greater will and less flexibility, largely because of new authority from the federal courts. That March the Fifth Circuit Court of Appeals had ruled against a school desegregation plan very similar to Hyde County's in a nearby southside Virginia school district. In *Green v. County School Board of New Kent County*, the federal court basically held that only school integration plans that eliminated the dual school system in practice were legal, no matter what the plans' motivations, goodwill, or theoretical efficacy.[69] This ruling, which most observers believed would be upheld by the Supreme Court, undermined "freedom of choice" plans throughout the South. Bolstered by this decision, HEW's Office of Civil Rights began in October to require final plans for eliminating segregated school systems, with successful implementation of those plans by September 1969.

The likelihood that failure to comply with HEW's requirements would lead to litigation with the Department of Justice and to the imposition of a desegregation plan drawn by the federal courts grew steadily. School officials particularly feared the prospect of desegregation blueprints imposed by judges. An increasingly common outcome of federal battles with recalcitrant school districts, a court-ordered plan would have effectively removed white officials' authority over the school district and could easily have opened up desegregation planning to local blacks. A federal lawsuit of the sort already filed in neighboring Beaufort County by the NAACP Legal Defense and Educational Fund could have the same result.[70] In addition to those concerns, federal courts more frequently were holding state governments responsible for helping local school districts evade desegregation. North Carolina's Department of Public Instruction had consequently grown more reluctant to support such school districts, and its financial and legal assistance in fighting HEW could no longer be taken for granted. Faced with these realities, the Hyde County school board made its first serious moves toward school desegregation.

Shaping School Desegregation

While black citizens may have hoped that school desegregation would be the opening wedge in breaking down broader patterns of racism in Hyde County, white school administrators were determined to limit its impact. Having been forced to bend to federal intervention by the fall of 1967, the school board would hereafter fight to channel this "social revolution," in Dodds's earlier words, into old patterns of social order and white supremacy. School desegregation need not disturb the race line otherwise, even with respect to educational administration. White authorities knew that carefully calibrated concessions could potentially strengthen their power to mold a school desegregation plan on their terms. The determination to shut down the black schools only symbolized the continuity of white control.

At its regular meeting on October 25, 1967, the Hyde County Board of Education resolved that school desegregation would subvert local democracy, threaten peaceful race relations, and destroy the quality of schooling.[71] The board members placed the blame for the anticipated debacle squarely and solely on the federal government. Then they passed several resolutions designed to placate HEW. On the advice of HEW's legal counsel and field staff, they moved first to eliminate two of the more glaring disparities between the Mattamuskeet School and the two black schools. Because Mattamuskeet had much better vocational shop facilities than Peay or Davis, the school board decided to bus black children to the white school for shop classes. The school board also created a biracial class of "gifted students" who would study English and history together at Mattamuskeet. The black students would be bused from their schools to the white institution specifically for those classes.[72]

Beyond those steps, the school board resolved to spend its next surplus funds to consolidate all three student bodies into the Mattamuskeet

School. In order not to use former black schools, southern school districts regularly invested enormous energy and money in building new schools or enlarging white schools. Their struggles to avoid sending white children to historically black schools often bordered on the ludicrous. Even when they had only recently built black schools and, aiming to avoid pressure to desegregate, had endowed them with first-rate facilities, white school boards again and again shut down the black institutions and sent their children to white ones. Closing black schools had come in many cases to symbolize the last stand of white control over education.

The Hyde County school board's plan to avoid utilizing the black schools would of course require an enormous building expansion at Mattamuskeet, and the school board did not discuss when funds for so ambitious a project might become available. The county was still repaying its debt on the bond issues that financed construction of Mattamuskeet and expansions at O. A. Peay in 1964. But board members believed that HEW should be satisfied with their latest compromises. They stipulated that their plan would only go into effect when HEW agreed not to initiate any court action that school term.[73]

Pressure to utilize the black institutions in a school desegregation plan grew greater yet when HEW did not accept the new concessions in early 1968. The problem concerned the large number of improvements necessary to enable the Mattamuskeet School to accommodate the 852 black students at Peay and Davis.[74] Mattamuskeet was in fact overcrowded with its own 514 students; the gymnasium and storage facilities were already employed as classrooms, and two new classrooms were under emergency construction. HEW simply did not believe the school could house a significant number of black students, and the Hyde County Board of Education simply did not have the money to enlarge Mattamuskeet. HEW's deadline for achieving meaningful school desegregation was less than a year away, and it seemed that sufficient expansion at Mattamuskeet could not occur by then.

Utilizing all three schools seemed like the only available course of action. Converting black high schools into lower grade schools was not uncommon in the South. HEW officials clearly believed it was the only way for Hyde County to implement an acceptable plan by September. The school board had exhausted its appeals at HEW and could soon anticipate a Justice Department lawsuit. HEW attorney Goldschmidt could not fathom why the board would not consider converting Peay and Davis into elementary schools and making Mattamuskeet the high school.[75] Even J. D. Williams, the school board's own legal counsel, did not understand the school officials' unwillingness to send white children to the two black schools, though he had observed the attitude throughout the South. "I have never been able to grasp the concept that white children will not attend a school simply because it . . . was . . . a Negro school," Williams wrote to George Davis and Allen Bucklew in May 1968. He suggested that the school board consider "renaming, repainting, and refurbishing" O. A. Peay and Davis and using them as elementary schools. He warned his clients that this was the only way to reach a settlement with HEW outside of the courtroom.[76]

Though HEW officials saw the logic of including Davis and O. A. Peay in a desegregation plan, their commitment to the black schools was another matter. Later that May, the school board proposed a new plan to HEW that excluded the black institutions but required state and federal endorsement. The willingness of state and federal agencies to support the school board would reveal that they shared many of the board's assumptions concerning the black schools and the black role in school desegregation. Through J. D. Williams, local school officials proposed to gradually transfer all black children from Peay and Davis to Mattamuskeet. They argued that this schedule would allow time to expand the school. If three or four grades transferred every year, the construction program would only have to accommodate a third of the black students every year. The first several grades could be transferred at the beginning of the 1968–69 school year, within HEW's deadline, and the two black schools would close entirely at the end of the 1969–70 school year. The board reasoned that the expansion could be financed by diverting 60 to 70 percent of the county's annual ESEA funds to the building program.

HEW did not require Hyde to use the black schools and acted satisfied with this new plan, including its three-year timetable. In a letter to a disgruntled parent, an agency spokesman later explained, "We realize . . . many school districts are abolishing the dual school structures by discontinuing Negro schools . . . , [but] we are not authorized to [prohibit] such actions if they are taken to eliminate the dual school system."[77] Neither the executive branch nor the federal courts required more than a unitary school system. Nor did they require black participation in decisions related to school desegregation, though HEW policy encouraged it, and they most often left the implementation of school desegregation to local white school boards.

Before HEW could approve the school desegregation plan, the Hyde County Board of Education had to seek permission from Raleigh to divert the ESEA funds necessary to finance the building program. ESEA funds originated with the federal government, but the states had the principal authority over their dispersal. Since the money was intended to support educational programs for children from disadvantaged backgrounds, spending it for a building program reflected a very liberal interpretation of the original legislation. However, federal courts had not yet prohibited the practice. Speaking for HEW, Goldschmidt found the diversion irregular and would not consent to help Hyde County school officials persuade North Carolina's Department of Public Instruction to permit it. Andy Vanore, the school board's liaison at the attorney general's office in North Carolina, was also pessimistic about the possibility of approval, but he left it an open question.[78]

Rejection of the plan to divert ESEA funds would almost certainly have kept the O. A. Peay and Davis schools open. But in fact, tentative approval was forthcoming almost immediately. State officials still sought to help local school districts handle desegregation issues in their own way. Having opposed school desegregation for so long, they were hardly committed to being fair to black communities during its implementation. Moreover, a series of federal court rulings in the spring of 1968 pressed them to desegregate quickly. In May the Supreme Court had found that school districts still having separate schools under voluntary plans indicated "precisely the pattern of segregation" that *Brown* had ruled unconstitutional.[79] Later that month, the court had specifically ordered North Carolina to accelerate school desegregation.[80] Finally, a Johnston County case that would soon give the state an affirmative obligation to see that desegregation occurred in local school districts was moving rapidly through lower federal courts toward the Supreme Court. A memorandum from the state's Department of Public Instruction to school superintendents had already declared unequivocally that school districts could find "no escape."[81]

The Department of Public Instruction did not permit the Hyde County Board of Education to divert from ESEA funds the $60,000 to $70,000 a year it had requested. The state agency deemed that amount too large a proportion of the county's $118,000 annual allocation. But state officials would allow a diversion of $32,000 a year to the building program, and they pledged another $30,000 a year for construction costs out of the state's pocket.[82] This money would enable the school district to finance twelve new classrooms at the Mattamuskeet School each year of the three-year program.

With this support at the state and federal levels, the Hyde County school board approved the desegregation plan at its May 24, 1968 meeting. Grades one through three would transfer from Peay and Davis to Mattamuskeet that fall. Grades one through eight would attend the school a year later. By the 1970–71 school year, all black children would be transferred and the black schools closed. The teachers at Peay and Davis would be transferred in a similar fashion.[83] The school board submitted the plan to HEW a week later, on May 31, and the Office of Civil Rights approved it for 1968–69 on July 3. HEW then informed the state's Department of Public Instruction that the school district could again receive federal funds and suspended its administrative review until the next year.[84]

In Hyde County, school officials worked furiously through the humid summer months to prepare for black students at Mattamuskeet. They soon developed a plan for two buildings, an elementary school and a high school, at the Lake Comfort site. They purchased new land in July and began to accept construction bids for the first classrooms.[85] To provide enough space for the new students by September, they rushed to acquire two mobile trailers and build four new classrooms; once again, however, they decided that classes would meet in the gymnasium.[86] They also made plans to convert the Davis School into a local branch of Beaufort County Community College and turn the O. A. Peay School into an office building in 1970.

The school desegregation plan finally approved by the Hyde County Board of Education, HEW, and state officials differed in no significant way from the majority of such plans elsewhere in North Carolina and other southern states. School desegregation was a remarkable and pivotally important accomplishment for the civil rights movement, but it did not merge black and white schools so much as obliterate black schools. In Hyde County, as in most school districts, desegregation had become a one-way street through which black students entered former white schools. White leaders had successfully preserved their control over the local schools despite having school desegregation forced on them. The possible threat to the broader race line in Hyde County also seemed minimal. The closing of the black schools indicated further that school desegregation apparently need not presage racial equality or black empowerment. Consequently, among white school leaders the conflict over desegregation seemed by the summer of 1968 to have been settled along familiar lines accepted by most citizens in other southern school districts.

CHAPTER 2

Tired of Having to Bear the Burdens

Abell Fulford, Jr., at first could not believe that the school desegregation plan accepted by HEW required closing the O. A. Peay and Davis schools. Though he was president of the O. A. Peay School's alumni association, Fulford had not known that such a plan was under consideration. Neither the school board nor HEW had consulted him, and Hyde County did not have local media that might have alerted him earlier. On hearing the news in early July 1968, Fulford immediately discussed the school closings with other alumni leaders, most of whom had studied under O. A. Peay himself during the three decades after 1930, when "the founder" had been a county school principal. Those men and women shared a strong devotion to the O. A. Peay School, and they agreed that the school board and HEW, according to alumnus Golden Mackey, "[did] not have the right to take something belonging to us."[1]

The threatened closing of Peay and Davis collided with educational traditions that had helped to sustain the Hyde County black community since Reconstruction. Regardless of white perceptions or intentions, for five generations black educators, parents, and children had conspired with considerable success to build schools that would prepare their students for intellectual achievement and racial advancement. After the school board decided to shut down Peay and Davis, local blacks began to fear that school desegregation was threatening—rather than enhancing—this tradition of achievement. They were not alone. Civil rights workers and government field staff had started to notice a new disquiet in black communities undergoing school desegregation. HEW's A. J. Howell warned in the fall of 1968 that "Negroes are tired of having to bear the burdens of integration."[2]

"A Sense of Mission"

For black Hyde Countians in 1968, the O. A. Peay School embodied a rich educational heritage that dated back at least a century. One has to begin looking that long ago to understand how they reacted to the threat of losing the school. When the school board decided to close Peay and Davis, the older black residents could still recall their parents' and grandparents' stories about attending classes in bush tents only a few months and years after gaining their freedom in the Civil War.[3] As a black educator said later, the commitment to education was "[in] our blood from way back."[4] By 1872, black residents had already built several one-room schoolhouses. They supported sixteen schools by 1886, twenty by 1896.[5] They cleared the land and erected the buildings with their own hands and somehow found money enough to supplement a teacher's salary and purchase a slate for most children. Furnished only with long benches and cast-iron stoves, the schools often served fifty students in a sixteen-by-twenty-four-foot room. School terms would later stretch to five and six months a year, but most schools at first offered only two six-week sessions for when the children were not working in the fields.[6] The struggle to feed and clothe a family had priority in those days when hunger lay waiting beyond every hard winter and poor harvest. Teachers and students "made do" with what they had, when they had it.

Those grade schools grew into a fundamental part of black life in Hyde County. Black citizens organized schools not only in the larger settlements of Fairfield, Engelhard, Swan Quarter, and Scranton, but also in remote hamlets like St. Lydia, Slocumb, Nebraska, the Cove, California, and the Ridge. The schools attracted students from as far as a child could walk. The Tiny Oak School, for example, founded in 1887 and located "o'er the quarter," drew black children from a four-mile radius, from Tiny Oak to Juniper Bay. Such schools figured prominently in the daily life of their surrounding communities. Local residents used the school buildings for square dances, basket parties, festivals, and other assemblies. Schools and churches often shared a building, and church congregations saw support and upkeep of the school as an extension of their Christian duty. Some mutual aid groups and lodges organized on principles of Christian charity, such as the Loving Charity Lodge in the Ridge community, also loaned their buildings for daytime use as schools.[7] By the end of the 1930s, black citizens supported as many as forty such grade schools in Hyde County, and the number did not decline significantly until black school consolidation in 1949.[8]

One of these community schools, located in Sladesville, evolved into the O. A. Peay School. Mary W. Cox and her older students cleared the land for the Sladesville Graded School in 1913. Three years later, the county's first "Negro supervisor," Rhoda Warren, began to campaign for a campus in Sladesville that would offer Hyde County's black children more than a grade school education.[9] The Alabama native clearly possessed extraordinary will, vision, and faith. While local men and women had built and maintained many grade schools, the establishment of the county's first black secondary school faced special difficulties. A handful of local families already sent children away to study at black high schools in Beaufort and Pasquotank counties. But most did not have the resources to clothe and supply children all the way through grade school, much less through high school.[10] Students who did not reside in Sladesville would also have to board with local families, which meant an added expense and often a prohibitive loss of help around the household. In addition, recruiting qualified high school teachers to so remote a locale would not be easy.

Most important, a black high school would receive only the most minimal public funds. In North Carolina few rural public schools, black or white, received adequate government support, but black schools still faced extraordinary disadvantages compared with white schools. As late as 1916, neither the state nor any of its counties had financed a single four-year public high school for black children.[11] Even in the grade schools, black teachers then earned only half what their white counterparts did—a far worse proportion, in fact, than before the rise of Jim Crow in the 1890s—and public investment per pupil in school property was four to one in favor of white children.[12] The secondary education campaign sweeping the white South had totally excluded black schools. Consequently, Hyde County blacks were forced to accept the same kind of "double taxation" that other black southerners had experienced since Reconstruction. They paid local taxes that public officials diverted to support the white schools, then made private contributions of cash, land, and labor to bolster their own schools.[13]

Rhoda Warren died in 1919, but she had sown seeds that bore fruit in ensuing years. While students temporarily attended classes at Zion Temple Baptist, an important Sladesville church founded only two years

Administration Building, Hyde County Training School. ("Memories of the Hyde County Training School Banner, 1940")

after the Civil War, black citizens remodeled and expanded the grade school in 1921. They renamed it the Hyde County Training School (HCTS) and offered nine grades the first year and eleven grades by 1928. The school would always struggle against official indifference and a scarcity of funds. Compared with the white high schools in Swan Quarter and Engelhard, the HCTS would always be allocated less money for equipment, books, bus service, staff, salaries, and upkeep. As the 1920s ended, the school still had neither the staff nor the resources to offer a twelve-year education.

Oscar A. Peay arrived at the Hyde County Training School in 1930 during the Great Depression. Originally from the Deep South, and a graduate of Atlanta University, the devout young teacher committed his life to the school, serving as principal until his retirement in 1961. Peay and his wife Mary Carter Peay, the school's mathematics teacher, recruited a group of talented and earnest educators who understood the poverty and racism that hindered blacks in Hyde County. Those men and women believed that education was the only route available by which their students and the community could "advance as a race," in former teacher Marjorie Selby's words. The HCTS teachers believed

Prof. O. A. Peay crowns the queen at the annual May Day Festival at the Hyde County Training School. (Selby et al., Hyde County History)

that they had to sustain "a sense of mission" not shared by white educators. They were preparing their students "to contribute to society [and] to help somebody."[14] They believed that the black community would depend on their students, and HCTS alumni long remembered the sense of obligation to make a contribution to the community that was instilled in them.[15]

Peay and his teachers believed that local social conditions required special sensibilities in and out of the classroom. They acquainted themselves with their students at home, in the community, and at church, and they tried to employ all of those institutions to improve the children's educations. The quiet rural atmosphere in Sladesville favored this approach. Located on a marshy peninsula between Rose Bay and the Pungo River, the village was small and isolated, and its life revolved around the new school. The HCTS teachers and local boosters acted as surrogate parents for the students, and they welcomed the young people into a tight-knit and caring community. Their concerns ranged from assuring that the students ate good meals to chaperoning dates. Even after the school moved to Job's Corner and students no longer boarded nearby, the HCTS educators still understood that parents who worked day and night at a seafood packing house, or who had moved north to find a job and left their children to be reared by grandparents, had entrusted them as much to oversee the students' general well-being and development as to teach the three R's.

Community and school life naturally intertwined, especially during the Sladesville years. Phillip Greene, a Peay protégé who became the school's principal in 1971, remembered that the founder required his students to attend Sunday school classes and regularly taught Sunday school lessons that complemented course work at the training school. Teachers attended church with their students and often visited the families where they boarded. Conscious of their roles as mentors, they allowed older children to accompany them to community events and even on daily errands that provided opportunities for conversation and guidance.[16] The school also became a community center for blacks all over Hyde County. Civic and church groups held adult classes, choir rehearsals, benefit concerts, and social events in the main building, and the HCTS staff organized clubs and other activities that included both students and unenrolled children.[17]

The HCTS teachers set high standards and constantly put new challenges in front of their students. According to the alumni, the teachers urged them to improve themselves and prodded them not to be satisfied with the limitations that Hyde County imposed. "You *can* do something," Peay and his teachers repeatedly told the students; "*You* can make it."[18] Though few of their students' parents had graduated from grade school, the educators encouraged the children to finish twelfth grade, which was first offered at the training school in 1934, and to continue their educations. Knowing that many students would migrate out of the South in order to find jobs or escape Jim Crow, they consciously sought to prepare them to excel anywhere. They reasoned that a white school in Hyde County might justifiably prepare children for a farming and fishing life, because many white students would inherit enough land or wealth to make a good living locally. A black school could not afford to nurture that illusion. But the teachers also emphasized a duty to Hyde County, and they fully expected the better students to return home to teach in the schools. A stern dress code, strict discipline, and daily prayer reinforced these high expectations.

The curriculum also supported such concerns. In most respects, "training school" was a misnomer. The school did not train domestic workers and oyster shuckers. The HCTS had originally been called a training school to mollify the local school board and northern philanthropists who donated part of the original construction costs. Documentation of the earliest curricula remains too sparse to draw firm conclusions about its character, but by the 1940s black educators had clearly oriented the school's curriculum toward the liberal arts and college preparation. The school offered home economics and agriculture classes, but standard coursework included English, chemistry, physics, a foreign language, and three levels of mathematics. The students' aspirations confirmed the nature of their classroom instruction. Of the fifteen HCTS graduates in 1940, for example, ten had career goals that required at least some college education. Five graduates planned to become trained nurses; three, teachers; one, a physician; and one, a pastor. Of the other graduating seniors that year, three hoped to become professional musicians; one, a stenographer; and one, a beautician.[19]

The paucity of county or state support required the Hyde County Training School to depend on the black community. Guided by the educators, especially vocational teachers B. W. Barnes and Seward Selby, the older students and many community volunteers improved the school facilities as high school enrollment grew from only eighteen in 1930 to more than a hundred three decades later.[20] Over the years, they landscaped the school grounds, drained and built up the playground, laid cement walkways, replaced walls, added a lunchroom, purchased buses, and spearheaded many other improvements. Community people regularly supplied the school with firewood, supplies, and equipment and often boarded both teachers and students. When the school relocated in Job's Corner in 1953, black citizens donated a major portion of the land. Parents and alumni later raised funds for the playground, athletic and laboratory equipment, books, cafeteria furniture, a new

Hyde County Training School faculty. Left to right: Senia Sheperd Johnson, Annie Bonner, John Raleigh Spencer, O. A. Peay, Rosa Mackey Bell, Beulah Kelsey McNair, Lucie B. Hargraves. Standing: Seward Selby, Rosaliner Hill Peay. (Selby et al., Hyde County History)

kitchen stove, and gymnasium curtains. With Principal Peay's en-couragement, community boosters supported the school through their churches and civic groups; they also organized an alumni association and a Parent Teacher Organization (PTO) to raise money for college scholarships and other school needs.

Founded in the early 1950s, the alumni association perhaps best reflected this school loyalty and commitment. The HCTS alumni first organized chapters locally and in Brooklyn, New York, where black Hyde Countians had been migrating in large numbers for generations. As more graduates moved north, they also organized chapters in several other Eastern Seaboard cities. The alumni chapters held local fund-raisers and reunions to support the school and the children "back home." Their members identified job and educational opportunities for HCTS students, and they often oriented recent graduates to new homes in Washington, Philadelphia, or Brooklyn. For men and women who had moved away from Hyde County reluctantly, the alumni association not only connected them to the training school but also soothed their homesickness for family and community down South. It was a powerful bond to their childhoods as well as to their native land. This bond bred a fierce loyalty. By the 1960s, the Alumni Homecoming had become the biggest social and cultural event in Hyde County. Every Memorial Day weekend, busloads of former classmates and educators returned home from across the nation to celebrate their achievements, the promise of the new students, and the tradition of struggle personified by the school.

At the request of black citizens, the school board renamed the Hyde County Training School in honor of O. A. Peay after his death in 1963. Under his leadership, the school had survived and become a nucleus of the black community despite terrible underfunding, racial discrimina-tion, and official neglect. By 1968, the O. A. Peay School was a source of inestimable pride to Hyde County blacks and symbolized their aspira-tions for education and racial advancement. Though the institution was obviously under the formal authority of the Hyde County Board of Education, black citizens believed that, in the most meaningful sense, the O. A. Peay School belonged to them.

Hyde County blacks had never intended to sacrifice those achievements or this legacy for the sake of school desegregation. They had hoped to merge their schools and way of schooling on equal terms with whites.

Anyone who considered the process seriously knew, of course, that compromises would be required. Certainly they, like many other southern blacks, had quite often discussed advantages and disadvantages of school desegregation in the years since *Brown*, but outside their community they usually remained silent about any misgivings. Prior to 1965, most black leaders in Hyde County had overcome any ambivalence toward school desegregation by considering its enormous potential for fostering greater racial equality and better schools. The potential gain had outweighed other concerns. By 1968, however, the calculus of what was going to be gained and what was going to be lost had shifted.

Large numbers of black citizens had been disenchanted by what they had seen of school desegregation between 1965 and 1968. They had observed the treatment of the few black children who attended Mattamuskeet during "freedom of choice," and they had not liked what they had seen. The discrimination and alienation felt by those children had given the white school a bad reputation among Davis and O. A. Peay students, some of whom expressed fears of being mistreated at Mattamuskeet. Many parents worried that their children would be consigned to a second-class status at the school. One rumor held that black students might be segregated within Mattamuskeet, possibly in the mobile home trailers that the school board was purchasing with ESEA funds.[21]

Black attitudes were also influenced by the way that white school leaders and extremists had handled the school desegregation process to that point. Ku Klux Klan and other anti-integrationist threats made many blacks both fear for the safety of their children and doubt the goodwill of white citizens generally. The failure of the Hyde County Board of Education to include black leaders in shaping the school desegregation plan was even more troubling. Black parents had begun to doubt that they would have significant influence over their children's educations or reasonable access to educators at the school. They believed that the school board had not shown respect for their opinions or their tradition of schooling thus far; how could they expect to receive any such respect when the children had to attend Mattamuskeet?[22]

They had also been learning that black school closings were likely to be accompanied by the demotion or dismissal of black employees. It was widely known that other school boards nearby had demoted black principals and dismissed black teachers during school desegregation. The demotion of James Ambrose, the respected principal of a black high

school in Beaufort County, was especially notorious.[23] Blacks expected
to see similar problems in Hyde County if Peay and Davis were shut
down. They worried about the educational consequences of losing
school leaders and teachers and about the prospect of not having as
many black educational leaders to connect the schools to their own
communities. Also, they could not help but be concerned about the
economic impact of closing Peay and Davis. The two schools were
among the largest local employers of blacks, and they also offered
the only available jobs requiring a college education. The North Carolina Teachers Association, the black affiliate of the NEA, had already
warned Hyde County's teachers to expect problems, and local black
educators indeed felt especially threatened by the plan to shut down
their schools. "There's only going to be one principal and a certain
number of teachers," one concerned instructor said, "and I don't believe
the whites are going to have any trouble getting first dibs."[24]

Most black citizens in Hyde County, as throughout the South, had
supported the NAACP's campaign for school desegregation. But by 1968
the serious threat to the black schools and the inequitable burdens of
school desegregation had begun to raise new concerns. More and more
blacks began to ask themselves how much they were willing to sacrifice
for school desegregation. Many began to feel that white officials were
forcing them to choose unnecessarily between their educational heritage and racial equality. Almost all blacks expected to lose something
during the implementation of school desegregation; merging two races,
classes, and traditions into the same schools would have always required
many trade-offs and sacrifices by black and white citizens alike. But the
more school desegregation resembled a complete subsumption of black
students into the Mattamuskeet School, the more Hyde County blacks
feared for their children and communities and reassessed the sacrifices
of school desegregation.

The calculation of costs and benefits naturally yielded different answers,
even among Hyde County blacks. Many local NAACP leaders, in an
important exception to the majority opinion, greeted the new desegregation plan with a combination of enthusiasm and relief. The thinking of
those NAACP leaders, in fact, probably reflected the reasoning common to most African American communities in the South. If this
reasoning had prevailed, it would have led local blacks to accept the

closing of Peay and Davis as an unfortunate sacrifice for school desegregation. Johnnie Midgette, Early Bryant, and other NAACP leaders realized the new plan was not equitable but recognized it as a major advance.[25] Fourteen years had passed since *Brown*, yet only a few black students attended classes with white children in Hyde County. In North Carolina overall, almost three-quarters of black students remained in single-race classes.[26] Under the school board's plan, black and white children would at least attend school together, and racial discrimination in education would presumably come to an end.

The NAACP leaders also believed that raising too many objections to the school desegregation plan might endanger other gains. The national political climate had changed dramatically since passage of the Voting Rights Act in 1965. Civil rights groups had lost much of their power, and many black leaders were reluctant to postpone school desegregation further. In North Carolina, Democratic presidential candidate Hubert Humphrey would soon finish a distant third in the 1968 election, behind both Richard Nixon and George Wallace, largely because of vehement white opposition to school desegregation. A political backlash could already be seen within Congress, and the Johnson administration had wavered in its support for school desegregation in order not to alienate southern white voters before the November elections.[27] Many civil rights leaders reasoned that black demands for fair school desegregation plans might feed this white backlash and threaten school integration itself.[28]

NAACP leaders also saw some educational advantages for black children in the proposed plan. They believed, for example, that a single large school would increase course offerings available to black students. They looked forward to their children having larger libraries, better equipment, and newer textbooks. In addition, converting the Davis School into a community college branch would have provided an unprecedented opportunity for blacks to receive some higher education without leaving the county.[29] Johnnie Midgette and other NAACP leaders believed those long-term advantages would eventually be more important than the short-term pain of losing the black schools.

"To Keep the Schools Open No Matter What"

Abell Fulford, Jr., and the other school activists who met at Mt. Pilgrim Disciples Church in Sladesville in the sweltering heat of early July did not agree with that view. Since learning about the proposed school closings, they had attended the next school board session and had discussed the situation with Superintendent Bucklew. They had also informed local black leaders in the PTOs, the teachers' association, the parent advisory councils, and the NAACP about the school closings.[30] Apparently none of them had been consulted by the school board either. This fact reinforced a cynicism about white goodwill that the assassination of Martin Luther King, Jr., had recently brought to the boiling point. The threat to Peay and Davis seemed like one more attempt to tarnish a noble cause—in this case, school integration—that had promised racial equality and fellowship. At the meeting in Sladesville, the black leaders decided that the school closings were simply too great a risk and too large an affront to accept without a fight. Though they supported school integration, they nevertheless balked at the price. The group agreed they must first quickly inform the rest of the black community about the school board's intentions and begin to organize for a new plan.[31] Since they hoped to change the plan before the beginning of the school year in September, there was little time.

Fulford was chosen to lead this effort. Though he had never been a civil rights or political activist, he was a well-respected church and civic leader. He lived in Job's Corner near the O. A. Peay School and had been a school booster since his own graduation from the training school in 1945. Following in the footsteps of his father, who had been a prominent local minister, Fulford was also one of the younger deacons at Job's Chapel Baptist Church and a leader in the Masonic Lodge.[32] He belonged to the local NAACP chapter, which his father had co-founded, but had never been very active in it. He was steady, reliable, and not easily provoked.

His employment with the North Carolina Mutual Life Insurance Company provided Fulford with several special advantages for the task before him. Based in Durham, North Carolina, Mutual was the largest black-owned insurance firm in the United States.[33] Mutual agents traveled door to door in even the most rural locales selling policies tailored to black families and collecting small monthly premiums. As the local Mutual agent, Fulford was something of a rarity in Hyde County. He had flexible working hours, did not have a local white employer who could retaliate against him for his activism, and was acquainted with almost every black family living between the Pungo River and Wysocking Bay.

Fulford contacted the deacons at every black church in the county and arranged to discuss the school desegregation plan with their congregations.[34] The churches were a natural forum for the school crisis. Black life in Hyde County, as in the rural South generally, revolved around the church and the school, the "preacher and the teacher." The churches and schools reinforced and supported one another and shared fully the burdens of education, spiritual development, and community service. Fulford and the other alumni leaders also knew that the church congregations possessed the organization, leadership, and commitment necessary to deal with the school closings.

During the last weeks in July, Fulford discussed the school desegregation plan at Sunday worship or weeknight prayer services in every black church in Hyde County. He first related what he had learned about the plan from school officials and told the congregations that the alumni leaders could not see good motivations or practical reasons behind the school board's decision to shut down O. A. Peay and Davis. Both schools were well located, relatively new, and in good condition. Closing the two schools would overcrowd Mattamuskeet and put many students in mobile home trailers. The building program might also result in greater county debt and higher taxes. In addition, the diversion of ESEA funds to construction would reduce educational programs for poor children. Fulford also explained that the school board had not consulted black leaders about any plan that required closing O. A. Peay or Davis. "Everybody was against closing the schools," Fulford remembered later.[35]

Fulford recruited two persons from each of the seven key congregations, involving every local denomination, to serve on a countywide committee charged with advocating a new school desegregation plan. The "Committee of 14" included eight women and six men who had all demonstrated leadership in church affairs. Several were church deacons. Most were domestic workers, farmers, and—in Fulford's words—other "regular poor people."[36] Educators, the only true black middle class in Hyde County, were not chosen because of their vulnerability to retaliation from the school board. Black teachers would, however, frequently attend meetings and serve as advisers. Ministers would have been natural choices in many southern communities, but not a single black minister resided within Hyde County in 1968. Served monthly or bimonthly by visiting pastors, the churches relied more regularly on their deacons, elders, and other lay leaders.

In Fulford's words, the committee members "were used to speaking up." Albert Whitaker, for example, had long been an outspoken member of the NAACP and of the PTO at the O. A. Peay School.[37] Pencie Collins and Rosa Adams were leaders among the crab pickers and oyster shuckers in Engelhard. Etta Mae Greene, a church deacon herself and the cafeteria director at the O. A. Peay School, had devoted her life to charitable activities. Rosa O'Neal and Fulford himself, representing Job's Chapel Baptist, were of course strong supporters of the alumni association. Chosen from a wide variety of churches, the committee members crossed the most important boundaries of geography, family, and class within the black community. "With those people," Fulford later concluded, "we organized the whole county."[38]

When members of the Committee of 14 visited with the superintendent on July 29, 1968, to express their opposition to the school desegregation plan, Bucklew paid little attention to their concerns and even refused them a formal copy of the plan.[39] The closing of the O. A. Peay and Davis schools remained a fait accompli to Bucklew and the school board. They were preparing frantically for the influx of black children at Mattamuskeet in September and hardly welcomed new complaints. They would not consider revisions of the desegregation plan and blamed HEW for any dissatisfaction. Other, more informal meetings with school officials had the same results.

At the request of several NAACP members, James Ferguson II, one of the most prominent civil rights attorneys in North Carolina, sent an investigator to Hyde County to meet with black leaders about the school situation. Ferguson had already played a pivotal role in the civil rights movement in North Carolina. He had led or been involved in most of the civil rights lawsuits arising in eastern North Carolina; he had been successful enough to have the Ku Klux Klan target him for assassination. He narrowly escaped death in 1965 when his car was bombed in New Bern, a hundred miles southwest of Hyde County.[40] Ferguson had repeatedly seen black communities dissatisfied over the terms of school desegregation, and he agreed to research the possibility of legal action to preserve Peay and Davis. He hoped that he could at least negotiate a temporary settlement with the school board.[41]

Through Ferguson and a few other contacts, the Committee of 14 educated themselves about the politics of school desegregation and the particulars of the Hyde County plan. They discussed their findings with their church congregations. Many of the new facts did not sit well with the black community. Parents grew particularly displeased when they learned that school desegregation would begin that fall with the youngest children, the students in the first, second, and third grades. Those children seemed too vulnerable to be the first exposed to the racial tensions within Mattamuskeet, and black parents could not help but feel that a policy so misguided could only be explained by white fears of miscegenation. News that HEW's guidelines did not require closing the black schools, as local officials had been declaring, confirmed their worst suspicions about the school board's lack of good intentions. They also learned that after the O. A. Peay School was converted to an office building in 1970, the school board planned to rename it: this move would be the ultimate symbol of obscuring the black educational heritage. The closing of Peay and Davis grew more unacceptable with every new piece of information.

On the morning of August 5, the Committee of 14 and several other black parents met again with Bucklew, Attorney Davis, and the school board members. The delegation presented to the school board a petition stating firmly that "no students grades one through three will enter the Mattamuskeet School from the O. A. Peay School under the present plan." The petition further decried the exclusion of blacks from any role in developing a desegregation plan. The black leaders told the school officials that any plan requiring the one-way transfer of black pupils to Mattamuskeet was unacceptable. The petitioners argued that HEW guidelines did not require specific schools to be left open or closed; consequently, both white and black schools should continue to be used. "We will not send our children to the white school under the present plan of desegregation," warned the parents, "[and] we will let the courts settle the desegregation of Hyde County schools [if] a more suitable plan is not worked out."[42]

The ensuing discussion proved brief and hostile. The black representatives were growing frustrated at the school board's refusal to disclose details or negotiate seriously. The school board was unaccustomed to black demands and was unresponsive, again blaming HEW for any problems. Several of the petitioners became furious. Albert Whitaker, a Fairfield farmer and storekeeper, asked the superintendent, "Didn't you promise to come back to us before making a decision?" Whitaker, an imposing figure of a man, glared down at the superintendent and told him that the parents were angry that "he had lied to us."[43] The school officials sat quietly and did not respond to him. At the end of the meeting, the school board reauthorized Superintendent Bucklew to assign black students in grades one through three to the Mattamuskeet School.[44]

The parents redoubled their efforts after that infuriating August 5 meeting. The Committee of 14 wrote HEW that same afternoon. In the letter the committee affirmed that Hyde County blacks desired school integration "provided white students were relocated as well as black," and they suggested geographic zoning as an alternative to the current plan. The committee also requested a written copy of the desegregation plan and a meeting with HEW staff to develop a better plan. The letter was accompanied by a petition protesting the school closings, signed by two hundred black citizens.[45] Another group of black parents—the advisory council for the O. A. Peay School—also immediately wrote a letter to HEW protesting the school closings. In their letter, Rosa O'Neal, John Greene, Curfew Harris, and Henderson Harris argued that the one-way transfer of black students into the Mattamuskeet School was clearly unfair. They informed Walter Warfield at the Civil Rights Compliance Office of HEW that the two black schools were fully accredited, and they argued that Mattamuskeet could not possibly hold even three grades of black students. Not trusting the school board, they inquired whether HEW had actually approved the school desegregation plan and, like the Committee of 14, suggested that geographic zoning would be a better policy.[46] Rosa O'Neal sent a telegram to HEW two days later reemphasizing the urgency of their situation.[47]

Successful negotiations with the school board seemed more and more unlikely. "We went to [them] several times," recalled Albert Whitaker, "and they said that was all they had to offer—so we decided to stop going to [them]."[48] The Committee of 14 instead devoted its energies to finding a strategy to compel the school board not to close Peay and Davis. The committee broached the issue with the Hyde County Board of Commissioners, but the commissioners were not receptive; in August they allocated an extra $18,000 to the school board to finance the construction of temporary classrooms at Mattamuskeet.[49] The committee also sent a delegation to visit public school leaders in Raleigh, but state officials refused to intervene.[50] By 1968, they had grown accustomed to a measure of dissent in black communities upset over the terms of school desegregation; they expected no unusual problems in Hyde County.[51]

The reaction from HEW was also discouraging. The federal government's position was relayed in an August 30 letter to Rosa O'Neal from Lloyd Henderson, the education branch chief in HEW's Office for Civil Rights. Henderson showed an awareness of and some sympathy for the black parents' concerns, but he also discussed the limited authority granted to HEW by the Civil Rights Act of 1964.[52] Henderson explained that HEW urged school boards to "inform their communities of proposed school desegregation plans," but he told O'Neal clearly that "it is not mandatory that they do so." The law, he explained, required a school district to provide equal educational opportunity to black and white children. But "the responsibility for selecting a workable plan toward the elimination of the dual school system rests with the school board," and only with the school board.[53] The Civil Rights Act did not require community participation in developing school desegregation plans, nor the retention of historically black schools in a school district. Moreover, HEW policy evidently did not even require making copies of a school desegregation plan available to the public; Henderson would not send Rosa O'Neal a copy of the plan for Hyde County. He advised her instead that "some inconvenience will be experienced by pupils of both races in the initial desegregation process." She should look forward to the future when "quality education will be available for pupils of all races." In the meantime, he suggested that she discuss the issue with the Hyde County Board of Education.[54]

James Ferguson did not have good news for Hyde County blacks either. His legal research confirmed HEW's position that the federal courts would be satisfied if the desegregation plan dissolved the dual school system.[55] The details remained under the school board's authority. He also realized that without firm precedent any legal challenge would not resolve the issue until long after the school board had closed O. A. Peay and Davis and invested large sums of money in Mattamuskeet. By then, a federal judge would be reluctant to reopen the two black schools. Ferguson informed black leaders in Hyde County that a lawsuit was not a good strategy. He apparently also attempted without success to initiate negotiations with the Hyde County Board of Education.[56]

"Finally," remembered Abell Fulford, Jr., "we did not have many options." The school board was not listening to black parents and had not offered any compromises.[57] Local school officials argued that the problem was not their fault; they still favored "freedom of choice" and suggested that black citizens address their grievances to HEW. Officials at HEW would not take responsibility for the school desegregation plan and pointed back to the Hyde County Board of Education. State officials also avoided taking responsibility. Neither state nor federal officials appeared particularly sympathetic. Confronted with few choices and little time, the black parents felt cornered. A school boycott, originally a threat designed to encourage the school board to negotiate with them, represented one of the few strategies left open. They decided that they could not send their children to the Mattamuskeet School under the present terms; even segregated education was preferable. Fulford described their thinking thus: "We decided that they couldn't implement their plan without students, so that we would boycott the schools until they listened to us, until they agreed to keep the schools open. That was our goal: to keep the schools open no matter what. We wanted integration but we would have taken anything so long as we still had our schools."[58]

"We Built That School Up There"

On a Saturday morning at the end of August, the Committee of 14 sent a delegation to visit Golden Frinks, the state field director for the Southern Christian Leadership Conference (SCLC), at his home in Edenton. The group also included Fred Simons, the principal of the O. A. Peay School, and two teachers, Phillip Greene and Donnie Blount. They traveled to the colonial-era riverport in Chowan County, seventy-five miles north of Hyde County, to persuade Frinks to help them to organize a student boycott to protest the school closings. None of them knew Frinks, but the SCLC's Christian principles, church orientation, and philosophy of "nonviolent, direct action" strongly appealed to them.[59] They had also admired the SCLC's co-founder and first president, the Reverend Martin Luther King, Jr., who had been assassinated only six months earlier.

Founded in 1957 after the famous bus boycotts in Montgomery, Alabama, and other Deep South cities, the SCLC had grown rapidly in the past decade. While the NAACP continued to have deeper roots in the small towns and countryside of eastern North Carolina than its younger counterpart, the SCLC had also become very important there by 1968. In fact, the SCLC had of late gained a reputation for using more aggressive tactics, but the two civil rights groups often existed side by side, usually sharing many members. Civil rights activism near Hyde County had also been supported by other, more radical groups, such as the Congress of Racial Equality, the Student Nonviolent Coordinating Committee, and the Southern Conference Education Fund. However, because these groups were beset by government harassment and internal divisions, their influence had waned markedly by this time. In eastern North Carolina, at least, their presence and prestige could not compare with that of Golden Frinks and the SCLC.

The Committee of 14 had first contacted Frinks after Fred Simons had discussed the school crisis with a Masonic Lodge brother, Milton Fitch of Wilson County, who happened to be the SCLC's state coordinator. Fitch and Simons had gotten acquainted at regional Masonic events and become friends over the years. After talking with Simons, Fitch had immediately called Golden Frinks and discussed the school closings with him. They were both very familiar with the problem. Throughout North Carolina, they had frequently witnessed black outrage and disillusionment with desegregation plans that closed schools and displaced black leaders. Often those feelings had led to local protests, though these protests were usually tempered by the promise of racial equality held out by school desegregation.[60] The two SCLC activists agreed that Frinks should meet with the black citizens, and the first meeting in Edenton went well. Though concerned about missing the SCLC's national convention in Memphis, Frinks agreed to meet with them again in Swan Quarter the next week.

Frinks did not have a good first impression of Hyde County. Accompanied by Alan Long, a teenage civil rights leader in Edenton, he traveled to Swan Quarter through countryside so desolate and communities so impoverished that he could not believe the prospects for a civil rights victory would be good. When he met the small crowd of black citizens, perhaps thirty in all, who were waiting for him at Job's Chapel, he did not feel entirely welcome or comfortable at first.[61] The elders of the church greeted him with a solemn dignity that evoked an earlier era, not 1968. Most of the assembly reminded him of the old country people who lived beyond Edenton, out by the Great Dismal Swamp, where they quietly worked the land and only reluctantly visited town. The Edenton townspeople often looked down on those rural blacks for their provincial ways and "old-time" demeanor. Frinks's afro and gold chains did not fit this atmosphere. A majestic elderly woman with a walking stick also sat silently in front of him, staring at him reproachfully throughout the meeting. He felt self-conscious and later remembered, "The only thing I was thinking about was [that] I had missed going to Memphis."[62]

After a benediction, the group explained to Frinks their feelings about the threat to Peay and Davis. Their point of view was clear: "We built that school up there," they told him; "they want to take it." The black leaders wanted Frinks to give them some direction and the support of the SCLC. However, Frinks thought they expected miracles. He was reluctant to encourage them or make commitments. The rural locale, the isolation, the lack of previous civil rights activism, and the short time before the opening of the school year all indicated to him that their problem could not warrant a great deal of his involvement. His words were discouraging.

After listening to Frinks endeavor to lower their expectations, the elderly woman in front of him rose slowly to her feet aided by the person next to her. Letha Selby was seventy-eight years old and commanded respect in Hyde County. Ms. Letha, as she was known, had taught in local black schools for more than forty years. Her high standards and unshakable will were legendary among her former students, who represented a significant part of the black adult population by 1968. Her example, however, had been her most effective lesson. She was a longtime deaconess and a founder of the Woman's Home Mission in the Disciples Church. She had been a founding member of the local NAACP and the first black woman in the county to vote. She had also raised three children, all of whom had become schoolteachers, and often reared other children whose parents could not care for them.[63] The church sat silent before her.

Pointing her cane directly at Frinks, Letha Selby admonished him angrily. "Listen here," she told him, "don't come down here telling us what we cannot do." She did not have to look behind her to know that she spoke for everyone in the church. "You tell us what you want us to do so that we will get our schools back," she demanded. "That is what we want."[64] Stunned by her fury and conviction, Frinks suddenly forgot about Memphis and began to take the meeting more seriously. He asked more questions. And he talked about the problems that he had seen black people encounter during school desegregation elsewhere. The crowd of black leaders asked him more questions about protest strategies, SCLC resources, legal rights, and other issues. Their resolution gave Frinks a new optimism, and he in turn gave his audience some hope that they could save their schools. They agreed to hold a mass meeting in the largest church in the county on the next Wednesday evening, just before the beginning of the 1968–69 school year. The Hyde County citizens strategized about how best to organize the county over the next four days, and the meeting concluded with prayer and song. On her way out of the church, Letha Selby shook Frinks's hand and promised him that he would not be sorry for coming to Hyde County.

Early the next morning, most of the black citizens who had attended the meeting at Job's Chapel discovered that their mailboxes had been knocked down during the night. Four or five men drove to Edenton to inform Frinks about the incident, and he visited Hyde County later that day. Ku Klux Klan or other white extremists had apparently learned who had been at the meeting the previous day and hoped to nip the protest in the bud. Frinks knew this kind of intimidation could indeed defeat a nascent movement. He immediately telephoned the U.S. Department of Justice, contacting officials with whom he had developed solid relationships through his work on other civil rights protests. FBI agents stationed in New Bern and Elizabeth City began an investigation that day and soon visited blacks who had been victimized and whites who might have information.

The agents made no arrests, but the incident represented the first time that law enforcement agencies had responded seriously to black concerns about racial intimidation in Hyde County. This fact impressed black and white citizens alike and considerably enhanced confidence in Frinks. Meanwhile, at church services that morning, members of the

Committee of 14 discussed the previous day's meeting and announced the mass gathering planned for Wednesday night. Word spread rapidly into the most remote hamlets and crossroads in the county. Crab pickers talked about the news around their worktables the next day, and field-workers traded views about the big meeting during midday breaks. The lodges, church societies, and school alumni methodically disseminated information about the meeting among their members, while many men and women took time to call or visit relatives who might not have heard. A flurry of long-distance calls also occurred between Hyde County and the school alumni leaders in Brooklyn and other cities; even if they could not be there, their voices would still be heard.

Frinks was not prepared for the scene at Mt. Pilgrim Disciples of Christ Church in Engelhard only three days later. A fishing village built on Far Creek, Engelhard had a two-block downtown and only seven hundred residents. When Frinks arrived that evening, the village looked like it could not contain the crowds. He could scarcely believe the throng of people who had come to hear him, especially in a county with only a few thousand black residents. Cars were lined up and down both sides of the street from the church to downtown; Frinks could not park anywhere nearby. In order to reach the church, he had to push his way through a large crowd that had overflowed out of Mt. Pilgrim. Inside, several church secretaries frantically wrote down names and telephone numbers. The pews had filled and people stood in the back and along the walls. Ushers opened the church windows so that the people outside could hear.

Late into the night, under the leadership of Frinks and the Committee of 14, this unprecedented crowd organized the school boycott. Throwing aside his earlier apprehensions, Frinks pledged the SCLC's support for the protest and promised that he would stand by them personally. Black citizens vowed that starting on September 4, the first day of the new school year, they would not send their children to class until the school board either included O. A. Peay and Davis in a new desegregation plan or left them open under segregation. Rhoda Warren, O. A. Peay, and all the black teachers and parents who had struggled against enormous adversity to educate their children in the black schools would doubtless have been proud.

CHAPTER 3

Once in Our Lifetimes

Golden Frinks was the most important civil rights organizer in eastern North Carolina in the 1960s. He had been a nightclub owner and secretary of the Chowan County NAACP in 1959 when a dozen high school girls had approached the NAACP indignant that they could not eat ice cream in the drugstore where they bought it.[1] Two years later, Frinks and those teenagers led months of protests against racial segregation at the drugstore, movie house, bus station, and other public accommodations in the small coastal town of Edenton. Frinks quickly learned the costs of challenging Jim Crow: he was threatened repeatedly, beaten by police, and arrested.[2] But the "Edenton Movement" produced some of the first civil rights victories in North Carolina, and as an NAACP volunteer, Frinks was soon involved in similar protests in other small towns around the Albemarle Sound.[3]

His relationship with the SCLC began during the Edenton Movement, when Martin Luther King, Jr., sent funds to help bail him and other civil rights demonstrators out of the local jail. Though the NAACP Youth Council led the Edenton Movement, King and other SCLC leaders followed the protests closely, and the Reverend Fred LaGarde, who was the SCLC's regional representative in northeastern North Carolina, must have frequently discussed the brash NAACP volunteer with them. LaGarde was the co-leader of the Edenton Movement, and Frinks attended his Providence Baptist Church.[4] When the SCLC first sought to employ a field organizer in North Carolina in 1963, King offered Frinks the opportunity. He soon sold his nightclub and joined the SCLC. Though Frinks was periodically assigned elsewhere in the South, he devoted himself most passionately to civil rights organizing in eastern North Carolina.[5]

Frinks proved to be an extraordinary civil rights leader. He had not attended college or served in the ministry, but the ex–truck driver and small businessman had a sharp mind and spoke with a roughhewn eloquence. His small town upbringing had shaped an outlook more in touch with rural blacks than that of many of the SCLC's leaders, who came predominately from the largest southern cities. Moreover, Frinks was committed, savvy, and able to inspire trust. Raised in North Carolina, he understood African American life and local politics. He also possessed both extraordinary courage and a streak of wildness that repeatedly unnerved white leaders and won civil rights victories. He combined those gifts with the patience necessary to organize well in rural areas. Frinks had learned early on that in order to have the tenacity to wear down white opposition to black civil rights, rural movements required not only singular moments of bravery or aplomb, of which he was quite capable, but also painstaking periods of education, the building of trust, and the creation of a "movement culture." His combination of "fire and ice" usually served local activists very well.

Between 1963 and 1968, Frinks had been a lightning rod for civil rights activism in eastern North Carolina. The SCLC was at the height of its national prestige, and local black leaders who respected its nonviolent philosophy and church orientation often sought his help. Frinks assisted civil rights struggles in countless small towns and crossroads, helping local citizens to challenge voting rights violations, police brutality, racial segregation, and Klan harassment. By 1968, he had already played a leading role in civil rights movements in Halifax, Washington, Martin, Bertie, Chowan, and Pasquotank counties.[6] Though these movements had all been seminal local events, they had not occupied the national spotlight or been a top priority for the SCLC.

During the Edenton Movement in 1961 and 1962, Frinks developed a pattern of activism that would become his trademark in later years. Led by Frinks and LaGarde, the Edenton protesters wore down Jim Crow with years of civil disobedience, picket lines, slowdowns, strikes, and boycotts. What most distinguished the Edenton Movement, though, was where it happened and who supported it. Unlike all but a few other major civil rights protests to that point, the Edenton Movement occurred in a rural, isolated area, not in a southern city. It drew its leadership and most vital support not from college students or an educated middle class but from poor, uneducated people. Children also played a prominent role in the local protests. The civil rights movement in Edenton received some national attention but never moved to the forefront of any civil rights group's agenda. But to many observers, Edenton showed that the tools of "nonviolent direct action" could prevail in the rural South.[7]

The Williamston Freedom Movement, which took place from 1963 to 1965, was the closest that a civil rights campaign led by Frinks had come to having truly national significance. In the spring of 1964, SCLC leaders in Atlanta sought a local civil rights movement that they could use to focus a national campaign for new voting rights legislation, much as black activism in Birmingham had been the SCLC's springboard for the Civil Rights Act of 1964. In Williamston, the seat of Martin County, black citizens had strong local leadership and had challenged Jim Crow very effectively in downtown businesses, the public library, hospital, and schools. The town leaders and a very active Ku Klux Klan had adamantly opposed all civil rights concessions. Frinks himself had been in jail under spurious charges for almost six months.[8] The SCLC clearly saw an opportunity to make a national stand in that small Tobacco Belt town. However, after narrowing the choices down to Williamston and Selma, Alabama, SCLC leaders finally chose Selma for the national protest.[9] "Bloody Selma" would become world famous; Williamston and Frinks, thus far, historical footnotes.

In the fall of 1968, Frinks realized that the SCLC needed new directions and new civil rights campaigns. The SCLC had lost influence within the civil rights movement to groups less committed to racial integration and more dedicated to black nationalism. The group had also turned away from the South. With little success, it had sought to address racism and poverty within urban ghettos, especially Chicago, and had not conducted a major campaign in the South since Selma. Finally, the assassination of Martin Luther King, Jr., that April had almost destroyed the organization, and many staff members still felt shellshocked by their leader's death.[10] The fate of the SCLC seemed very uncertain at that moment. Frinks believed that Hyde County had the potential to revitalize the organization. He hoped the school boycott would give it a renewed presence in the rural South. He also believed that this local school protest had national implications that could dovetail with the resurgence of black nationalism.[11]

The Rise of a Protest Movement

Fifteen hundred black men, women, and children marched in Swan Quarter on Sunday, September 2. The protest had been announced in every church that morning, and the crowd had already overflowed the grounds around Job's Chapel and the O. A. Peay School when Golden Frinks arrived with several SCLC co-workers and one or two college students from Elizabeth City. Looking out over the broad open plains and salt marshes, the visitors could scarcely believe so many black people lived in Hyde County.[12] The procession stretched out far from the church toward its destination at the Hyde County Courthouse in downtown Swan Quarter.

The pastoral calm of the fishing village on a Sunday afternoon was broken by songs of protest. White citizens who lived in the heart of town witnessed the march with wonder and concern. Most of them were unfamiliar with the details of the school desegregation plan and had few insights into the process that had shaped it. Many did not share the school board's obsession with closing Peay and Davis, even if they opposed school desegregation itself, and did not understand why the two black schools had to be shut down. Some would have opposed the school closings if given a choice. But a civil rights demonstration, much less one of this size, was unheard of in Hyde County. When the protesters marched back to Job's Chapel, they left a disturbed and anxious village behind them.

Two days later, on the first day of the new academic year, few black children attended the Mattamuskeet School, the O. A. Peay School, or the Davis School. Their parents and grandparents had finalized plans for the school boycott at community meetings at Job's Chapel the previous night and early that morning.[13] The church network established by the Committee of 14 smoothly communicated last-minute details all over the county. Only a handful of black parents sent their children to Mattamuskeet. In a show of solidarity with the younger children, the large majority of parents with children assigned to O. A. Peay and Davis also kept them out of school. Only twelve students attended the Davis School, and only thirteen appeared at the O. A. Peay School.[14] Black citizens held a second protest march that afternoon and a mass meeting that evening.

While the school boycott, marches, and mass meetings continued day after day, boycott leaders tried to negotiate a new school desegregation plan. On Wednesday, September 5, Abell Fulford, Jr., and four other local activists carried a petition and a compromise proposal to HEW's Office of Civil Rights (OCR) in Washington, D.C. The delegation presented OCR's A. J. Howell and David Richardson with a petition that protested the "unfair racially motivated operation" of Hyde County schools and blacks' exclusion from the shaping of a desegregation plan. They argued that the school board had created the plan without considering "the Negro child, community, or those who may have been an inspiration [to the children], the Negro [educator]."[15] They also proposed that black parents would send their children back to school if at least the O. A. Peay School was included in a desegregation plan. They would be willing to sacrifice the Davis School if absolutely necessary.

The Hyde County delegation warned Howell and Richardson that racial tensions were rising back home and they feared that violence could break out if HEW did not intervene soon. The two federal officials promised to speak with school leaders in Hyde County, but they explained that the local school board still had authority over the exact character of school desegregation. Howell remembered in an interview the next year that he "told them that if the school district chooses to phase out a Negro school to comply with the [Civil Rights] Act, HEW has to accept that."[16] In a memorandum to his supervisor, though, Howell made clear that "this did not seem to satisfy them."[17]

Black leaders also met with the Hyde County Board of Education back in Swan Quarter. The school board had discussed the boycott with Attorney Davis on September 3, and Bucklew had also spoken with Dr. Charles Carroll, the state superintendent of public instruction.[18] In a letter to Gov. Dan K. Moore the next day, Carroll stated bluntly that "conditions in Hyde are not good." At Carroll's suggestion, Bucklew invited David Coltrane, the chairman of Governor Moore's biracial Good Neighbor Council, to visit Hyde County to help mediate a settlement. Though they held a special session with Coltrane and school boycott leaders, the local officials showed little willingness to negotiate and blamed HEW for the protests.[19] They told the black leaders that HEW was forcing them to close their schools and that they had an obligation now to comply with the current desegregation plan.

Black enrollment did not increase appreciably during the first half of

September. Racial tensions mounted daily. Howell at HEW telephoned Superintendent Bucklew a few days after his visit from the boycott leaders and discussed their proposal with him. Bucklew was not persuaded, however, by the proposal to close only the Davis School and pair O. A. Peay and Mattamuskeet. He felt confident, in Howell's words, that "utilization of [only] the formerly white school would provide for the best educational set up."[20] Indeed, he and the school board had lost patience with HEW. They had been telling the federal government since 1965 that neither white nor black citizens in Hyde County wanted school desegregation; they now felt that the school boycott vindicated their position and wanted HEW to handle the problem. The alternative—school integration using all three schools—remained unmentionable. Yet Bucklew was also clearly shaken by the school boycott. He told Howell that the situation seemed very volatile, and he sounded uncertain and genuinely worried about what might happen next. He also mentioned that he had received what he considered a "threatening letter" from some black citizens.[21]

Despite their anxiety, Bucklew and the Hyde County Board of Education did little to ease racial tensions. The school officials were frightened and psychologically shaken by the school boycott. They had been accustomed to having total power, and the mass protest had turned their world upside down. Farmworkers and oyster shuckers over whom they had exercised unchallenged authority had suddenly demanded a share of power and control over the schools. "In private discussion," recalled Dr. Dudley Flood, who was later one of Gov. Robert Scott's envoys to Hyde County, "you could physically see the fear in them."[22] Flood and other observers believed that this dread of social change unnerved the school board members to the point that they could not act rationally. "They were so preoccupied with that fear," remembered Flood, "that it began to skew the whole picture. . . . Having what was right done was secondary to the encroachment on their power."[23] It seems that the strain soon took its toll. Bucklew and two of the five school board members were convalescent within three months.

The boycott transformed daily life in Hyde County. With the help of SCLC co-workers Milton Fitch and James Barrow, Frinks led protest marches and mass meetings almost every day. An average of 150 to 200 demonstrators marched most afternoons from Job's Chapel to the Hyde

County Courthouse in Swan Quarter.[24] Many days, protests occurred in Engelhard as well as at the county seat. The school boycotters also conducted longer marches through the countryside: Swan Quarter to Scranton, New Holland to Engelhard, Lake Landing to Fairfield. Every Sunday afternoon they held a larger march and a mass meeting in Swan Quarter.

Confrontation was not the point of those first protest marches. The demonstrators scrupulously followed instructions from state troopers not to walk directly on the public roads, and they did not try to provoke arrests or engage in civil disobedience.[25] Both SCLC and local boycott leaders believed that even though such tactics might become necessary, greater trust, refined goals, and better cooperation must come first. They realized that the marches and community meetings had several purposes at this point. Those events taught the black community more about civil rights activism and about school desegregation issues. They served to recruit more people into the movement, and they helped black activists gain greater experience in working together. Frinks and Fitch, in particular, consciously encouraged a "movement culture" that could sustain the school boycott through confrontations, threats, and the frustration of temporary defeats that inevitably lay ahead.[26]

To this end, school boycott leaders held community meetings almost nightly after the protest marches, rotating the location among the county churches.[27] Years later participants still remembered their exhilaration and energy at those gatherings. Singing and worship formed the heart of every meeting. Guest speakers, often civil rights leaders visiting the school boycott, frequently gave inspirational or educational speeches. Frinks and other SCLC activists often conducted workshops on civil disobedience. Other times, several meetings happened at once within a church. Small groups caucused and later reported to the larger session. While a youth group met to plan the next protest, for instance, the adults would organize another delegation to Raleigh or sing gospel and movement songs. Most decisions were brought to the full gathering, discussed openly, and made by consensus. They handled threats against any of the activists, internal problems, and other controversies in much the same way. "Everything was aired at the meetings," Alice Spencer recalled, and everything seemed new, important, exciting, often revelatory.[28]

One almost has to visualize mass meetings at isolated churches like Pleasant Grove, Snow Hill, or Old Richmond to appreciate their import

Job's Chapel Baptist Church. (Selby et al., Hyde County History*)*

to the rural people who attended them. Surrounded by swampy waste-lands and a few homes on a creek bank, most of these small country churches had dwindling congregations, with an unusually high propor-tion of elderly members because so many younger people had migrated out of the county. None of them had full-time or local ministers, and many churchgoers only saw the pews even half-filled when former members and relatives returned to Hyde County for homecoming. Now, all of a sudden, the churches could barely hold the large crowds. The vibrant music and oratory and the tumult of activity brought new life to both the churches and their remote communities. Beyond the possibility that they could preserve Peay and Davis, these scenes filled many black Hyde Countians with a more general sense of promise and hope.

Something seemed to be happening every moment during those early weeks of the school boycott. Crab pickers and oyster shuckers, whose shifts often began in the middle of the night and finished in late morning or midday, frequently came to Job's Chapel directly from the fish houses in Swan Quarter, Engelhard, and Rose Bay. SCLC leaders were staying in the rectory, and the church had become the daily center of school boycott events and the rallying point for protests directed at the county government in Swan Quarter. At almost any hour, black citizens who showed up at Job's Chapel could count on being drawn into a strategy session, a protest, a fund-raiser, or a workshop. Other churches and school groups were also preoccupied by the boycott. Even mutual aid societies like the Order of Love and Charity and lodges such as the Masons and Eastern Star devoted their energies to the school boycott, organizing fund-raisers, donating materials, arranging transportation, readying churches for meetings, and providing food and chaperons for student protesters.

By the start of the school boycott's fourth week, black activists had yet to make progress in their negotiations with the school board and HEW. Faced with so intransigent a school board, they grew disturbed that their protest had attracted little attention beyond Hyde County. The Raleigh *News and Observer*, the leading newspaper in most of North Carolina, had run a small article about the school boycott on its first day, but had not mentioned the protest since then.[29] SCLC organizers believed that they could never succeed without the publicity necessary to generate support beyond Hyde County.

Local officials and law enforcement agents expressed gratitude for this lack of press attention. They believed the absence of news coverage had prevented the racial crisis from escalating further. Capt. R. F. Williamson, the highway patrol's district officer responsible for Hyde County, informed his superior in Raleigh that "we have . . . been fortunate thus far in this group not receiving the usual publicity."[30] Williamson assigned only two state troopers to keep the marchers under surveillance because he believed that in the past Frinks had stepped up protests when more patrolmen were on duty. Moreover, his officers and Hyde County sheriff Charlie Cahoon had, according to Williamson, "been able to obtain the cooperation of the white population" to avoid confrontations with the demonstrators. The civil rights marches went pointedly "unnoticed" by most white citizens, and SHP or SBI agents had even persuaded the Ku Klux Klan to cancel a mid-month rally in order to avoid violent clashes that might attract media attention or public sympathy to the school boycott.[31]

Besides not receiving publicity, the school boycott had lasted longer than most black citizens could possibly have expected at the first mass meetings and protests. Parents were naturally very concerned that the children had missed so much school. In mid-September, the Committee of 14 consequently made two important strategy decisions. First, the committee members resolved to use more confrontational tactics in order to draw greater attention to the boycott. Protesters would do whatever necessary to disorient white leaders and provoke confrontations that would receive media attention, build public sympathy, and compel negotiations. Second, they also revised their short-term goals, informing the school board and federal officials that they would willingly accept the kind of "freedom of choice" plan that had been operative in Hyde County between 1965 and the spring of 1968. The most immediate advantages of sweeping aside the HEW-approved plan would have been the at least temporary salvage of the O. A. Peay and Davis schools and an immediate return of black children to classes. Racial segregation would have again been the rule in Hyde County schools, but black activists had judged segregation to be a short-term solution more tolerable than the loss of Peay and Davis. A permanent solution could be worked out when the children were back in classes.

The change in strategy was soon apparent. On Tuesday, September 17, a group of black students sat in at the Hyde County Board of Education's offices in Swan Quarter.[32] The first two days of the protest were uneventful. On the third day, though, several of the demonstrators joined a group of first, second, and third graders and their parents on a march to seek formal admission for the young children at the O. A. Peay and Davis schools. At about one o'clock, twenty-five to thirty teenagers rejoined the sit-in outside Superintendent Bucklew's office on the second floor of the Hyde County Courthouse. They had been singing protest songs for almost an hour and a half when Sheriff Cahoon and two state troopers moved to evict them.[33] The students at first left voluntarily, but they immediately attempted to reenter the building. When they tried to force their way in the front door, Trooper Jerry Jenkins fired two bursts of Mace over their heads.

The acrid, burning gas dispersed the demonstrators immediately, but the use of Mace signaled the beginning of a more confrontational stage in the school boycott. Black parents were outraged that the chemical spray had been used against their children. According to an SHP inter-

Golden Frinks (nearer) and Milton Fitch, Sr., amid a protest rally at the Hyde County Courthouse, Swan Quarter, November 1968. (The News and Observer Collection, Division of Archives and History, Raleigh, N.C.)

nal memorandum, the commanding officer in Hyde County that day, Lt. L. J. Vance, also believed "that the use of Mace on this . . . occasion was not necessary," and he ordered his officers to attend counseling sessions on the proper use of the gas.[34] One likely reason for his dismay was that the *News and Observer* described the incident on page three the next morning.[35]

The clash at the courthouse incited a flurry of new protests. The school boycott leaders held more church rallies, marches, sit-ins, and other demonstrations, sometimes several times a day. On September 22, the next Sunday afternoon, more than 1,500 people—as much as half of the county's entire black population—attended the weekly mass meeting in Swan Quarter.[36] Distrust of white leaders had only deepened with the use of Mace on the children. "We want to maintain these schools on a segregated basis," Golden Frinks told the rally, "so the white man will recognize and respect the black man." He and James Barrow blamed HEW for not allowing local citizens to develop a new school desegregation plan. "We want HEW to get the devil out," Frinks told the crowd. "Let us make our own plan," he insisted.[37]

The protests grew more confrontational daily. On September 25, Sheriff Cahoon used tear gas to disperse more than a hundred teenagers and younger children picketing the Hyde County Courthouse.[38] It was the third demonstration that day alone. Cahoon told a news reporter that the young people had tried to "take over the courthouse," and he called the demonstration "the rowdiest yet."[39] He again refrained from arresting the activists, but the situation was becoming difficult for him. In Raleigh, SHP officials assigned more troopers to monitor the civil rights protests in case Cahoon and his deputies needed their help.[40]

Cahoon needed their assistance the very next day. Ninety blacks, mostly school children, tried several times to occupy the courthouse, and it required ten state troopers wearing helmets and carrying riot sticks to block their entry. The protesters sang and prayed by the courthouse steps for two hours, then marched back to Job's Chapel.[41] Now well into their fourth week of the school boycott, they pressed school and law enforcement officials harder almost every day. Both black and white observers believed the situation could explode at any moment.

State Policy

On September 5, 1968, the state superintendent of public instruction, Charles Carroll, had sent Governor Moore a memorandum summarizing the status of school desegregation in eastern North Carolina.[42] In Beaufort County, for example, he reported that school desegregation was "fairly normal," although the U.S. Supreme Court had revised the local plan only a few days earlier. In Martin County, black citizens had organized a school boycott the previous week to protest black school closings, but a temporary reinstatement of "freedom of choice" had induced parents to send their children to class again. In New Hanover County, the school board had shut down the Williston High School and transferred hundreds of black children to white high schools with what Carroll called only "minor difficulty." Black parents had protested the closing of the venerable institution; finally, though, they had begrudgingly accepted it. In that school district, however, some white parents now complained that their children had been placed with black teachers. In Pitt County, a federal court was overseeing school desegregation, yet the opening of schools appeared "near normal" except in two rural communities where most white parents had refused to send their children to former black schools.[43] This panoply of racial tensions was expected and did not overly concern the state officials. Hyde County was another story.

Carroll and Governor Moore's staffs believed that the Hyde County school boycott would probably not last long or grow very serious, but they already recognized the potential danger. Of course they had some fiscal concerns about the school boycott. They did not relish providing full state funding for Peay and Davis if only two dozen students attended classes.[44] But the paramount questions to them were the school boycott's political and racial implications. Many other black communities had protested school closings in the last year or two, most vehemently in Williamston and Roanoke Rapids, and the potential was growing for the school boycott to ignite more such protests beyond Hyde County lines.[45] They feared this kind of racial conflict could have an impact on school desegregation throughout North Carolina. The willingness of black communities to tolerate assimilation into white schools and not to require a balanced merger of black and white schools was a central unwritten tenet of local and state policy. State officials realized that the Hyde County school boycott could raise black expectations and spark a new wave of protests and demands from blacks dissatisfied with the repercussions of school desegregation on their communities. These protests could aggravate antagonism among white citizens and possibly trigger federal intrusion. State officials consequently believed that a prompt and quiet settlement to the school boycott was absolutely necessary.

The Good Neighbor Council's David Coltrane visited Hyde County immediately and met with local officials and school boycott leaders. Created by the previous governor, Terry Sanford, the council assisted black and white citizens in negotiating local solutions to school desegregation and other racial conflicts. It had many local chapters but was under the authority of the governor's office, and between 1965 and 1968 the council reflected Dan K. Moore's relatively moderate racial views. In Swan Quarter, Coltrane quickly realized that racial tensions and distrust were too high for successful negotiations. He recognized that the only common ground between the protesters and the Hyde County Board of Education was their mutual interest, for very different reasons, in returning to "freedom of choice." On September 9, Coltrane tried to convince HEW to permit a temporary return to the 1965–68 school plan, which would have again allowed O. A. Peay and Davis to remain open to black students in all grades. As he told William Mammarella, who took his call at the Office of Civil Rights, Coltrane thought that "through more communication between the white and Negro communities" Hyde County blacks "might accept desegregation of grades one through eight" at the Mattamuskeet School the next year.[46] He apparently believed that over the 1968–69 school year the Good Neighbor Council could organize a local chapter that would lessen racial tensions, improve trust, and smooth the transition to school desegregation sufficiently that black citizens would in time accept the loss of Peay and Davis in exchange for other concessions.

During the same week, the Hyde County Board of Education also requested permission from the OCR to return indefinitely to the 1965–68 plan.[47] However, the federal officials denied the request almost immediately on the grounds that the earlier plan had already failed to desegregate the school district. Weary of taking the blame for the school closings, OCR personnel notified local education leaders by telephone, letter, and telegram that "we had no objection to the use of all the schools on a desegregated basis." Mammarella also stressed to Coltrane that they had not instigated the plan to close the black institutions. Ruby Martin, the OCR's director, even wrote to SCLC leaders in Atlanta to defend HEW, explaining that her office had encouraged (but not required) the Hyde County school board to use the black schools.[48]

On September 18, the Hyde County Board of Education called a special session in Swan Quarter to discuss the desegregation crisis with black parents and state officials. Carroll, a number of his assistants, and Ralph Moody, an assistant state attorney general who had been a "segregation specialist" in the Hodges administration, attended the meeting. After a lengthy discussion, the parents still would not consent to settle the boycott until, in their words, the school board "agree[d] to assign students solely on the basis of Freedom of Choice."[49] This stance of course represented an ironic convergence of interests. The school board had been satisfied with the 1965–68 "freedom of choice" plan and only under compulsion had required school desegregation. Thus everybody at the meeting blamed HEW for the current plan. Sounding oddly co-conspiratorial, in fact, Moody even suggested that black parents file a legal suit against the Hyde County Board of Education to have a federal court void the desegregation plan accepted by HEW. Theoretically, they could have then returned to "freedom of choice." Black leaders did not take the suggestion seriously, and Bucklew would instead ask that HEW permit a return to the old plan; again, HEW summarily denied his request.

As the school boycott continued into October, state officials strengthened their efforts to bring about a settlement. David Coltrane and Preston Hill, his assistant at the North Carolina Good Neighbor Council, tried almost daily to negotiate between the parents and school officials. Charles Carroll and J. Everette Miller, the associate superintendent of public instruction, were counseling Bucklew and the school board and helping to shape the governor's strategy toward the protest. They had also invited race relations specialists from North Carolina State University to consult with the two sides. According to the school board's October 4 minutes, this team "was working almost constantly trying to get the Negro children back in school," yet was making little progress in bringing about negotiations, much less a settlement to the crisis. [50]

The Moore administration and the Hyde County Board of Education also contemplated whether or not to enforce the truancy laws. In early September, Bucklew had sent black parents a letter explaining the truancy laws and warning them that prosecution was a possibility. [51] The parents refused to open the letters and returned them to the post office with "Return to Sender" written on the envelopes, but school officials did not initiate legal action. [52] First of all, state leaders had strong doubts about the constitutionality of the North Carolina truancy laws. In fact, Attorney General Robert Morgan believed the statutes were constructed so poorly that they would probably not withstand a serious challenge. [53] Given the truancy statutes' potential usefulness as a threat against other parents, Morgan, a future United States senator, recommended not testing them until they could be amended by the state legislature. In addition, school board members were not particularly disposed to compel black parents to send their children to the Mattamuskeet School. Prosecution would be expensive, troublesome, and tedious. It would likely inflame black citizens further. Most important, the boycott was delaying school desegregation, which the school board had always opposed anyway. The local political leaders blamed HEW first, and black parents second, for the crisis. Having complied with all federal laws themselves, they believed that the ethical burden of black student truancy sat with parents and HEW.

Because state government leaders could not or would not force black parents to send their children to school, they redoubled their efforts to bring about negotiations. In the last few days of September, after great exertion and several failures, David Coltrane finally persuaded black leaders and white school officials to confer. On September 30, he and Leon Ballance, a school board member, agreed to organize a small conference for the next afternoon. The gathering included the school board, the county commissioners, the school principals, the "Negro Committeemen" and PTO presidents of the Davis School and the O. A. Peay School, and Coltrane and Preston Hill from the Good Neighbor Council.[54] After meeting for more than three hours, the group concluded that they would try again to convince HEW to allow a return to "freedom of choice," this time by dispelling suspicions that this was just another ploy for white school leaders to avoid school desegregation.

Black leaders consequently agreed to circulate a petition requesting the school board to return to "freedom of choice" for an interim period. Coltrane understood that the school board would then allow black children to attend Peay, Davis, or Mattamuskeet, and black parents would in turn enroll their children in classes again. According to a Coltrane memo to Governor Moore, the cooling-off period would probably extend until the end of 1968. He believed strongly, however, that the school board should not request permission from HEW. When the federal agency was confronted with a fait accompli, Coltrane speculated, "the question will be, what will HEW do?" He believed HEW would not interfere before 1969. "After tempers have cooled," he optimistically informed the governor, "the Board of Education in cooperation with the Negro leaders will develop an acceptable School Desegregation Plan" before HEW interceded further.[55]

Two days later school boycott leaders submitted the petition, which had been signed by 75 percent of black parents in the school district.[56] However, they had also added a caveat to the document that did not sit well with the school board. If HEW rejected the petition and continued to require desegregation immediately, they insisted that both white and black schools be utilized. Contrary to Coltrane's expectations, the school board then did not take any unilateral action but instead included the petition in another request to HEW that the school district be allowed to revert to "freedom of choice."[57] Misrepresenting their level of harmony with black citizens, the school leaders reported to HEW that black parents "were strongly opposed to the integration of their children with the white children at the Mattamuskeet School." Their unity could only be exaggerated so far, however. The school board also confirmed its belief to HEW that, if school desegregation was inevitable, closing Peay and Davis remained in "the best interest of all of the children."[58]

Coltrane knew that HEW would not approve a return to "freedom of choice" if approached directly by the Hyde County Board of Education. HEW had been quite clear in this respect. The keys to the October 1 strategy had been to act without HEW's approval and to develop a workable plan by December 31, before the federal agency could react.[59] The state officials working to negotiate a settlement were overwrought following this failure of strategy. On October 9, Coltrane informed Governor Moore that "the school situation in Hyde County looks almost hopeless." He bitterly blamed the "deplorable situation" on "the bad leadership of Golden Frinks and J. V. Barrow, an arbitrary group of Negroes, an arbitrary School Board, and an arbitrary HEW."[60]

State leaders still held out a hope that they could persuade federal officials that Hyde County presented "an unusual situation . . . and that time is needed for a cooling off period," but HEW formally rejected the request for a third time on October 18, the seventh week of the school boycott.[61] Lloyd Henderson again declared that HEW would not object if they amended the plan to include O. A. Peay and Davis.[62] This news was hardly what the state or local leaders wanted to hear. For the remainder of October, until a heart attack killed him on October 31, Coltrane worked feverishly to convince black activists to end their protest, apparently exhorting Frinks even from his deathbed to settle the school boycott. But the boycott and other protests continued week after week without a noticeable decline in black participation. After HEW's refusal to return to "freedom of choice," the school board held no direct negotiations with the Committee of 14 and had virtually no further contact with HEW for the remainder of the school year.[63]

The Children

The rural character of Hyde County presented serious obstacles to sustaining such a large boycott effort. Unlike in the southern cities where more famous civil rights protests occurred, black citizens did not live in a central location. No more than about 10 percent of the black population resided in any single village, in fact, and many rural families did not own automobiles or telephones. SCLC and local activists consequently worked very hard to assure good communication in the growing protest movement, enlarging school boycott leadership and extending it further at the local level. By augmenting the Committee of 14 and its church network, Frinks helped to organize a larger, countywide planning committee with several dozen members. This group met frequently, usually at Job's Chapel, to coordinate protest activities and to plan fund-raising events, negotiating strategies, media relations, and the many other chores required by the school boycott.[64] Black leaders also organized support committees in their neighborhoods. Those committees performed tasks that ranged from scheduling carpools to arranging local activities for children. To some observers, it seemed that "everybody was organized."[65]

At first, the school boycott leaders included few children. Their parents had brought them to protest meetings and made the decision to withdraw them from school. Early in the boycott, however, hundreds of young people became activists and leaders, often demonstrating more dynamism and creativity than their parents. They enjoyed the challenge and excitement of developing new strategies, discussing local politics, and searching for solutions. They also had more time than their parents to devote to those activities. They would eventually plan most protests, and they usually comprised the majority of demonstrators.

The young people gradually assumed many of the day-to-day responsibilities for running the boycott. Teenagers Alice Spencer and Charlie Beckworth, for instance, eventually kept the financial books for the entire movement, with help from two other young women. Ida Murray, in her early twenties, coordinated transportation.[66] Linda Sue Gibbs, a teenager from Scranton, directed a choir that sang movement songs during meetings and protest activities. A youth group also participated in the movement planning committee. Most parents, on the other hand, devoted themselves more to creating broad policies for the school boycott and to supporting the protest activities of their children.

When daily events did not revolve around Job's Chapel, the children often attended "movement schools" organized in seven local churches. From the beginning of the boycott, black parents had naturally been concerned that their children were missing so much school, and many parents also needed day care for younger children.[67] The movement schools offered the children an alternative education and a supervised environment. At least as important, they also helped to build community unity and to strengthen the movement culture. The schools affirmed both the independent tradition of black education in Hyde County and the new sense of black pride emerging during the school boycott. Retired school teachers, college students, and sympathetic visitors taught the older students, and high school students usually worked with the lower grades. Though they were held sporadically and were not always well organized, the movement schools had more than four hundred children in mid-October, with the number of students per site ranging from twelve to one hundred.[68]

The school boycott activists briefly sought to obtain state certification for the movement schools. Certification would have given them the authority to promote students and would have been a symbolic victory for black schooling. Following the same procedures utilized elsewhere by the white citizens organizing "Christian academies" to avoid school desegregation, black leaders requested certification in early October from the state Department of Public Instruction. A team of inspectors from the Division of General Education visited the schools on October 11 but found none of them in compliance with state standards. Director Niles Hunt found the school activities "improvised" and lacking "the elements usually found in a public school," such as regulation books, state-approved teachers, and proper equipment.[69] Black parents never made accreditation a priority, but the movement schools remained in irregular operation throughout the year.

By the end of October, the school boycott had replaced the daily tenor of life in Hyde County with protests, workshops, and meetings. The school boycott had also changed the black community's sense of itself and was having a profound impact on hundreds of individuals' sense of personal identity. Black citizens, especially the children, developed a self-conscious awareness that they were living in a historic moment. They were determined that they would, in one's words, "stand up once in our lifetimes."[70] They had the help of the SCLC and the attention of state and federal officials, and they had never before come together so well as a community. The young people felt that Hyde County had never before had this extraordinary potential for social change, and they were afraid to let the moment slip away from them. "If we do not do something now," Dudley Flood remembers the children saying, "it will never happen." He was impressed that "they had become convinced that they *owed* it to future generations."[71]

With this attitude, the young people threw themselves into the civil rights struggle, ignoring the risks and devoting their souls and every moment of every day to it. "You walked, talked, ate, thought, . . . *lived* for the movement," explained Alice Spencer; "it was all you did."[72] Thomas Whitaker, who would have been a senior at the O. A. Peay School that year, later described that he "felt like [he] was giving [him]self completely to something larger and more important than [him]self."[73] He and many others discovered energy, ability, and commitment in themselves and each other that they had never imagined before. "We were all brothers and sisters then," they proudly recalled, and this awakened community spirit made them only more determined to hold onto their schools.[74]

Nine weeks into the boycott, negotiations remained at a standstill, and the huge majority of black students were still not in class. The effort to pressure HEW to permit a return to "freedom of choice" had made uneasy allies of the school board, state officials, and black protesters, but it had ultimately been unsuccessful. Officials at HEW would not require citizen participation, equitable desegregation, or the use of black schools, but they also would not allow the school district to abandon desegregation. Frustrated at the failure of negotiations, state political leaders feared that the school boycott signaled a new era of higher expectations for school desegregation and new militancy within disillusioned black communities.

Hyde County blacks questioned the wisdom of school desegregation even more when they observed the school board's stubborn refusal to utilize O. A. Peay or Davis and then witnessed the tear gassing of student protesters. During such moments of disappointment with the white

establishment, the school boycott's original goals were sometimes replaced with the desire to have Peay and Davis to themselves again. Black
citizens usually considered a return to the 1965–68 "freedom of choice"
plan a tactical strategy, a temporary goal that would let the children
attend the black schools until they reached a permanent settlement. Yet
at other times it seemed a safer, more reasonable answer in itself.
Indeed, the O. A. Peay and Davis schools had only grown more important to black families during the boycott. Now the two schools also
embodied their struggle for civil rights, come at long last to Hyde
County, maybe never to come again. They believed that they might
never live in a more important moment.

CHAPTER 4

Another Birmingham?

As great flocks of migrating tundra swan settled onto Lake Mattamuskeet for the winter, the school boycott seemed to take off. Hyde County blacks were pushing political leaders harder than ever, and racial tensions were growing rapidly. The two youngest school board members, Walter Lee Gibbs and Tommy Jones, had privately shown interest in negotiating with the Committee of 14, but board chairman Silverthorne, the two older board members, and Superintendent Bucklew adamantly refused to deal with the protest leaders. When a delegation of thirteen black parents expressed their frustration about the impasse in negotiations during a school board meeting on November 4, school officials simply informed them that they would follow the desegregation plan already approved by HEW. They expressed no interest in further negotiations.[1] More than 90 percent of their children were still participating in the school boycott, but black citizens sought desperately to escape the obscurity that seemed to enclose their struggle. In November and December, however, they would compel the world to listen.

A county government agency sparked the protests that would draw national attention to the school boycott. On November 1, the director of Hyde County's Department of Welfare, W. A. Miller, warned thirty-one families that the department would rescind the benefits allotted for their school-age children if the children did not enroll in classes by December. The welfare funds in question did not necessarily amount to a great deal of money. Often the funds equaled only the $3.50 a month that eligible children received for school supplies, though they could be somewhat higher if a child had special health care needs. But these children were very poor even by Hyde County standards. Though school attendance was indeed a legal requirement for the state funds, the idea that Miller would intimidate such vulnerable families appalled

Hyde County blacks. In addition, the welfare agency already had a reputation for not employing blacks and for discriminating against its black clients. The threat inflamed old wounds.[2]

Golden Frinks and the other SCLC leaders did not at first appreciate the depth of this anger, but they soon adapted their protest strategy to accommodate it.[3] On the afternoon of Friday, November 8, 150 young people occupied the county welfare office in Swan Quarter.[4] Calling themselves "the Martin Luther King Crusaders," the children informed county officials that they would not vacate the building until Miller withdrew his warning.[5] County and state law officers removed the demonstrators using Mace and tear gas, but the Crusaders continued the agitation across the street. They renewed their protest on Veterans Day, the next Monday morning. At about 9:30 A.M., twenty-four young activists occupied Allen Bucklew's office on the second floor of the Hyde County Courthouse and demanded a meeting with him. Meanwhile, more than a hundred students demonstrated and sang protest songs outside the courthouse.[6] Bucklew met briefly with the students at about two o'clock, but afterward they again refused to leave the building, and Bucklew requested that law enforcement officers evict them.

According to United Press International (UPI) correspondent Jack Loftus, who witnessed the scene, Sheriff Charlie Cahoon and three state troopers wearing gas masks threw smoke and tear gas grenades into the second-story room of the courthouse and slammed the door, then held it shut for at least two minutes. Other witnesses later confirmed Loftus's report.[7] Pandemonium broke out among the two dozen children trapped within the gas and smoke. Some of the "young bulls"—in the words of a witness—managed to break out, but the law enforcement officers confined most of the children within the building.[8] Many ran to the windows gasping for air. In the blind push of bodies, seventeen-year-old Mamie Harris fell or jumped out of a window. She broke her pelvis on hitting the ground two floors below and was rushed to the Beaufort County Hospital in Washington. Other protesters leapt more carefully and were not hurt.

The incident outraged the demonstrators and almost provoked a riot. Black leaders strained to calm Foraker Harris, Mamie's father, and some of the older children. "We ought to tear this place down," teenager Jimmy Johnson cried out.[9] SCLC and local leaders both felt the situation was almost beyond their control, and they feared somebody might become violent.[10] When the tear gas cleared, several parents and children had restrained their angriest companions, but demonstrators still blocked every road through town. They pounded on cars and pleaded with state troopers to arrest them.[11] Two girls lay across a car's hood. Six teenage boys were finally arrested for impeding traffic—the first arrests in the ten-week-old school boycott.[12] Fred Simons, the principal at the O. A. Peay School, later reported that a group of boys also entered and vandalized the school, knocking over chairs, pulling books off shelves, and taking food out of kitchen freezers. By six o'clock, a nine-man patrol squad had arrived from Greenville to reinforce the one dozen officers already in Hyde County.

The injury to Mamie Harris put the school boycott on the front page of the *News and Observer* for the first time. Across the nation, news editors who read Jack Loftus's UPI reports assigned reporters to Hyde County. The *Washington Post*, the *New York Times*, and the major television networks sent reporters and photographers immediately. A correspondent from the British Broadcasting Corporation (BBC) arrived within the week. *Jet* magazine and other black publications also sent reporters, and several school boycotters appeared on NBC's "The Today Show" in New York City. In Swan Quarter, city journalists joined the odd crowd of state troopers, FBI agents, courthouse regulars, and idlers mingling in the gravel parking lot and general store outside the Hyde County Courthouse.[13] They kept the school boycott in the national news during the next two weeks.

After Mamie Harris's injury, school boycott leaders decided to organize demonstrations that would provoke arrests—enough arrests, they hoped, to overcrowd the small county jail and compel negotiations. SCLC had often used the tactic successfully elsewhere. One hundred twenty-five people marched the next day from Job's Chapel to the Hyde County Courthouse. Rather than walking on the road shoulder, they marched directly on the highway, then walked around the courthouse singing and chanting in front of a line of state troopers wearing steel helmets.[14] When they locked arms and spread out in a circle across both lanes of the road, the troopers arrested fifty-two of the demonstrators.

The children crowded into the musty brick jail appeared "rather composed" to SHP officers. They decorated their cells with pink curtains that afternoon and continued to laugh and sing "Ain't gonna let no nightstick turn me around" while several dozen junior high–age youths

Police escort student protesters into the county jail, Swan Quarter. November 1968. (The News and Observer *Collection, Division of Archives and History, Raleigh, N.C.)*

stood outside the jail singing freedom songs.[15] The jail was already so overcrowded that Sheriff Cahoon released the thirty girls that evening. State troopers warned their headquarters in Greenville and Raleigh that they expected more demonstrations and arrests, and Cahoon requested permission from law enforcement agencies in other counties to use their jails if necessary.[16]

The school boycotters held more protests and provoked further arrests daily. Older black citizens demonstrated outside the county jail the next day in support of their children and grandchildren.[17] When they marched back out of Swan Quarter toward Job's Chapel, a smaller group of about twenty-five young people led by James "Little Brother" Topping, a teenager from Lake Landing, marched into town carrying chickens, a gesture intended to goad the law officers into arresting them.[18] They prayed and sang movement songs in front of the courthouse, then gathered in a circle on the main road, where state troopers arrested eighteen of them.[19] A thirteen-year-old rushed to catch up with her friends, calling out "Hey, wait for me, Mr. Trooper, I want to be arrested too!"[20]

The day after the "chicken protest"—Thursday, November 14—30 to 40 teenagers conducted a demonstration by blocking traffic and tossing a basketball in the intersection of Oyster Bay Road and Highway 264. The Highway Patrol arrested 34 of the protesters, jailed 11 girls and 2 boys, and released 20 under the age of sixteen as juveniles. The Hyde County Jail had been filled and the sheriff now scattered the arrested demonstrators among small town prisons sixty to ninety miles away, in Greenville, Washington, Plymouth, Williamston, Windsor, and Tarboro.[21] The clerk of court also increased bail bonds from $25 to $200.[22]

One hundred marchers, including many parents and toddlers, held a prayer service at the courthouse the next day.[23] Willie Bolden and Joe Hammond from the SCLC's national headquarters in Atlanta joined them there. Marching back toward Job's Chapel, fifteen to twenty teenagers left the procession and began skipping rope on the highway. When state troopers arrested them, they dashed rambunctiously toward the jail until a squad of troopers interceded and corralled them into an orderly line.[24] The protests had already filled so many of the closer jails that Sheriff Cahoon transferred a dozen girls to the Greene County jail in Snow Hill, more than a hundred miles west of Swan Quarter. Business leaders in some closer towns had grown worried that the prisoners would inspire demonstrations by local blacks, and at least two sheriffs would no longer accept detainees from Hyde County.[25]

Because the arrests had also depleted the ranks of the demonstrators, Frinks had to organize fewer acts of civil disobedience and involve more adults and younger children. Still, the protests occurred incessantly, day after day. On Saturday, November 16, two hundred people marched from Job's Chapel to the Hyde County Courthouse without trying to provoke arrests. They sang freedom songs and listened to several protest speeches instead, then they returned to Job's Chapel for a meeting.[26] The next afternoon Frinks led a similar march of almost four hundred people, including many adults and several dozen preschool children.[27] On Monday, November 18, Cahoon arrested twenty-one marchers, almost half of whom were under sixteen.[28] On Tuesday, Wednesday, and Thursday, small groups of young people marched without incident from Job's Chapel to the Hyde County Courthouse. According to an SHP internal memorandum, most looked under the age of sixteen.[29] On Friday, November 22, twenty-three boys and girls staged a "read-in," reciting from school books while blocking traffic in Swan Quarter. State

One of the daily protest marches from Job's Corner to Swan Quarter, November 1968. (The News and Observer *Collection, Division of Archives and History, Raleigh, N.C.)*

troopers arrested the entire group and imprisoned the ten children over sixteen, putting the total number in jail at over 160.[30]

By mid-November, Sheriff Cahoon believed that most white people in Hyde County had reached "the boiling point." State law agents agreed. They observed that white citizens were very restless, and they feared that violence would erupt at any moment.[31] Many whites resented that their black neighbors had gotten school desegregation, to quote a service station manager in Swan Quarter, "crammed down our throats by those folks in Washington" and had then decided "they don't really want it anymore."[32] Cahoon pleaded with those he called "the more easily inflamed whites" to let him, his deputies, and state troopers handle the racial conflict. But as Cahoon told a newspaper reporter, "tempers are short on both sides."[33] A black teacher observed that everybody, black and white, seemed to be carrying guns, and state officials from the Department of Public Instruction soon requested special permission from the General Assembly to drive unmarked cars without state license plates because they feared snipers.[34] SCLC leaders decided to· spend most nights away from the county to avoid trouble. Yet on November 13, police arrested two white men carrying high-powered rifles and making threats against the school boycotters outside Frinks's new quarters at the Holiday Inn in Washington, North Carolina.[35]

Avoiding violence had become a daily challenge for whites and blacks, law enforcement officers and civilians alike. "We had some blacks who wanted to start something violent," Albert Whitaker recalled, but black community leaders "always headed it off." They tried informally to calm their more contentious white neighbors as well.[36] A number of white citizens eased racial frictions by soothing the most upset among them. Some white Hyde Countians also quietly reduced tensions by communicating their sympathies to black acquaintances. One white man, for example, secretly met his black neighbor in a field between their homes early that fall. He told the black man that he sympathized with the school boycott's goals and knew the two of them would remain friends long after the school boycott, but that he "was going to stay out of this mess" publicly. There must have been many other such meetings, or the school boycott could never have remained so peaceful. One white bus owner, in fact, often transported black children to protest meetings on the sly, and black marchers even saw a few whites wave at them in support.

Sheriff Charlie Cahoon himself did a great deal to reduce racial tensions. Renowned for his smelly cigars and cool head, Cahoon knew virtually every soul in Hyde County. He had been county sheriff for nineteen years and was a member of one of the oldest and largest local families. His family relations and experience gave him the ability to calm tempers effectively, and he went out of his way to relax the white citizens most hostile to the demonstrations. Cahoon was also, as one of the most devoted black demonstrators later called him, "a compassionate man" generally respected by white and black citizens.[37] He constantly worried about violence. Though he rarely lost control of a situation, he did not try to humiliate the protesters, and his manner did not often invite vindictiveness. On occasion the sheriff even allowed arrested demonstrators to leave his jail to attend mass meetings at night.

Cahoon never gave the school boycotters any public support, but out of the public eye, he blamed the Hyde County Board of Education for causing the boycott and Bucklew's racial attitudes for the failure of negotiations. He also empathized to some degree with the black community's concerns. He argued privately that the school boycott would have never occurred if political leaders had first consulted with black citizens about the school desegregation plan. These attitudes, along with his support for the appointment of a black person to fill a school board vacancy later in the year, revealed a sensibility well suited to easing racial tensions without prompting more violence.[38] At this point, a veteran civil rights reporter observed that most Hyde County whites showed more curiosity than hostility toward the protesters, unlike the whites in almost every other place that she had worked in the South.[39] Yet Cahoon and other leaders of both races still held together at best a fragile, vulnerable peace.

The Outside World's View of Hyde County

During the volatile days of November and December, the school boycott attracted both support and criticism from outside Hyde County. The issues and conflicts underlying the protests were interpreted to the rest of the country primarily by the news media. Many newspapers implicitly blamed Hyde County blacks for "changing their minds" about the desirability of school integration. The *News and Observer*'s most thorough feature story on the school boycott had a headline that read, "Negroes Reject Integration."[40] Like many others, this article emphasized the ironies of a civil rights protest against school desegregation but did not distinguish clearly that the boycott opposed a racist plan, not school desegregation itself. Many news writers portrayed a villainous HEW decidedly too ignorant of southern people, white and black, to intervene usefully in local matters. This image concurred, of course, with the Hyde County Board of Education's interpretation of events. Other reporters downplayed the racial conflict and argued that the school boycott was fundamentally a school consolidation fight, albeit one with racial implications. "What is happening to several thousand Negro citizens of Hyde County," wrote one newsman, "has happened to perhaps hundreds of thousands of rural white citizens in recent years."[41]

More astute editors, such as those at the *Charlotte Observer* and the *Washington Post*, realized that civil rights activists in Hyde County could change the rubric of racial politics nationally if they inspired enough black communities to follow in their steps. These journalists saw that the boycott reflected new and evolving attitudes about school desegregation, including strong undercurrents of ambivalence toward the loss of historically black schools. A few even recognized the threat that discriminatory school desegregation plans posed to the cultural integrity of black communities. The *Charlotte Observer* opined that black North Carolinians "themselves are having doubts and second thoughts about the shape of the new relations they are after." On November 15, the same editors wrote that Hyde County should be viewed as a "laboratory case . . . [where] we can see the complex and often confusing state of racial attitudes in much of North Carolina." The demands of the civil rights movement were changing, the editorial went on, and what was acceptable earlier in the decade was becoming intolerable in 1968.

Illustrating this evolution in racial politics, the *Washington Post* contrasted the school boycott with an infamous five-year shutdown of public schools only a decade earlier. In Prince Edward County, Virginia, white leaders had chosen to close all public schools rather than send white children to class with black children. Now Hyde County blacks had chosen not to attend public schools rather than accept desegregation on racist terms. It was a striking transformation in black and white expectations. Now the fundamental political assumptions about school desegregation were being challenged not by whites but by blacks. In this kind of media coverage, at least, they had clearly gotten their message across to the rest of the nation. An editorial in the *Charlotte Observer* warned political leaders that the school boycott "better be understood for what it is—a situation that can repeat itself in scores of other North Carolina counties."[42]

There were at first few signs from political leaders in Raleigh that they had heard the Charlotte newspaper's warning. In fact, few political leaders could be found in Raleigh after the November elections. Gov. Dan K. Moore, whose term would expire in January, was in Rio de Janeiro on an "extended tourism promotion" tour. His successor, Lt. Gov. Bob Scott, was vacationing outside the state.[43] The new General Assembly had not yet chosen a Speaker of the House or president pro tem of the Senate. In this leadership vacuum, Governor Moore's aides monitored SHP and SBI reports and sent the Reverend Aaron Johnson from the Good Neighbor Council in Belhaven to meet with Hyde County leaders. Moore appointed in absentia a new GNC chairman, Dr. James Taylor, a retired psychology professor and black leader in Durham whose first priority was the school boycott.[44] Moore also requested that his most trusted assistant, Charles Dunn, visit Hyde County to encourage negotiations between school officials and boycott leaders. Dunn, a future SBI director, had developed what he later called a "working relationship" with Frinks during other civil rights protests.[45]

When both Dunn and GNC field staff failed to bring about negotiations, Dr. Taylor grew frustrated that the school boycott leaders refused to soften their demands. In a public television interview on November 17, Taylor acknowledged that Golden Frinks had made an important statement about school desegregation, but he also accused him of refusing to negotiate in good will and of irresponsibly harming the children's educations. He even suggested that the news media should try "a conspiracy of silence" to deny Frinks attention and public sympathy.[46] Other prominent black leaders who were worried about backsliding away from school desegregation agreed with Taylor, and several also tried, possibly at his request, to intervene in the school boycott. For example, Dr. Reginald Hawkins, a Charlotte dentist who had led the recent campaign to desegregate health care in North Carolina, expressed sympathy with the black citizens during a visit to Hyde County.[47] But Dr. Hawkins also wanted boycott leaders to negotiate more flexibly with the school board, and he tried to allay concerns about losing Peay and Davis.[48]

Other civil rights leaders supported the school boycott with enthusiasm. Activists from the black state colleges in Elizabeth City and Fayetteville showed their solidarity during visits to Swan Quarter in November. The Reverend Leon Nixon of New Bern, Bennie Rountree from Pitt County, Sara Small of Williamston, and other civil rights leaders from eastern North Carolina also participated in marches and protest rallies. A representative of the Southern Conference Education Fund briefly joined the protests, and rumors held that Stokely Carmichael, leader of the Student Nonviolent Coordinating Committee (SNCC), was planning a visit as well.[49] Several state and national church groups also expressed support for the school boycott, and liberal clergymen from Raleigh to Boston drew attention to the school problems in Hyde County from their pulpits.

The protesters also welcomed support from the O. A. Peay School Alumni Association in Brooklyn, New York. A chief destination for Hyde County immigrants at least since early in the twentieth century,

Brooklyn remained an important "second home" to many black families. So many former Hyde County residents lived in Brooklyn, in fact,
that the alumni association occasionally held its annual reunions in
Brooklyn instead of Swan Quarter, and hundreds of alumni would
travel north to attend the event. Young people frequently joined relatives in the city to find work, flee Jim Crow, or further their educations.
Some never returned, while others only stayed north briefly to visit
family or to work a summer job.

This north/south link was propitious in 1968. Brooklyn minorities
were in the midst of the nation's largest community school movement,
centered in the borough's Ocean Hill–Brownsville section.[50] While
circumstances in Hyde County and Ocean Hill–Brownsville differed in
significant ways, the central issue of community control over education
was very similar. In the midst of this highly charged controversy, the
Brooklyn alumni had certainly thought seriously about the issues raised
in Hyde County. As a result, they empathized even more deeply with
their southern kinfolk, and in the Reverend Lloyd Burrus's words at a
November 20 benefit, they took special satisfaction that "the folks back
home feel their children will be better educated at the hands of black
teachers and principals."[51] During the fall of 1968, the Brooklyn alumni
pledged their financial and moral support to the school boycotters and
held at least two large fund-raisers for them.

Three Efforts to be Heard

Back in Hyde County, school boycott leaders realized that they needed
new strategies in order to sustain the momentum and visibility of their
protest. The dispersal of arrested demonstrators to so many jails outside
of Hyde County had diluted the jail-in's impact. Approximately half of
all black high school students were already in jail, in fact, leaving few
volunteers available for more arrests. State troopers and local police had
also become more careful to avoid dramatic confrontations that would
increase media interest. In addition, after state troopers moved into
Swan Quarter and began regularly attending the local Baptist and
Christian churches, they found that the more militant white citizens
grew more receptive to their pleas to avoid conflicts with black protesters. The last of the national media had consequently left Hyde County
by November 22.

The waning of media attention was not the only problem with the jail-in. Parents had not minded when their children occupied the local jail. They knew Sheriff Cahoon, visited the jail frequently, and often carried homemade food to the children. It was different after the county jail filled. Many parents grew worried then about having their children imprisoned in strange jails so far distant from Hyde County. Many North Carolina jails had a reputation among blacks for racist violence, and the threat seemed somehow to grow more real the farther away their children were.

School boycott leaders consequently decided to forsake their strategy to overcrowd the jails. On Sunday, November 24, they posted bail for the arrested demonstrators. The youngsters reunited in Swan Quarter that afternoon and joined more than four hundred of their companions in a celebratory march and demonstration at the Hyde County Court-house.[52] Their release, though, posed new problems for sustaining public interest and increasing political pressure on school officials. Between Thanksgiving and Christmas, the boycott received little media attention and showed no signs of inducing negotiations with the school board. Frustration occasionally prompted black citizens to try more militant protests, some of them poorly conceived and ill fated. It also brought out divisions within the SCLC over how to handle Hyde County, as well as doubts about the national SCLC's commitment to the school boycott. As the year faded into winter, the protesters struggled to be heard—by the school board, by political leaders, even by the SCLC in Atlanta itself. Though demonstrations continued daily, three occasions illustrated the tenor of this struggle especially well.

The first incident was Ralph Abernathy's visit to Hyde County on Tuesday evening, November 26, when Frinks received neither the moral boost that he had expected nor a promise that the SCLC would substantially increase its support. Several hundred people staged a demonstration that afternoon to welcome the SCLC president from At-lanta.[53] Abernathy arrived by private plane around eight o'clock at a small airstrip near Engelhard. An hour later, addressing a crowd of more than six hundred in the O. A. Peay School's gymnasium, he pledged greater resources to the school boycott and warned political leaders that more arrests would occur without a settlement. According to witnesses, though, Abernathy appeared "visibly weary and ill."[54] He could barely

The Reverend Ralph Abernathy addresses a crowd at the O. A. Peay School.
(The News and Observer *Collection, Division of Archives and History,*
Raleigh, N.C.)

complete his speech and afterward was not strong enough to meet with
the school boycott leaders.

Physicians determined later that night that Reverend Abernathy had
pneumonia.[55] Prescription drugs that he had taken to lower a raging
fever had even impaired his ability to think clearly. The SCLC leader
spent the evening at the Holiday Inn in Washington and felt too ill the
next morning to visit Hyde County again. Frinks pleaded with him to
make at least a token appearance to encourage the school boycott
leaders.[56] But A. T. Johnson and Willie Bolden, the SCLC staff members accompanying Abernathy, insisted that their leader should return to
Atlanta immediately to recover from his illness. Abernathy left open the
possibility that he would return soon but made no promises, and Frinks
found little solace in this gesture of the SCLC's commitment to the
school boycott.

Before leaving North Carolina, Abernathy and his lieutenants did
briefly discuss the SCLC's protest strategy with Frinks, Barrow, and
Milton Fitch. The local SCLC workers sought Abernathy's support,

including more staff and funds, to begin large-scale arrests that would "make Hyde County into another Birmingham."[57] They hoped the SCLC would choose the school boycott as the focus of a national campaign to redress the racial injustices that black communities experienced during school desegregation. However, Abernathy did not share their enthusiasm for the effort, and he discouraged Frinks from provoking more mass arrests. Still shaken by internal dissension, recent program setbacks, and the death of Martin Luther King, Jr., Abernathy and the SCLC were making few commitments in any direction that fall. They may well have been further daunted by the complexity of the issue involved—criticism of school desegregation—and by the lack of visibility in such a rural locale. The prospect of making Hyde County "another Birmingham" thus only seemed more remote when Abernathy left North Carolina, and Frinks and the other school boycott leaders grew even less confident in the SCLC's support.

The second incident happened on Thursday, December 5, at the O. A. Peay School itself. Protests had been held in comparative calm every day since Abernathy's visit two weeks earlier. Only brief occupations of the Surplus Food Store and the Employment Security Commission in Swan Quarter had almost prompted arrests.[58] With so little progress toward negotiations, a handful of black parents decided to inquire whether high school seniors who returned to school could graduate that spring.[59] Apparently without consulting with school boycott leaders, they met with Allen Bucklew, Fred Simons, and the O. A. Peay guidance counselor on the morning of December 5.[60] As the meeting got underway, several dozen young people marched singing and chanting to the O. A. Peay School and disrupted classes. They entered the school's front door and playfully wandered the hallways. When admonished by state troopers and SBI agents, most of them left the building and continued the demonstration outside. Sixteen boys, however, locked themselves into Principal Simons's office and piled file cabinets, tables, and chairs against the door and office windows.[61]

Simons rushed from the superintendent's office and immediately dismissed the students in class, but demonstrators attempted to block the parking lot exits in order to prevent buses from leaving the school grounds. Law enforcement agents dispersed the protesters and forced their way through the makeshift barricades to arrest the boys within the school.[62] Meanwhile, the Davis and Mattamuskeet schools had received bomb threats, and Bucklew ordered all three schools closed by noon. Tensions grew so high that no teachers and only fifteen students reported to the O. A. Peay School the next day.[63] The building occupation profoundly disturbed school administrators and also reflected nascent divisions among the school boycotters. Most black citizens considered the protest and bomb threats heavy-handed and misguided.

The third incident occurred a week later, during the district court session in Swan Quarter. Blacks had demonstrated on a daily basis the previous week in either Swan Quarter or Engelhard. Twenty-eight more teenagers had been arrested for blocking traffic, and two SCLC activists, Allan Long and A. T. Johnson, were arrested for "contributing to the delinquency of minors" when they led acts of civil disobedience that included children under sixteen.[64] When district court convened on December 11, Judge Hallet Ward, Jr., who rotated among a number of county courthouses from his Washington home, discovered the cases of 166 demonstrators on his docket.[65] Other than blocking traffic, the 187 charges included disrupting school, the two cases of contributing to the delinquency of minors, and one incident of vandalism.[66] This docket provided quite a contrast to the handful of cases that circuit-riding judges usually found in Hyde County.

Before an overcrowded courtroom on December 12, Judge Ward found the first seven teenage boys on trial guilty, gave them suspended four-month prison sentences, and placed them on probation. When court officers requested that the people in attendance stand for his exit, black citizens neither rose from their seats nor said a word. The judge repeated the order, but the crowd was again silent and immobile, and Ward then ordered Sheriff Cahoon to remove the protesters. Though outraged, Ward did not hold them in contempt in order to avoid heightening tensions during the remainder of the court session.[67]

Judge Ward was not so patient when district court reconvened in Swan Quarter on December 18. Confrontations, including another attempt to block the buses at the O. A. Peay School, had occurred daily during the court recess.[68] When Ward found twenty-nine more activists guilty that morning, seventy-five young people returned to the courtroom during the lunch adjournment and demonstrated against the verdicts by stomping their feet and singing movement songs.[69] They were still at it when the judge reentered the courtroom at two o'clock, and they neither halted nor stood when Sheriff Cahoon called the court back into session.[70] Ward found everybody not standing—ninety-nine people in all—in contempt of court and had them carried to jail by state troopers.[71]

The courtroom protest backfired on SCLC leaders. More state troopers immediately reinforced the two patrols already on duty in the county. Law enforcement officials scattered the young men found in contempt of court among several jails in other eastern counties, but transferred the women to the state prison in Raleigh, which was not only 175 miles away but was also the prison for the worst female criminals in North Carolina.[72] The protest was bad public relations for the school boycott, put the young women in a worrisome situation, and left the demonstrators in jail during Christmas. A dismayed Golden Frinks told news reporters that he had "lost control of the situation," having been out of the courtroom momentarily when the sit-in occurred.[73] He publicly blamed four SCLC field workers from Atlanta and Chicago for organizing the protest.[74] Serious problems among the SCLC staff in Hyde County and a lack of direction from Atlanta had become apparent. During the next day's court session, black citizens avoided the Hyde County Courthouse, leaving the courtroom empty except for the defendants and court officers.[75] Frinks announced a cessation of protests until after Christmas.

The Dilemmas of Black Educators

The school boycott challenged no one more than the black employees and students still at the Peay, Davis, and Mattamuskeet schools. School life during the boycott was strange and disorienting for them. Though buses ran their usual routes and teachers reported for their normal duties, the schools were almost empty. Well into the fall, the O. A. Peay School operated six buses for a total of nineteen students.[76] Phillip Greene, then a sixth-grade math, science, and health teacher, often had fewer than four students in his classes at O. A. Peay.[77] Another teacher, Daniel Williams, sat alone in his classroom for six weeks, then had only one student for another six weeks.[78] In late November, a frustrated gym teacher still did not have enough students to form two basketball squads.[79]

The daily protests, classroom disruptions, and occasional bomb threats created a stultifying atmosphere for the few students who attended Davis or O. A. Peay. A Davis School teacher believed that both students and teachers performed poorly "because they do not know from day to day what to expect."[80] Most of her students had not wanted to attend school and felt left out of the boycott. Moreover, the black students often felt harassed by the school boycott activists, who tried to convince them not to attend classes. Mounting racial tensions even led some of them to worry for their personal safety. Their studies naturally suffered, and that spring only one out of every six high school seniors received their diplomas.

Teaching and learning also proved difficult at Mattamuskeet. Marjorie Selby, who had been transferred from O. A. Peay to the former white school with several other black educators that fall to teach the lower grades, observed that the handful of black students were discontented there. She found them "not happy at all." Most had come to school because their parents either received welfare or were state employees who feared losing their jobs and pensions.[81] White teachers and students also disliked the fearful, unproductive environment at Mattamuskeet that year.[82] While boycott participants found their protest to be a remarkably rich learning experience in itself, these students accomplished little in the public schools. Visiting educators called the Hyde County schools an "educational catastrophe."[83]

The school boycott also confronted black teachers, administrators, and service workers at O. A. Peay and Davis with very difficult personal and professional choices. They were torn by their professional obligations, the demands of white school officials, and their community's expectations that they provide moral leadership. The two principals, Fred Simons and Charles Boone, undoubtedly felt the most pressure and suffered the most pain. The competing pressures and expectations taxed both men. Simons seemed especially shaken during these months. "The whites are against me," he complained to a news reporter in November. "They can't understand why I can't get these kids back in school." Many white leaders indeed believed his students would reenroll if Simons fully exerted his prestige and influence. They accused him of supporting the boycott because he would certainly lose his job if the O. A. Peay School was closed.[84]

A few black citizens, on the other hand, believed that Simons was trying too hard to please school administrators. They sought his help in strengthening the boycott, encouraging him to halt the operation of the buses or even to suspend classes altogether. "My own people are turning against me because they think I'm collaborating with the enemy," he lamented. "I don't run Hyde County schools," an exasperated Simons tried to explain that fall. "I take orders from a superintendent and a school board."[85] This explanation did not satisfy some black citizens, who believed he placed his interests before those of the community. Simons felt trapped between factions, and the situation virtually overwhelmed him, as it might have most people. His co-workers soon observed that the friendly, sociable principal was losing much of his personal vitality and his will to work through the racial dilemmas confronting him. By the end of 1968 he acted as if the school crisis had, in one's words, "[taken] something out of him permanently."[86] "Sometimes," Simons was quoted, "I just wish I could go to sleep and wake up someplace else."[87]

The teachers also faced a difficult situation, especially as Simons began to suffer from more paranoia and isolation. By late November, the principal had lost considerable trust in his staff and had stooped to eavesdropping on his teachers over the school intercom system.[88] He warned them in a November memorandum to "be more careful in how you participate in activities that will reflect adversely on those persons (me), who . . . are responsible for your being here this year." He suspected that the teachers discouraged children from coming to school, and he called their behavior "unbelievable [given] as close as we have been as a staff."[89] In a later memorandum, he accused the faculty of trying to persuade or coerce student bus drivers not to run their routes. His hurt and disillusionment were evident in every word of those documents.

On October 1, Simons sent his staff a memorandum reminding them of their "individual obligations." It instructed them to perform their regular duties, to teach their handful of students, and not to get involved with the school boycott during working hours.[90] In at least two staff meetings, Simons apparently intimated that teachers and service workers might have to choose between sending their own children back to school or losing their jobs.[91] Bucklew himself sent a memorandum to black educators later in the month. "A number of teachers and other school personnel are actively supporting movements not conducive to the best educational opportunities for the students in Hyde County," the superintendent warned. He enclosed with the notice a copy of the state law concerning dismissal of public school teachers for inappropriate conduct.[92]

School employees who openly supported the boycott risked dismissal. The manager of the O. A. Peay cafeteria was a special target for school officials because she belonged to the Committee of 14. Etta Mae Greene had been employed at the O. A. Peay School for fourteen years, and her cafeteria had the highest performance rating in the school district. In early October, however, Simons allegedly threatened to dismiss Greene unless she enrolled her children in school. He also wanted her to persuade other parents to send their children to class.[93] After she refused, Mrs. Greene was fired on October 25, officially for not accepting a transfer to Mattamuskeet.[94] Another cafeteria worker, Ida Murray, had been dismissed in early September when she attended a protest rally during school hours.[95] School administrators also threatened employees who attended boycott meetings in their off-duty hours.[96]

Most black school workers did not participate so openly in the boycott. They often attended the mass meetings, though, and they contributed money for bail bonds, lawyers, and other school boycott needs.[97] Nonetheless, some black leaders expected more from them. During the flurry of protests in late November and early December, SCLC staff pleaded with the teachers to strike in order to shut down the schools entirely. Pushing for a teacher strike during a meeting at Job's Chapel in late November, SCLC field worker Willie Bolden told the crowd, "We want to know which side of the fence [the teachers] are on."[98]

Explaining why he kept teaching at the O. A. Peay School, a frustrated Daniel Williams regretted that "people . . . could not understand our situation for some time."[99] He and other teachers felt enormous pressure to walk out in support of the boycott, yet they also knew their careers in the school district—and livelihoods in Hyde County—would be jeopardized by such a stand.[100] By Thanksgiving, they found it almost impossible to continue coming to school. They also suspected that Bucklew would reassign them to Mattamuskeet if Peay and Davis did not have significantly more students by the start of the spring semester in January. If that happened, a large number of the teachers would have felt obliged to refuse the transfer, in their words, "to save face in the community" rather than leave Peay and Davis. According to an internal NEA memorandum, they believed that Bucklew was "looking for an excuse to dismiss any or all of the Negro teachers," and they feared their refusals to accept a transfer would provide the justification, as it had with Etta Mae Greene.[101]

Hemmed in by this dilemma, the black educators turned to their state professional organization for help. The North Carolina Teachers Association (NCTA) was not a formal labor union but a voluntary association of black teachers. The all-black NCTA and the all-white North Carolina Education Association were both affiliated with the National Education Association. Because state laws severely limited the rights of public employees to strike or organize labor unions, the strength of the NCTA derived from political and advocacy efforts, not negotiations or strikes. E. B. Palmer, the NCTA president, sympathized with their problem but counseled Hyde County's teachers not to walk out of the schools. He suggested that they instead articulate publicly their support for the school boycott's goals through their local chapter, the Hyde County Teachers Association (HCTA). This move would hopefully satisfy black activists yet spare the teachers from having to surrender their jobs without a fight. If the school board ignored their grievances or retaliated against them, they could next request an NEA investigation that might protect the teachers' jobs.

On November 25, the HCTA passed a series of resolutions placing black teachers solidly with the demonstrators. The resolutions called for the school board to involve all sectors of the community in developing a new desegregation plan that would utilize Peay, Davis, and Mattamuskeet.[102] The teachers also demanded that the school board retain black personnel at their current pay and professional status after school desegregation. If the school board did not take action, they threatened to request NCTA and NEA sanctions against the school district and to "bring to bear all of their collective strength" to force the school board to develop a new desegregation plan.[103] Thirty-nine black teachers announced their new stand by marching three days later from Job's Chapel to the Hyde County Courthouse.[104] Then, at a December 2 meeting, Etta Mae Greene appeared with the HCTA officers and several other black citizens to inform the school board of the resolutions.[105] The group also expressed its dissatisfaction with the diversion of ESEA funds away from poor children's programs.[106]

The black teachers heard no encouraging words from the school board that night and at first only felt the pain of their dilemma more acutely. HCTA president Daniel Williams and the other executive officers faced new harassment from school officials. The demonstrations and bomb threats at Peay and Davis the next week further increased the pressure on the educators. Both SCLC leaders and law enforcement agents believed the teachers would be compelled to walk out any day in order to demonstrate their disillusionment with school officials.[107] Their situation grew untenable when Bucklew deducted their pay and threatened them with dismissal for not reporting to the O. A. Peay School the day after the bomb threat and building occupation on December 5.[108] The teachers did not strike but instead met on December 19 with an NEA investigator and on the next day requested a formal inquiry into the school crisis. Both the NCTA and NEA endorsed the investigation in early January, and the NEA arranged to send a team into Hyde County during the spring.[109]

The HCTA resolutions and the NEA investigation were political, not legal, maneuvers. The black teachers had no bargaining agreement with the school board. But threatening the school board with public censure and professional accountability may have given them a measure of job security. Those actions also made their lives easier within the black community by putting them publicly behind the school boycott. Future developments showed that they had indeed reduced the pressure enough to carry them through the year, and the large majority of black educators and service workers would remain with the school district after the school boycott. Embattled principal Fred Simons, however, would take early retirement in the summer of 1969.

The Hyde County school boycott was overshadowed late in 1968 by the Vietnam War and the impending arrival of the Nixon administration in Washington, D.C. Widespread resistance among whites to busing black students into their neighborhoods, another of school desegregation's one-way streets, occupied the national spotlight more than the struggle for racial equality. It also muffled the growing number of black voices challenging racism in school desegregation. White anxiety over interracial education again commanded the attention of political leaders more than these black concerns did. Nevertheless, the school boycott had for a time brought national attention to Hyde County and to the black school closings occurring throughout the South.

This achievement was important, but it was not enough to preserve the black schools in Hyde County. Wearied by the school board's refusal to negotiate, blacks activists now sought new ways to generate support for the O. A. Peay and Davis schools. The prospects for more protests seemed ominous over the Christmas holiday. Black and white frustrations were growing deeper and more dangerous, and racial tensions could still have torn the county apart. Black educators balanced precariously between the school board and activists. Moreover, real problems were evident within the SCLC. Its leaders had announced Christmas Eve sympathy demonstrations for the jailed young people in Raleigh, Tarboro, Gatesville, and Warrenton, but failed to follow up on them.[110] More leadership trouble surfaced when Washington's sheriff jailed Frinks overnight for bouncing a small check to the Holiday Inn.[111] Their school boycott was eighteen weeks old, but Hyde County's black citizens clearly had more obstacles to overcome for the sake of the O. A. Peay and Davis schools.

CHAPTER 5

The Marches to Raleigh

Winter is always hard in Hyde County. The weather seems to magnify a hundredfold the poverty and rural solitude. Cold northeasterly winds and rains regularly come down from the North Atlantic, sweeping over the low barrier islands and salt marshes. A few long-haul fishing crews venture into the rough seas beyond the Outer Banks, and oystermen and shuckers scrounge out a meager living from local bays. Otherwise the county becomes economically dormant. Farms and many seafood packing houses shut down for the winter, and country families largely withdraw from society until spring. Many quietly stretch beans, fatback, and a bit of wild game into the next growing season. One would barely know somebody lived in many of the isolated homes if it were not for the lean plume of chimney smoke. The whole county appears empty and still, with few automobiles on the roads or people in town. It is hardly a promising season for civil rights demonstrations. During the winter of 1969, the black struggle for the O. A. Peay School and the Davis School became an endurance test.

Inclement weather was only one of several problems confronting black citizens looking ahead through the winter and spring. The school boycott had already lasted half a school year, more than eighteen weeks, by the first of January. Many Hyde County citizens had been exhausted by the racial tension and turmoil, and prospects looked bleak for new negotiations. Even some local white leaders now admitted privately that Superintendent Bucklew would never allow blacks to influence a desegregation plan. He still discouraged virtually all concessions.[1] When board chairman Cecil Silverthorne suffered a heart attack in December, the chance of serious negotiations with the Hyde County Board of Education prior to his recovery or replacement grew more unlikely yet.[2] A few black parents felt so discouraged that they sent children away to live and attend school with relatives elsewhere for the remainder of the year.

In addition to the stalemate in negotiations, the school boycotters had other serious concerns midway through the academic year. More than a hundred protesters, mostly teenagers, remained incarcerated over the holidays, many of them in jails over 150 miles away. Their families worried about the young women especially, because they had heard reports of miserable living conditions at the Women's Prison in Raleigh. Local blacks were also troubled by the national SCLC's lukewarm support for the school boycott. Neither Ralph Abernathy nor other leaders had visited Hyde County since late November, and important strategy disagreements remained unsettled between local SCLC organizers and the Atlanta leaders. Moreover, the national media had apparently lost interest in the school boycott. Without that publicity, the protest could not sustain public support or increase the pressure on political leaders. Golden Frinks doubted that the national media would renew its interest unless the SCLC committed resources to a larger campaign there.

Between Christmas and the middle of January, local black activists and SCLC leaders reexamined their commitments, strategies, and goals in Hyde County. Though they held small marches and demonstrations every day the weather permitted, they concentrated more on using a series of special meetings to chart the school boycott's future.[3] First, the Committee of 14 and other local black leaders discussed the school crisis all day on New Year's Eve.[4] A few days later, Ralph Abernathy sent the Revs. Bernard LaFayette and Oliver Taylor, two of his most experienced assistants, to Hyde County to evaluate the SCLC's commitments. After working two weeks with local activists, they convened a gathering of national staff and state leaders in Swan Quarter to resolve disagreements and unify their strategy toward the school boycott. More than a dozen SCLC activists visited Hyde County, including veteran James Bevel, a leader of the Selma march and the Nashville Movement; Sara Small from Williamston; and the Reverend Leon Nixon from New Bern.[5]

On the afternoon of January 16, those SCLC leaders welcomed home the last sixty-seven demonstrators jailed under the contempt-of-court order.[6] They then joined a mass meeting at a local church where black citizens debated and prayed over the school crisis until midnight. It was the largest meeting in six weeks; a state trooper reported that automobiles were lined up on both shoulders of the road for a quarter mile.[7] Finally, to clarify their own commitments to the school boycott, the SCLC leaders caucused by themselves the next day at a Holiday Inn in Williamston.[8]

Though a reliable record of these several deliberations does not exist, one could see their results immediately. Publicly, SCLC leaders announced that the Hyde County school boycott was no longer a local issue but a civil rights struggle of state and national significance. In reality, their commitment to this idea was not quite so clearcut. The SCLC had decided to invest greater resources, but certainly not on the scale of the major national campaigns at Birmingham and Selma or the recent Poor People's March on Washington. Frinks himself still believed that Hyde County could become "a Birmingham" if the SCLC would commit itself. At the Williamston summit, however, other SCLC leaders disagreed with him. A few had never felt comfortable with a major protest against black school closings; it seemed to endanger school desegregation itself. Furthermore, though everyone had praised the extraordinary perseverance and unity of black Hyde Countians, at least a few people questioned how Frinks had guided the school boycott. Those individuals blamed him for his reluctance to negotiate more flexibly, and several men, especially Reverend Nixon, apparently challenged his leadership.[9]

Real strategic and philosophical differences did exist. To some degree, however, SCLC's internal problems bred discord. In the aftermath of Martin Luther King, Jr.'s assassination, SCLC had suffered a troubled year of tactical failures, low staff morale, and financial difficulties.[10] Though not completely confident in Golden Frinks, the national leaders realized that they could not afford to back down at this point. They needed a victory in Hyde County; another defeat for the SCLC would have been disastrous. Thus they decided to rededicate the SCLC's resources toward a successful closure to the school boycott, but they avoided the full-scale national campaign envisioned by Frinks.

This strategy reform had several ramifications. First, the school boycotters soon halted the local demonstrations that had been held almost daily for five months. Black leaders promptly communicated this turnabout to law enforcement agents. A January 22 SHP memorandum indicated that state troopers would no longer need the prison bus or more than one officer stationed in Hyde County.[11] Second, Frinks announced a march to the state capitol in Raleigh the next month, an effort that would attract more widespread public support for the school boycott and spark civil rights activism in other parts of eastern North Carolina. Third, the national SCLC allocated more funds and personnel to the school boycott. Oliver Taylor, Willie Bolden, and Bernard LaFayette stayed in Hyde County to oversee the SCLC's new commitments, and they were joined periodically over the next few months by Hosea Williams and other organizers from Atlanta.

Beyond broadening the battle for Peay and Davis, school boycott leaders had also made several other important decisions. Both national SCLC leaders and some black parents had pleaded with Frinks and his co-workers to find a way to get the children back in class through negotiations while they relied more on political activism to preserve the O. A. Peay and Davis schools. The assignment of Bernard Lafayette and Oliver Taylor to Hyde County was intended partly to assure the presence of more negotiation-oriented staff. Efforts to bring about a diplomatic solution thus took on greater importance in late January. SCLC leaders immediately rescheduled a meeting with Gov. Robert Scott that they had postponed indefinitely as recently as January 9. They also arranged for January 24 the first negotiating session in months with the Hyde County Board of Education and planned a meeting with Craig Phillips, the new state superintendent of public instruction, in Raleigh on January 28, ten days before the March on Raleigh.[12]

A Growing Civil Rights Movement

The school boycott changed in other important ways that winter. Hyde County life still revolved around their struggle for the O. A. Peay and Davis schools, but black citizens also organized to secure other civil rights. The school boycott had been an extraordinary classroom. Blacks had been immersed for half a year in analyzing and questioning the root causes of the school closings. At countless meetings and informal gatherings, they probed the nature of the social order that gave five white men—the Hyde County Board of Education—the authority to shut down their schools. How, they asked themselves, had they gotten to this point, and what could they do about it now? Black citizens learned from every discussion and ordeal, as well as from the civil rights leaders who shared experiences of organizing elsewhere in the South. They gradually developed a remarkable intellectual confidence, critical ability, and political sophistication. The lessons of the school boycott led them inevitably to challenge longstanding racial injustices, including segregation and political powerlessness, that they identified as the underlying sources of the school crisis. They not only questioned the injustice of the world around them but also believed that they could do something about it. Energy and ambition, especially among the young, seemed irrepressible.

Between late January and June, black activists forged a broader movement, always reinforcing the school boycott, that brought forth a steady stream of civil rights activism and community self-help projects. They organized a voter registration drive, and they campaigned to have blacks appointed to the two vacancies that opened on the Hyde County Board of Education when members resigned for health reasons.[13] Protesting low wages, seasonal workers refused to harvest the early cucumber and flower crops that April and May.[14] Black citizens also staged several demonstrations and consumer boycotts. They targeted the East Carolina Bank and other local businesses that did not employ blacks, continued to adhere to Jim Crow, or had retaliated against workers who publicly supported the school boycott.[15] In addition, the school boycotters petitioned the Nixon administration to make low-interest loans available for black families to homestead and develop the vast acreage of federally owned land in the county.[16]

While younger activists led the new civil rights protests, the older generation of black citizens developed Poor Peoples Incorporated (PPI), a nonprofit community development organization. Backed financially by northern churches and philanthropists, PPI activists organized several quilting cooperatives and two small groceries by the summer of 1969.[17] An emphasis on economic justice seemed natural for the older activists. They understood that poverty could be as oppressive as Jim Crow or disenfranchisement, and to strengthen these enterprises they could also draw on a strong local tradition of economic self-help cultivated during the age of segregation. Though not a long-term financial success, PPI boosted the school boycott during the last half of the year. At a time when the boycott seemed like it might never end, PPI's successes and the local civil rights victories provided the black community with an important sense of accomplishment.

The story of Marie Hill is a good illustration of the way their new confidence and political awareness led the school boycotters to embrace broader civil rights issues, even far from home. While several Hyde County youths were imprisoned in Edgecombe County over the Christmas holidays, they occupied a cell next to a young stranger named Marie Hill. When Linda Sue Gibbs asked Hill why she was in jail, the sixteen-year-old girl told them that she faced execution for murdering a white man. Outraged at North Carolina courts for sentencing a child to the electric chair, they cried and commiserated with her.[18] Over the holiday the Hyde County prisoners grew close to the condemned girl. When released from jail in January, they convinced the other school boycotters that they should pressure Governor Scott to stay their new friend's execution. "Save Marie Hill" became another battle cry for the young activists. With the help of many other black Carolinians, they eventually brought enough public attention to the plight of Marie Hill that Governor Scott reduced her sentence.

Throughout the spring school term, the young people carried this conviction and energy into the rest of North Carolina with a missionary zeal. Golden Frinks remained the SCLC's field organizer for all of North Carolina, and publicity from the school boycott only increased the demands on him from other black communities. He was able to respond to them more often after the cessation of daily protests in Hyde County, and the young activists accompanied him everywhere. A Committee of 14 member recalled that they traveled "wherever people were having problems like ours."[19] But they got involved in more than school desegregation conflicts. Strengthened and seasoned by experience, the school boycotters joined community marches against police brutality, picketed downtown businesses that still failed to serve black customers, and aided black student protests throughout North Carolina.

The young people also participated in a black labor movement sweeping across North Carolina. To build an agricultural and manufacturing economy that relied on low wages, business leaders had for generations resisted union activism. As a result, the state had long had the nation's lowest rate of unionized workers. Black workers had made important inroads establishing unions in a few Piedmont cities, but they remained almost entirely without unions in the rural east. It was not for want of trying. Only two decades earlier, tens of thousands of black workers had organized labor unions in the wood products, tobacco, and slaughterhouse industries in eastern North Carolina. Like participants in earlier labor campaigns, however, they met with harsh and relentless repres-

sion, including mass dismissals, violence, evictions, and other reprisals.[20] White business and political leaders had prevailed in the end.
Miserable pay, segregated work, and dangerous conditions remained the
rule for black laborers into the 1960s.

From the late 1960s into the mid-1970s, however, the civil rights
movement inspired a new effort to organize labor unions in eastern
North Carolina. These campaigns became the centerpieces of civil
rights protest in several towns, especially Rose Hill, Beaufort, Washington, and Wilson, and they formed an important component of black
activism in most areas.[21] The Hyde County school boycotters bolstered
labor organizing campaigns like the volatile strike that March at the
Atlantic Veneer Company in coastal Beaufort by describing their own
struggles at union rallies and helping union activists to organize door-to-
door in black communities.

The children often left their parents in the morning and did not
return home for several days. "They knew what we were doing," recalled
one young school boycotter, "and they supported us."[22] Vanderbilt
Johnson remembered that his three children disappeared for days and
weeks consecutively. He often carried them and their companions fresh
clothes and moral support on his weekends off work. His wife and other
mothers sent food to the children at every town, picket line, and jail.[23]

The Marches to Raleigh

Though moving in many other directions, the school boycotters kept
the two marches to Raleigh as their central focus during the winter and
spring of 1969. They hoped the marches would galvanize public support
for the school boycott, inspire other civil rights protests, and foster a new
momentum for negotiations. Preparing for the marches required an
enormous effort. Under the leadership of Milton Fitch, who coordinated the marches for the SCLC, the Hyde County activists had to
arrange transportation, find places to stay, and prepare food for an entire
week. They had to meet with local civil rights groups along the march
route, and for their own protection they had to discuss their plans
thoroughly with state and local law enforcement agents. They also went
to great lengths to ensure continuing support for the school boycott
before leaving the county.[24]

The first march, called simply the March on Raleigh, began at Job's

Participants in the March on Raleigh enter Belhaven, February 11, 1969.
(*The* News and Observer *Collection, Division of Archives and History,*
Raleigh, N.C.)

Chapel on the dismal, rainy morning of February 9. More than 125
demonstrators walked west on Highway 264 followed by a caravan of
fifty-five automobiles, U-Haul trailers, and buses carrying food, bed-
ding, and chaperones.[25] Over the next six days, they traced a two-
hundred-mile route to the state capitol, parading through towns and,
between them, boarding cars and buses.

   The marchers spent the first two nights at black churches in Belhaven
and Washington, two coastal towns not far from Hyde County. They
traveled the next three days through the heart of the Tobacco Belt and
spent the evenings in Greenville, Farmville, and Wilson, the largest
tobacco markets in the world.[26] Along this route, local black residents
displayed signs of solidarity. Many walked in the Hyde County procession through their town, and civil rights groups held support rallies in
Belhaven and Greenville.[27] In Wilson, several hundred black students
boycotted high school for a day to join the march, then accompanied
them part of the way to Raleigh.[28]

   Racial tensions in Raleigh were high. Outside of Hyde County, the
school boycott had become something of an enigma, gaining a larger-

than-life aura. Many people remained astonished by its endurance and still could not fathom the blacks' rigid unwillingness to sacrifice Peay and Davis for school desegregation. While the school boycott usually struck a sympathetic chord among black Carolinians, for whom it evoked fond memories of other alma maters, to many whites it seemed as mysterious as the Hyde County swamps. State political leaders and other curious citizens crowded downtown to watch the procession, and fearful town officials prepared for the worst. Every available police officer was on duty. Three dozen state troopers stood nearby in case they were needed. Riot police wearing bullet-proof vests and antiterrorism gear waited at the Municipal Building, and National Guardsmen were on standby alert at the State Fairgrounds.[29] Large numbers of plain-clothed SBI and FBI agents wandered the crowds and closely monitored the march.

Bolstered by busloads of demonstrators from home on the final day, six hundred marchers arrived in Raleigh on Friday afternoon, February 14. A crowd of supporters led by several hundred black students from Shaw University and St. Augustine's College welcomed them to the capital.[30] Following six children carrying a casket with a sign that read "Save our soul sister Marie Hill," they proceeded slowly into the heart of the government district. They laid the casket on the Great Seal of North Carolina on the terrazzo in front of the State House, then held a long rally with a keynote speech by the Reverend Andrew Young, who was then SCLC's executive vice-president.[31]

During the last part of the rally, Young and school boycott leaders met with Dr. Craig Phillips at the state Department of Public Instruction and later with Governor Scott. At an earlier meeting on January 28, ten days before the March on Raleigh, the local black leaders had requested that Phillips support a return to "freedom of choice" in the Hyde County schools until a more equitable plan could be worked out.[32] They communicated a new flexibility that apparently reassured the state superintendent, who told the press that he had developed more confidence in the "concerns and motivations" underlying the school boycott. He pledged to work directly with black leaders and the school board to find both short-term and long-term solutions to the school crisis.[33]

At the meeting during the March on Raleigh, Phillips told the Hyde County delegation that he supported a temporary return to "freedom of choice," as well as black participation in shaping a permanent desegre-

The Hyde County marchers enter Raleigh. (*The* News and Observer *Collection, Division of Archives and History, Raleigh, N.C.*)

SCLC leaders at the March on Raleigh. Left to right: Golden Frinks, the Reverend Andrew Young, and Bennie Rountree. Back row: Durham activist Irving Joyner and an unidentified student protester. (The News and Observer Collection, Division of Archives and History, Raleigh, N.C.)

gation plan. He was, he said, "cautiously optimistic" that the school boycott could end soon, though the agreement negotiated at this meeting required the support of HEW and the local school board.[34] Probably influenced by new, more conservative leadership appointed by President Nixon, HEW had quietly shown some signs that it might allow the school board to return temporarily to 1967–68 conditions. HEW still insisted, however, that the Hyde County Board of Education take the initiative.[35]

The momentum that was evident in Raleigh ebbed in Hyde County the following week. Several state officials, including Jerome Melton from the Department of Public Instruction and Fred Cooper from the Good Neighbor Council, joined a closed meeting that next Monday night between black leaders and local school officials. It was the first of several conferences between February 17 and 22 to discuss the plan supported by Craig Phillips.[36] The local school leaders seriously considered contacting HEW, but finally decided not to. There is little record of those meetings, but school officials evidently had no problem agreeing to a return to "freedom of choice" for the remainder of the school year. Their objection to the proposal was based instead on black demands for fuller participation in developing a new desegregation plan.

The school board was prepared to make a few concessions to the black community. The board members agreed to open the O. A. Peay and Davis schools more fully to boycott activities. They pledged to appoint a committee of parents representing Peay, Davis, and Mattamuskeet to work with them to solve the racial crisis. They also discussed with black parents ideas for assisting high school seniors to graduate that summer. They offered to allow the students to make up English and history requirements in the spring and summer or to create a six-week summer session for seniors who only needed an English credit.[37] These last compromises would indeed have been very important. Disappointed black parents soon learned, though, that Bucklew was only prepared to grant "provisional certificates," not real diplomas, to children who participated in the programs.[38]

The school board never actually formed the new citizens' committee as promised. The Hyde County Board of Commissioners instead appointed such a committee itself in late February. The committee included Curfew Harris, Marjorie Selby, and the Reverend Booker Boomer, all well-respected black leaders, and an equal number of relatively liberal white citizens, among them the minister from Amity Methodist Church near Engelhard.[39] They met weekly in February and March but never had the necessary authority with either black activists or the school board to play a useful role. The committee eventually faded away without taking firm action or even making recommendations.[40] Its work represented the final effort to negotiate a settlement during the school year.

When they returned from the first march to Raleigh, school boycott leaders began to organize a second almost immediately, timing it to commemorate the first anniversary of Martin Luther King, Jr.'s assassination.[41] The Mountain Top to Valley March would approach the state capitol from the opposite direction than the March on Raleigh. The school boycotters planned to travel, again mostly by bus, 250 miles in eleven days, from Asheville in the Blue Ridge Mountains east to Raleigh. But the march was marked by tragedy before its first step. On March 24, a carload of youths—one of several "advance teams" that had spread out along the route to organize local support—swerved into a pickup truck on a highway in Wilson, one hundred miles west of Swan Quarter. Lucy Howard and Clara Beckworth, teenage girls from the Slocumb community, were killed on impact. The three other passengers were injured but not gravely.[42]

Hyde County blacks were profoundly shaken by the car wreck. Years later many people remembered the accident and the subsequent weeks of mourning more vividly than any other moments during the school boycott. The two girls had spent their last weeks away from home organizing civil rights demonstrations with the students at Johnson C. Smith College in Charlotte. They were returning to the coast, about to stop at Milton Fitch's house for the night, when the accident happened. The scene of the wreck itself had been strewn with testimony of their commitment to the black freedom movement: antipoverty pamphlets, posters of Martin Luther King, Jr., and placards saying "Save Marie Hill." Undoubtedly their families and some other people must have wondered if the sacrifice was worth it. However, most grew more determined to see the school boycott through, in Fitch's words, "not wanting to let Clara and Lucy down" by failing to honor their example.[43]

The Mountain Top to Valley March proceeded on April 4. The group of about seventy-five marchers followed a meandering course from Asheville to Raleigh. They moved rapidly by bus and on foot through the textile and furniture mill towns of the Piedmont, frequently changing their itinerary to respond to local events. In Madison County and Statesville, they helped black activists to consolidate school desegregation campaigns. They walked picket lines with textile workers striking at Cannon Mills in Kannapolis. White civic leaders greeted them as civil rights heroes in Valdese, and the Black Panthers welcomed them into Greensboro with open arms. In Asheville, on the other hand, black ministers shunned them, apparently concerned that outside activists would upset their own civil rights activities.[44]

The most memorable episode of the march occurred in Concord, where the Ku Klux Klan waited in ambush for the Hyde County demonstrators. As the marchers neared the Klan, a sympathetic local white minister frantically spread word of the impending clash to black students at a high school and at Barber-Scotia, a black Presbyterian college. Hundreds of the students quickly left their campuses to join the Mountain Top to Valley March, and the Klan shrank back before their

A Hyde County protester in Raleigh. (The News and Observer *Collection, Division of Archives and History, Raleigh, N.C.)*

overwhelming numbers.[45] The rambling marchers spurred civil rights activism in several other Piedmont towns. However, their erratic course, flexible timetable, and fluid goals built little momentum for larger demonstrations at their Raleigh destination or for exerting political pressure on the governor or General Assembly.

The Mountain Top to Valley marchers arrived somewhat disheveled in Raleigh on April 18, three days later than planned. Racial tensions were even higher in the capital than when the school boycotters had last visited, and they inflamed an already tense community. A year earlier, the assassination of Martin Luther King, Jr., had caused massive black protests in North Carolina, prompting curfews statewide and the occupation of Wilmington, Goldsboro, Durham, and Greensboro by the National Guard.[46] Now the anniversary of Reverend King's assassination had sparked a new wave of violence and vandalism in Raleigh, as in many other North Carolina cities, and a recent incident of alleged police brutality had also angered blacks residents.[47] The Hyde County youths joined their protests, including a peaceful march of several hundred from the Walnut Terrace housing project into downtown Raleigh, and initiated their own nonviolent demonstrations as well. However, their stay also coincided with a series of fire bombings at the bus station, two state liquor stores, and several other public places.[48] The Hyde County protesters could scarcely attract attention to the school boycott in so besieged a city.

Though most school boycotters returned home after a few days of protests in Raleigh, several dozen remained in town for more than two weeks. What was left of the Mountain Top to Valley March degenerated further, having already lost too much of its focus and clarity of purpose. Desperate to keep the school boycott in the public eye, the Hyde County activists attempted protests that were too ambitious to succeed so far from their local support. Frinks conducted protests at the state capitol, obstructing public roads and even access to the General Assembly, and he also led several acts of civil disobedience in the business district.[49] He planned to establish a "tent city" near the downtown area, but Raleigh officials refused him the necessary permits. At the end of April eighteen youths were arrested for blocking traffic, and Frinks himself was charged with contributing to the delinquency of minors after police arrested two boys under the age of sixteen for interfering with traffic on April 25 and 26.[50] The young people were not given prison sentences, but district court judge Ed Preston, Jr., gave Frinks a very stiff one-year sentence on May 7.[51] The sentence was appealed immediately but signaled the end of the campaign to occupy Raleigh.

While SCLC organizers and the young activists marched on Raleigh, spring had arrived back in Hyde County. The tundra swans began passing overhead in graceful formation, departing Lake Mattamuskeet for the far north. Crop planting, gardening, and the launching of fishing boats soon replaced the winter solitude. The sweet fragrance of the swamps and salt marshes coming back to life could have inspired hope in anybody, and important changes in school leadership that spring indeed seemed to warrant at least a cautious optimism. Supt. Allen Bucklew announced his resignation for health reasons. Principal Fred Simons decided to take early retirement from the O. A. Peay School. The Hyde County Board of Education elected a new, more moderate chairman, Earl Pugh, and the Hyde County Board of Commissioners was in the process of selecting two new school board members to replace the men who had resigned for health reasons. Some kind of break-through seemed inevitable. Though those changes in school leadership effectively precluded negotiations until the new leaders were in place, they raised hopes that the crisis would be resolved in the summer.

HEW also gave the school boycotters cause for hope. To the Office of Civil Rights, the standstill in negotiations and the arrival of a new superintendent indicated that the Hyde County Board of Education would have problems complying with its desegregation plan for the second school year. The next year of the plan required all first through eighth graders to attend Mattamuskeet. On April 28, skeptical HEW staff inquired about the school board's intentions for the 1969–70 school year. Lloyd Henderson from the Office of Civil Rights suggested that the board revise the old plan and use the O. A. Peay and Davis schools on a desegregated basis.[52] Though most local residents and school officials agreed that some kind of change was necessary, the Board of Education decided to hold its course until the new superintendent arrived in late June, and at a May 5 meeting reaffirmed its commitment to the current desegregation plan.[53] The threat that HEW would not tolerate another year of stalemate lingered, though, and contributed to a sense of urgency that the crisis should be settled over the summer. The school boycotters knew that a withdrawal of HEW support for the current desegregation plan would at this point work to their advantage; it would undermine the school board and almost certainly lead to the preservation of Peay and Davis.

The school boycott was still strong when the 1968–69 school year closed in early June. Black students had missed an entire year of classes, and some older children who might have graduated had instead left the county or found jobs, but black leaders declared that the sacrifice had been worth it. [54] Sustaining the school boycott through the last half of the year had been a remarkable act of endurance requiring them to overcome poor weather, jail, the deaths of Clara Beckworth and Lucy Howard, and their own fears for the children's educations. Yet black citizens had carried their struggle twice to the state capitol in Raleigh, and they had supported and frequently sparked civil rights activism throughout North Carolina. They had certainly influenced black and white expectations about school desegregation. In addition, the school boycott had grown into a full-fledged civil rights movement within Hyde County, allowing local citizens to address racism in economic and political spheres as well as education. Now, at the start of summer, the black and white citizenry expected a few months' reprieve from the intensity of the school boycott. They welcomed time to heal the wounds of racial conflict and to get acquainted with new school leaders, but they already looked ahead with apprehension to the first day of classes in September.

CHAPTER 6

The Hour of Harvest

On July 4, 1969, a sniper fired two shots into a carload of blacks passing by a Ku Klux Klan meeting in Middletown, a rural crossroads three miles south of Engelhard.[1] Though a bullet shattered their windshield, the four young passengers escaped unharmed and drove directly into town to alert Sheriff Cahoon. The sheriff at first seemed unperturbed by their story. He lingered at the local cafe while news of the incident flashed through the eastern part of the county.[2] When Cahoon and state trooper L. J. Vance finally arrived in Middletown thirty minutes later, dozens of well-armed blacks had already surrounded the Klan hall. About 125 black citizens soon confronted 80 Klansmen. From several counties, more state troopers hurried to Middletown and formed a line between the two groups, but the outraged blacks would not disperse and tried to force their way into the rally. According to an SHP internal report, they "were [even] discussing among themselves which [police] officers they were going to get in order to go through them into the Klan meeting."[3]

The standoff continued for two tense hours, with angry threats exchanged constantly, until the Klan leaders proceeded with the traditional cross burning despite the crowd that still surrounded them. "Immediately after the cross was set afire," reported a state trooper at the scene, a shot was fired and a barrage of gunfire erupted between the two groups.[4] The Klansmen discharged high-powered rifles, automatic weapons, and handguns. The blacks relied on hunting rifles and shotguns. "It was like a war," one stunned police officer later told a news reporter.[5] Law officers in riot gear quickly stormed the hall and subdued the Klansmen. A bullet grazed a twelve-year-old black girl, Debra Collins of Engelhard, and buckshot wounded several police officers, but nobody had been seriously hurt. The police arrested seventeen Klansmen and finally scattered both black and white combatants. Dozens of black gunmen were later charged and fined for their involvement in the showdown. Though not the death knell for the local Ku Klux Klan, the Middletown confrontation marked its retreat back into the shadows. The era of open-air KKK rallies, public toleration, and racist violence with impunity had ended.

The Ku Klux Klan was only one symbol of broader racial oppression that had grown intolerable by the summer of 1969. The shoot-out in Middletown revealed that a transformation had occurred in Hyde County. Only a year earlier, race relations had been mired in the traditions of the Jim Crow era. The school boycott had changed the county profoundly in ways still evolving that summer. There could be no retreat into disenfranchisement and segregation, no return to black deference and powerlessness. School desegregation too would inevitably be different than it had been the previous year, but its exact character, including whether Peay and Davis would be saved, remained in doubt. The fate of the black schools would be determined during the summer and fall of 1969.

The school boycott had worn down political leaders, both locally and in Raleigh. They were willing to encourage both serious negotiations and greater black participation in school matters, but they also wanted to take no chances that the boycott would extend into a second year. In the summer of 1969, they consequently wielded both a carrot and a stick to settle the racial crisis. They combined important concessions, extraordinary school reforms, and new flexibility with threats, police intimidation, and harsh penalties intended to undermine black leaders and divide the black community. While those efforts had an impact, the Hyde County activists would prevail as the school boycott came to an end.

Visionaries, Planners, and Thinkers

The administration of Gov. Robert Scott exerted its own influence over the school crisis early in the summer of 1969. The school leadership changes in Hyde had left the door open for Raleigh to intervene. The governor had little formal responsibility for local desegregation plans, but state officials steadily deepened their involvement. They feared that the school boycott might arouse other black communities when classes convened that fall. At the North Carolina Department of Public Instruction, state educational leaders were already hearing local school admin-

istrators declaring, "We don't want a Hyde County here." They consequently sought new ways of involving black citizens more fully in school
desegregation planning. "If it can happen in a little place like that," a
state official remembered worried school leaders telling him, "no telling
what could happen here."[6]

State superintendent Craig Phillips and the governor's office had
made two pivotal decisions late in the spring that helped to prevent
the school boycott from continuing into the next academic year. First,
they convinced R. O. Singletary, the forty-one-year-old principal at La
Grange High School in Lenoir County, to replace Allen Bucklew as
Hyde County's superintendent. Singletary was well respected for how
he managed school desegregation in La Grange. He supported community involvement and citizen participation, but he was also prepared to
use a firm hand to accomplish the task. Phillips believed Singletary was
the perfect man for the difficult job in Hyde County.

The state superintendent also directed a new team of school desegregation experts to work with Singletary. Governor Scott had formed the
Division of Desegregation Assistance early in 1969 to satisfy a federal
court order arising out of Johnston County. This court order gave North
Carolina an affirmative obligation to facilitate desegregation in local
school districts. The Scott administration probably would have created a
similar state office anyway. Hyde County alone had demonstrated its
need: the school boycott had exhausted the bureaucratic mechanisms
used by governors Terry Sanford and Dan K. Moore to defuse racial
crises. State political leaders also acknowledged that they had not been
"prepared psychologically" for the school boycotters' perseverance or for
the complexity of the schooling issues the boycott raised.[7] They realized
now that new approaches to school desegregation were necessary.

The Scott administration shaped the Division of Desegregation Assistance during the spring of 1969, when the Hyde County school boycott
was the focus of civil rights activity in North Carolina. The school
boycott clearly influenced its staff, mission, and approach. Phillips
appointed Robert Strothers, his special assistant, to direct the division.
Strothers, a white man, had joined the Department of Public Instruction after leaving the school superintendency in Greene County, a rural
county in eastern North Carolina's Tobacco Belt. Dudley Flood, a black
native of Hertford County and principal of a Pitt County school, was
appointed the assistant director.[8] Both men had grown up in eastern

North Carolina and had pursued school careers not far from Hyde County. Both were familiar with school desegregation issues. They empathized with Hyde County citizens about the complex problems before them and understood the attachment that black families held for Peay and Davis. Dudley Flood, in particular, appreciated this devotion. He still considered his own student days at a black school as among his fondest, most loving memories, and as a source of great pride and inspiration. Nonetheless, both Flood and Strothers opposed any civil rights protest that put so large a burden on children. The school boycott was their division's first real challenge at easing local communities through the traumas accompanying school desegregation, and they virtually lived in Hyde County during the next several months.

Singletary arrived in Hyde County in the last few days of June. Bob Strothers and Dudley Flood followed almost immediately. Local citizens greeted them with measures of both skepticism and hope. While Singletary acquainted himself with his school board and administrators, Flood visited school boycott meetings and church services and met privately with the Committee of 14, the NAACP, and other black leaders. Strothers worked principally with white citizens and their leaders, trying to grasp their attitudes toward school desegregation and black protests. He and Flood worked slowly at first, listening and learning about Hyde County society, the specific issues that gave rise to the school boycott, and the various factions that might help or hinder a settlement.

Flood and Strothers gradually laid a foundation for negotiations between the local school leaders and the boycott activists. With Singletary and the Hyde County Board of Education, they discussed ways to improve public relations and citizen involvement. They mapped out strategies for negotiations and public meetings. They shared relevant experiences from other school districts. And in time they convinced the board that there were grounds for negotiation that did not imply surrender to the black protesters.[9] Then they relayed proposals back and forth between white and black leaders, opening channels of communication that had not existed during the previous year.

The state officials observed that the Committee of 14 and other adult black leaders usually preferred to have issues brought to them for discussion and a yes or no decision but less often generated new proposals or answers to school problems. The young people, on the other hand, wanted to create solutions to the school crisis. They were especially impressive to Flood. He later remembered that the children showed extraordinary interest in every phase of reaching a settlement. He found them "incredible visionaries, good planners and thinkers."[10] When an impasse was reached, he counted on the children to find a way out of it. While their parents sometimes shushed them for their forthrightness, the children openly challenged school officials during negotiations. They demanded evidence, saw through false promises, and pushed aside efforts to avoid tough issues, going straight to the heart of the school dilemmas. Flood was astonished by their intellectual drive and curiosity, stronger than those among any students he had encountered in his career. Though hardly immune to their criticism, he recalled that "you really felt like you could do some teaching if you had kids like them."[11]

The major negotiations revolved around the very nature of school desegregation. For the boycotters, keeping the O. A. Peay and Davis schools open was preeminent but was hardly the only concern. Having scrutinized for a full year the broader implications of merging Peay and Davis with Mattamuskeet, they articulated their grievances and concerns with a refined clarity. Most concerns were related to black power and participation in the school district. The school boycott activists believed that only by having an equitable share of power over school policy, educational administration, and teaching could they assure that desegregated schools would promote intellectual achievement, pride, and social responsibility for black children. Only then, they reasoned, could new, biracial schools share in the strengths of Peay and Davis and become, like them, vital agents of black cultural and community survival.

With that basic vision steadfastly in mind, the Committee of 14, Frinks, student leaders, and other school boycott representatives negotiated with the Hyde County Board of Education over the details of a broad range of issues. They wanted assurances that black principals, teachers, and service workers would not lose their current jobs or be demoted during school desegregation. They sought a firm commitment from the school board eventually to employ a black principal at the Mattamuskeet School and black administrators at the Hyde County Board of Education's office. They demanded that blacks have more control over and participation in ESEA programs and that a class in African American history be taught. They insisted on equal opportunities to participate in extracurricular activities. They advocated for policies against tracking black students into lower-level classes, which amounted to racial segregation within schools, as well as for monitoring procedures to ensure that teachers did not discipline black children unfairly. The school boycott leaders also proposed that administrators structure parent and student participation more fully into school governance at Peay, Davis, and Mattamuskeet.

The black negotiators demanded further that the Hyde County Board of Commissioners appoint a black person to the next vacancy on the school board. If Peay and Davis were converted into elementary schools—a new compromise that seemed reasonable to black citizens—they would not accept any name but that of the O. A. Peay School's founder. They hoped to keep their sports teams' names, mascots, and trophy cases. They wanted a guarantee that alumni of the segregation-era black schools would continue to have access to their academic records. Finally, they sought assurances that the two schools would remain available for Homecoming, Founder's Day, and other black community events. Across the South, the failure to recognize or address precisely these issues tarnished school desegregation and led, in many cases, to mass alienation from the newly desegregated schools. In Hyde County, these matters would be acknowledged and discussed relentlessly. Negotiating these critical issues occupied local school officials, school boycott leaders, and state representatives throughout the summer and well into the next school year.

Superintendent Singletary tackled the difficult school boycott issues soon after his arrival in Hyde County. He displayed a refreshing flexibility toward the racial crisis, encouraged by the state facilitators, the more moderate tone of the school board, and the fledgling negotiations with black leaders. He and the school board admitted in late June that the school district would not be ready to implement the next phase of its desegregation plan by September. They informed HEW that more time was necessary, in their words, to "improve human relations" and "present facts to citizenship on possible alternatives [for] future direction of education."[12] They also acknowledged that their building expansion plans had been too ambitious. HEW had recently prohibited school districts from spending ESEA funds for construction, restricting their use instead to educational programs. The school officials consequently did not have the money necessary to enlarge Mattamuskeet to hold several more grades of black students. At a special session on June 30, the school board requested another year from HEW to transfer additional grades from the two black schools to Mattamuskeet.[13]

On June 30, school board members committed themselves publicly to consider alternative plans for desegregation. They announced that they would develop new options and confer over their advantages and disadvantages with every interested civic group and individual. The school officials also agreed that they would discuss the possible plans with boycott leaders in order to develop a better basis for negotiations and for black participation in this process. This game plan represented a remarkable turnaround from the previous year, of course, reflecting the school boycott's success, the mood of the citizenry, and the character of the new leadership. School officials concluded, "The Board wants to move in the direction that the majority of the people would like and support."[14]

School leaders examined several new desegregation plans over the next two weeks. Singletary appointed a biracial Better Education Committee to review the possibilities with him, and he also consulted with HEW and the state officials.[15] By July 10, he had become convinced that school desegregation should not start with the youngest children.[16] As an interim arrangement, he and the school board instead decided to transfer black students in grades four through six to the Mattamuskeet School for the next year and to allow the first through third grades to return to Peay and Davis. HEW had no problems with this amendment to the plan.

By the middle of July, after much deliberation and research, school leaders had narrowed their choices to two desegregation plans. At three meetings on July 16, they presented the two options and evaluations of their costs and benefits to black leaders, the school advisory councils, and county teachers. Singletary and the school board reported that they still preferred the existing desegregation plan. "Plan 1," as they called it, would have shut down O. A. Peay and Davis and transferred all black students to Mattamuskeet. In defending the plan, they emphasized the greater efficiency of centralized administration, libraries, bus systems, and teacher supervision. The closed black schools would also provide much-needed office space and room for a community college branch. In addition, they stressed that classes held under one roof would assure "equal education for all students."[17] However, the school officials also noted several important drawbacks to Plan 1. These included longer bus routes, the social mixing of elementary and high school students, and a total student population at Mattamuskeet exceeding 1,400 students, very large for a rural school district.

The school leaders professed that Plan 1 remained the best choice. But they acknowledged that the plan was not feasible unless they could raise enough funds to build twenty-eight new classrooms and to purchase land adjacent to the Mattamuskeet School. They calculated that the building expansions would cost almost half a million dollars, plus additional debt service totaling more than $350,000 over twenty-five years. To finance the project, they had already received tentative approval from the Hyde County Board of Commissioners to include a $500,000 bond issue in the local elections that November.[18] Plan 1 could be implemented only if the electorate passed the bond issue.

If the bond issue failed, "Plan 2," basically the option advocated by black citizens, was the "only other alternative." This plan would utilize all three facilities, converting Peay and Davis into elementary schools and Mattamuskeet into the county high school.[19] Though Plan 2 was not its first choice, the school board did not hesitate to elaborate strong arguments in support of this alternative. It required no new construction and only low-cost renovations that could be financed with a modest one-year tax increase. Bus routes would be substantially shorter for many children, and elementary and high school students would be separated socially. For a small investment in renovations, they also believed that Mattamuskeet could accommodate a two-year night program in vocational or college education, probably affiliated with the technical school in Beaufort County. Hard-pressed to identify disadvantages, school leaders concluded that Plan 2 would provide "good schools for years to come."[20]

The two plans had been formulated cleverly and with political astuteness. This path strategically removed the decision from school officials' hands and put the matter of the school boycott, and the future of Peay and Davis, to the electorate. School leaders assumed that the large majority of black citizens supported Plan 2 and would oppose the bond issue. But since white citizens comprised three-quarters of registered voters, they would have the final decision.[21] Many local observers now believed, however, that within bounds, whites would choose whatever would restore peace in their community. Even if white voters supported

Plan 1, their convictions would have to be vehement enough to counter-balance the prospect of higher taxes. Hyde County residents were still retiring the debt incurred when taxpayers financed the construction of the Mattamuskeet School, and the new bond issue would require another tax increase of nearly 25 percent. Consequently, the bond referendum placed the advantage of less taxation on the side of black citizens, but did not compromise the position of school board members among their white neighbors by forcing them to give in publicly to black demands.

Placing the future of the school district before the local electorate was incomparably more democratic and sensitive to black concerns than the heavy-handed approach that had sparked the school boycott a year earlier. But black voters remained in the minority, and many boycott leaders felt uncomfortable with this approach. "They have the power to open all three schools," contended Etta Mae Greene, "so they should do it."[22] Frinks and other SCLC leaders worried that the school boycott would lose too much momentum between July and November for them to organize new protests if the bond issue succeeded. Many blacks also distrusted school officials so thoroughly by this point that they suspected back-room dealings might close Peay and Davis even if the bond issue failed.[23] More than four hundred black citizens expressed their opposition to the referendum at a mass meeting in Engelhard on August 8, and they resolved to renew the school boycott in September unless the school board assured them that Peay and Davis would remain open. There was a small group of dissenters, led by the local NAACP leaders who had originally opposed the boycott, but the large majority of blacks remained firmly behind the goal of retaining their schools.

Leaders of both races strongly agreed that they needed more time to select a plan and implement it before black and white children attended classes together. Meeting in an unprecedented joint session on August 19, the Hyde County Board of Education and the Committee of 14 decided that another year of "freedom of choice" was the wisest course.[24] By postponing desegregation, they hoped to avoid a school boycott in 1969–70 and sought to assure school desegregation with biracial support in 1970–71. They also believed that the cooling-off period would help to reduce racial tensions.

Soon thereafter, Singletary, board member Walter Lee Gibbs, and two delegates from the Committee of 14 traveled to Charlottesville,

Virginia, where a special HEW review panel heard their petition to return temporarily to "freedom of choice." Though presented with white and black leaders in agreement, the HEW hearing officers felt compelled by their departmental regulations and legal precedents to forbid further delays in desegregating the Hyde County schools. They denied the petition. Singletary was so concerned that local blacks would blame the Board of Education that he had two HEW representatives join him to explain the decision at a community meeting at the O. A. Peay School in late August. Their justification for the denial was by then largely immaterial to black activists. With the new academic year almost upon them, they had to decide quickly whether to postpone the school boycott while waiting for the results of the November election. Their protests had already earned black citizens enormous, often fundamental reforms in school desegregation policy. But sending their children to Mattamuskeet without a firm commitment from the school board to utilize Peay and Davis was very difficult to contemplate after so many sacrifices.

Intimidation and Scare Tactics

Black citizens were not left alone to resolve this dilemma. While they welcomed new concessions and more participatory approaches to desegregation policy, they also confronted renewed efforts to intimidate them, discredit the school boycott, and divide their community. Singletary bluntly threatened his teachers with dismissal if they supported the school boycott or refused to send their own children to class.[25] While including black parents in more school decisions, the new superintendent also warned them that he would vigorously prosecute parents who failed to enroll their children that September. He showed signs of a seriousness never exhibited by Allen Bucklew, even employing a truancy officer—the first ever in Hyde County—to enforce the attendance law.

School officials also exacerbated and manipulated divisions within the black community. Singletary tried subtly to discourage more militant activism, for example, by appointing individuals who had not been boycott leaders to represent the black community on several biracial school committees. A group of black dissenters that emerged publicly in August was an even more serious concern. On August 8, Early Bryant, an NAACP leader who had originally opposed the school boycott, sent Governor Scott a petition he and fifty-six other black citizens had signed decrying the "corruptive influence" of Golden Frinks. In an accompanying letter, Bryant pleaded that "steps should be taken to eliminate [Frinks's] harmful influence from North Carolina." Requesting an investigation by the state attorney general, the petitioners alleged that Frinks misused donations and intimidated some local people into supporting the school boycott.[26]

The petition undoubtedly grew out of a year of great frustration for the few blacks who did not support the school boycott. Bryant in particular was disturbed not only at the deferment of school desegregation, for which he had long fought, but also at losing his status among local civil rights leaders. Indeed, he, Johnnie Midgette, and the other NAACP leaders who had not joined the school boycott had often felt like exiles in their own community over the past year. For some of them this isolation had been far more difficult to bear than the Ku Klux Klan harassment that they had withstood so bravely during their campaign to desegregate the schools. During the school boycott, the most militant black activists had ostracized them, and their children had sometimes been harassed for attending classes. It had been a very hard year for them, and the thought of more protests to further delay their dream of interracial schools seemed almost intolerable.[27]

The SBI later concluded that Bryant had no basis for his allegations. Few black citizens considered him a malicious man, though, and many believed that whites manipulated his frustration in order to discredit school boycott leaders, either by suggesting the letter or even by writing it.[28] According to an SBI internal report, Bryant had neither evidence nor specific accusations against the SCLC leaders.[29] Later that autumn he admitted to SBI agents T. W. Caddy and G. D. Phillips that "everything [I] know is strictly hearsay," and he cautioned them that other signers would not discuss the petition.[30] He acknowledged that he had always opposed the school boycott and had been suspicious of its leadership, especially Frinks, but he was unable to give them a single lead. Sheriff Cahoon and his deputies also had no information that suggested corruption among the SCLC leaders.[31]

Whether or not Early Bryant himself had been manipulated, the Scott administration used his letter and the petition in order to discredit Golden Frinks exactly when the SCLC leader most needed public support and when local blacks had to decide whether or not to send their children to school. The governor's aides waited until September 1, two days before the opening of school, to release the August 8 letter to the media.[32] At Governor Scott's request, Fred Cooper, now chairman of the Good Neighbor Council, met the next day with school leaders in Swan Quarter and afterward asked the SBI to hold a formal investigation into Frinks's conduct. A banner headline in the *News and Observer* the next morning read, "Scott Calls for SBI Probe of Frinks' Actions in Hyde."[33] Editorials in other newspapers blamed the SCLC for "interfering" in Hyde County. Neither the media nor the Scott administration observed that the allegations had not been supported by evidence and came from a small minority of black citizens who had always opposed the school boycott. Instead, they suggested that the charges were made by black protesters disaffected with the SCLC leaders.

The public announcement of the Bryant petition and SBI investigation momentarily jeopardized the credibility of Golden Frinks. He was already in a vulnerable position. His conviction and one-year sentence that May remained under appeal, and the superior court in Raleigh might have been influenced by new charges against him. A seasoned veteran of civil rights jailings, Frinks knew that a prison sentence would not be a useful gesture now. The accusations also threatened his public support. Though more experienced observers of the civil rights movement were skeptical of any unsubstantiated charges against black leaders, the broader public might well have believed that the SBI's inquiry indicated guilt. Moreover, Frinks's ill-fated efforts to occupy Raleigh had left a bad impression even on many of his liberal supporters in North Carolina. It was not a good moment to have questions raised about his leadership.

No less significantly, the SCLC leadership in Atlanta wavered in its support for Frinks at this critical moment. On hearing the allegations against their field director, the national leaders asked him to report to Atlanta immediately to discuss the situation with Andrew Young and Hosea Williams. They apparently wanted Jim Harrison, the SCLC's controller, to visit Hyde County in order to review the financial books. While Williams explained to a newspaper reporter that the group was "bound to look into any charge of irregularity," headlines like "SCLC Investigates," which appeared in the *Charlotte Observer*'s September 3 issue, did not bolster confidence in Frinks or his reputation.[34]

The SBI did not conduct its investigation in response to the Bryant petition until October, but evidently government agents had already been bearing down on Frinks and other school boycott leaders. According to their internal reports, the FBI or the SBI—or perhaps both—had been moving deftly to discredit black activists prior to the new school term. For most of the year, both the FBI and SBI had agents stationed in Hyde County. Even military intelligence officers had joined their surveillance activities on several occasions. FBI agents routinely monitored SCLC national leaders with wiretaps and other methods and sent regular updates on SCLC activities to their Hyde County agents, who in turn relayed information on the school boycott to FBI offices in Washington, D.C., and Charlotte, North Carolina. In terms of archival evidence, the question of whether—and, if so, how extensively—FBI and SBI involvement went beyond surveillance remains unclear until the summer of 1969. In early August, Assistant Attorney General Jerris Leonard ordered the FBI to investigate the "possibility of racial violence" during the opening of schools that fall. On reviewing state files, the FBI focused its North Carolina investigations on Hyde County and a handful of other school districts.[35]

Only a single document describes the investigation, and it is unclear whether this memorandum originated with the FBI or the SBI. Not on any letterhead but now attached to SBI records at the North Carolina State Archives, the document instructed unspecified agents to investigate Frinks and the Committee of 14 before September 2, 1969. In the undated memorandum, an FBI or possibly an SBI agent in Hyde County informed a superior elsewhere or his liaison with the other agency that "you should have as many men as possible down here for a few days."[36] The document listed the Committee of 14 members and instructed the agents to ask "questions . . . implicating the above people and Golden Frinks and his Associates."

In this document, the unnamed agent instructed his colleagues to look closely at the school boycott's finances. He urged them to ask who had contributed money, how much these donors had contributed, and how black activists had spent the donations. He wanted the agents to ask black families if they had taken part in the school boycott and who had encouraged their participation. The entire investigation was to be completed by September 2, the same day that the Scott administration publicly called for an SBI investigation. FBI records indicate that some kind of investigation occurred in Hyde County, but portions of key documents have been deleted, making it impossible to determine whether the FBI investigation was the same probe outlined in the SBI files. Whether or not evidence of criminal activity was found—and apparently it was not—any remotely similar investigation would have intimidated some black citizens and encouraged divisive rumors.[37]

The opening of the next superior court session also had a strong impact on the school boycott's future. Convening court early in September, Judge J. William Copeland heard the appeals of approximately eighty young people found guilty in district court of blocking traffic. He sentenced the protesters to six months in prison but suspended their jail terms on one important condition: the convicted students must immediately enroll in and attend school in Hyde County.[38] In addition, the judge gave active sentences ranging from sixty days to six months to seven boys and six girls who had broken previous probations by rejoining the demonstrations.[39] Since those young people and their families were among the most committed activists, these terms of probation and the prison sentences were a serious blow to further protests.

With Frinks under attack and having to travel to SCLC headquarters in Atlanta to discuss the accusations against him, black leaders met on the second day of classes, September 3, and decided to postpone the school boycott until the November election. Many parents had already chosen to give the bond referendum a chance to resolve the crisis. Approximately three hundred black children, substantially more than on any day in 1968–69 but still only about one-third the total black student population, had enrolled in classes the previous day. The threats against parents and educators, the restrictive conditions of probation, and the efforts to discredit their leaders had prompted some black residents to send their children back to school. Most, though, were so bone-weary with racial tensions and fear for their children's educations that they pinned their hopes on the new biracial committees and on an electoral victory in November. If the election disappointed them, they could revitalize the school boycott then.

A Referendum on the School Boycott

The special election on November 5 did not disappoint black citizens. Hyde County voters defeated the bond referendum by a four-to-one margin.[40] Without the bonds, the Hyde County Board of Education could not afford to expand Mattamuskeet to serve all black and white students. A new desegregation plan had to utilize the O. A. Peay School, the Davis School, and the Mattamuskeet School. The school boycotters had accomplished their most important goal. The historically black institutions would survive school desegregation, a precious achievement in the South.

In interviews two decades later, white residents shed light on why they rejected the bond referendum. Many people of course opposed the sizable tax increases necessary to enlarge Mattamuskeet, more than they opposed using Peay and Davis. Volunteering to pay to shut down the black schools would have required a degree of open racial animosity that most Hyde County whites simply did not have or could not afford. In addition, though, most white voters also felt that too much school consolidation had already occurred. The school board's Plan 2 allowed the large majority of young children—the black and white students who would attend Peay and Davis—to make shorter bus trips and cut as much as forty minutes of travel time daily. The greater accessibility and ease of community involvement that would exist at smaller, more local schools far outweighed any lingering anxiety about sending their children to a formerly black institution. Indeed, many white citizens still felt bitter about the consolidation plan that had closed the East Hyde School in Engelhard and West Hyde School in Swan Quarter in 1963. The opportunity to use Peay and Davis meant that they too, not only the black community, would again have a community school instead of having all their children centralized in Mattamuskeet.

Other white residents indicated that the bond referendum exposed a longstanding rift between white leaders and the white citizenry. They argued that the majority had not had a prior opportunity, such as an election or public hearing, to express their opinions about using Peay and Davis. In their eyes, the school boycott had revealed a crisis in local democracy and represented the failure of a few powerful men to represent the interests of either black or white citizens.

The conviction displayed by their black neighbors had also genuinely touched some white voters. If they had, out of ignorance or prejudice, failed to appreciate the importance of the Peay and Davis schools, the boycott had certainly instructed them otherwise. As it was now clear that they had to accept school desegregation, a number of local whites could

The Student Planning Committee, Mattamuskeet School. (Selby et al., Hyde County History)

even empathize with black concerns over losing the two schools. Many still felt anguish not only over losing East Hyde and West Hyde but also over the loss of even smaller community schools earlier in the century. All of these sentiments contributed to the white rejection of the bond referendum. By the fall of 1969, most whites voted to support a school desegregation plan that would finally end the black protests and racial discord.

The bond referendum assured that Peay and Davis would remain open, but much of the character of school desegregation remained to be negotiated before the beginning of the 1970–71 school year. A "Student Planning Committee" composed of equal numbers of white and black students, including many school boycott activists, advised school leaders on every aspect of merging their two educational traditions, sets of expectations, and cultures within the Mattamuskeet School. They shaped school policies on issues as fundamental as tracking and curriculum matters and as symbolic as graduation ceremonies and mascots' names. In some respects, the Student Planning Committee stepped into a void left by educational leaders so anxious to avoid further unrest that they seemed reluctant to make even mundane decisions without parent or student participation.

Throughout this year and in future years, the Student Planning Committee would also lay vital groundwork to bring the two races together at the Mattamuskeet School. With the support of their fellow students and the school administration, for example, the committee later required all candidates for student body offices to have running mates of another race. A white candidate for student body president thus had to recruit a black student as a running mate before he or she could be elected to office, and vice versa. Similarly, the committee members structured the yearbook and many other extracurricular activities to assure equal black and white participation. They understood that these activities provided a good chance for young people to come to know and respect one another. On the other hand, the Student Planning Committee decided that both black students and white students would, at least for a transition period, have their own homecoming and prom queens, graduation speakers, and yearbook honorees in order to defuse potential racial conflicts and to preserve their respective school heritages.[41] Such steps had an enormous importance in making school desegregation work. They also reflected capable, biracial school leadership that had learned over the course of the boycott how significant such issues could be.

Black and white leaders negotiated a host of other school desegregation issues that fall and spring. The negotiators included an exceptional number of groups: school administrators, the school board, the Committee of 14, the Student Planning Committee, the Hyde County Teachers Association, the biracial Better Education Committee, and the three school advisory councils. The issues ranged from teachers' job security to the extent of parent participation in school policy making. By the end of the 1969–70 school year, these groups had reached an extensive agreement. Black educators would not lose their jobs because of school desegregation. School administrators guaranteed that black principals would remain at O. A. Peay and Davis, pledged to hire a black assistant principal at Mattamuskeet, and promised that black candidates would receive priority when Mattamuskeet needed to recruit a new principal. The negotiators also agreed to make permanent the parent and student committees developed during the later phases of the school boycott. The Student Planning and Better Education committees would continue to advise teachers and educational leaders, and they would strive to allay parents' fears that biracial schools would deprive them of a strong voice in their children's educations. Administrators also agreed that all three schools would be available for black community events such as Homecoming and Founder's Day. Other agreements provided

ESEA reforms and an African American history class. Last, but hardly least important, the O. A. Peay School would retain the name of its founder.

The preservation of Peay and Davis meant that school desegregation would not be a one-way street in Hyde County. This arrangement gave black citizens a power base within the new configuration of schools, assuring them a strong voice in educational policy. Blacks would not have to fight white educators for jobs or leadership status. Black students were not required to "fit into" white schools, and their parents did not lose their intimate bond with the schools and a black tradition of education. Keeping Peay and Davis open guaranteed that Principal O. A. Peay's and teacher Letha Selby's contributions to black education would not be forgotten. As historian James A. Anderson wrote about similar school leaders, "The hard work of these educators seemed far more heroic in the hour of harvest than it did during the years of cultivation."[42] Out of their segregated schools, so many of which were needlessly sacrificed to school desegregation, came a generation of men and women with the intellectual skills and moral strength needed to lead the civil rights struggle in America.

Blacks and whites would have other problems to overcome as they learned to study and work together in the Hyde County schools. School desegregation would be an arduous, painstaking task for years to come. Nonetheless, the successful outcome of the boycott meant that black and white people shared equally the heavy burdens and wondrous benefits of school desegregation. The merger of the student bodies at O. A. Peay, Davis, and Mattamuskeet would inevitably change the black school experience, but the process did not have to subvert a rich educational heritage or its sustaining role in black culture. Indeed, students would now have the chance to learn from the best in both school traditions. These were, in the end, the ultimate successes of the Hyde County school boycott.

Epilogue

I first attended the homecoming for the O. A. Peay–Hyde County Alumni Association in the spring of 1983, when I was still a labor and community organizer in my native coastal North Carolina. I had always liked Hyde County. When I was growing up on the far shore of Pamlico Sound, I often visited the county and had even lived in Lake Comfort one winter. During those trips, I had gradually been drawn into two grassroots protests led by local fishermen and seafood packing workers. It was then that I came to know many of the people who appear in this book. My presence at an alumni homecoming, however, was an accident. I was visiting a friend near Lake Mattamuskeet when his neighbor, with the hospitality for which Hyde County residents are justly renowned, invited both of us to attend the homecoming banquet that night. I did not know anything about the event but gladly accompanied my friend.

Originally organized for alumni of the Hyde County Training School (what the O. A. Peay School used to be called), the annual homecoming had by then grown to reunite black alumni from all the county schools, past and present. That Friday night the crowd overwhelmed the cafeteria at the O. A. Peay School, and chartered busloads of alumni from Norfolk, Philadelphia, and Brooklyn were still coming during the evening. If the length of their journey kept them from the banquet, the alumni could still attend family and church reunions, the parade through Swan Quarter the next morning, a dance the next night, and a special worship service Sunday morning. It was an extraordinary celebration, and I could scarcely believe the size of the crowd in so sparsely populated a county.

That night I watched the alumni honor educators of the past, recognize personal accomplishments, and raise funds to support new students. They also discussed a remarkable civil rights protest that had saved the O. A. Peay and Davis schools a generation earlier—an event of which I was ignorant, despite my knowledge of educational and civil rights history. I would discover later that this event's existence and significance had long been overlooked. That homecoming tradition, which still flourishes, was the beginning of this book.

What became of the school boycott activists and their schools in Hyde County? The answer is a lesson in both the plight and promise of the rural South. The agrarian decline that began a century ago has continued over the last generation. Less than 5,500 people remain in the county, and growing numbers of abandoned farmsteads and boarded-up stores shroud the land. The breathtaking plains of salt marsh and the grim monotony of corporate farmlands far overshadow the few villages.[1] Looking out across the broad open landscape, one can wonder who is left to worship at so many churches or to tend their graveyards so carefully.

The countryside reveals no signs of a more promising future. Though timber companies still own local forests, their trucks steadily carry both the logs and the jobs away to distant mill towns. Even the seafood packing industry, long a mainstay of the economy, has begun to employ Mexican migrants instead of local workers.[2] While Hyde County residents go to great lengths to find employment, commuting hours to wash dishes or clean motel rooms on the Outer Banks, more and more young people have to move away. Only the annual family, church, and school homecomings disclose that Hyde remains the spiritual home for vast numbers of its departed children.

Hyde County is not an isolated case. In the 1980s, a depression spread across rural North Carolina and the rest of the rural United States. While the Old North State's total population boomed by more than 12 percent that decade, the growth concentrated in urban and tourism centers. Nineteen counties in the coastal plain and the Appalachians lost population, as did rural areas everywhere.[3] Nothing hurt those local economies more than the farm crisis. The ten counties surrounding the Pamlico Sound, including Hyde, are indicative. In one five-year period, between 1982 and 1987, the number of farms declined by 25 percent; half those counties suffered population losses from 1980 to 1990.[4] The farming, fishing, and timber economy is dying, but a new economy has yet to take shape. Many local people are caught in the bind between the two worlds. Rarely treated well by the old economy, poor people especially find themselves exploited or expendable in the emerging one.

The Hyde County schools have remained vital in this vanishing rural world. The O. A. Peay School especially has been a monument of stability and continuity of educational struggle. Though fully embracing its new responsibilities to white children, the school is still the cornerstone of black cultural life. Homecoming, Founder's Day, gospel concerts, and other community events are held at the school. O. A. Peay's portrait still hangs in a place of honor, and Phillip Greene, whom Peay hoped would one day succeed him, served as the school's principal for two decades beginning in the early 1970s. A fully integrated faculty has been teaching there on average for more than twelve years, a remarkable testament of stability and commitment, and has created a caring, academically strong institution in touch with parents and the wider community. Parents praise the O. A. Peay School's quality highly, and state education officials consider it a model rural school.

"The color line," writes the distinguished African American historian John Hope Franklin, "is alive, well, and flourishing in the final decade of the twentieth century."[5] His observation certainly holds true for Hyde County, where race still has a powerful hand. The school boycott, however, opened many new doors for black citizens. James "Little Brother" Topping was elected the first black county commissioner in 1976, and Doris Weston broke the racial barrier at the Hyde County Board of Education in 1980. Near Lake Mattamuskeet, a black family owns one of the few local motels and restaurants. Blacks have professional jobs in every county agency, and a black woman directs the local welfare agency.

Yet for all of the impressive changes, blacks still face enormous obstacles to true racial equality. Neither the school boycott nor civil rights legislation has altered the historical disparity in landownership and wealth that has remained the root cause of black poverty and powerlessness. Those tenacious inequalities have left many black citizens at the edge of economic despair and have sustained subtle vestiges of Jim Crow to the present day.

While race continues to shape local life in complex ways, race relations have improved significantly, largely because of school integration. The first generation of white students to study under black principals and teachers from the first to twelfth grades recently graduated from the Mattamuskeet School. It is also the first generation in which black and white children grew up in the same classrooms and played on the same sports teams. This experience at Peay, Davis, and Mattamuskeet has nurtured a profound improvement in racial attitudes in the younger generation, if not always among their elders, and a few white high school students have even begun to attend the Saturday night dance during the black alumni homecoming. The older generation has also shown encouraging signs of racial reconciliation. Unlike in so many places, white families have not forsaken the public schools by organizing a private academy or church school. Compared with other North Carolina counties, Hyde residents have provided financial support for high spending per pupil in the public schools, usually a good indicator of strong local support for public schooling and desegregation.[6] Today white school boosters support black sports stars and class valedictorians at the Mattamuskeet School.

The experience of school integration has also laid a foundation for blacks and whites to work together in other ways. Meaningful interracial cooperation remains noteworthy anywhere in the United States, but several important strides have been made in Hyde County. One instance merits special mention. Along with people from northeastern Beaufort County, Hyde residents have organized a biracial community group called the Community Developers of Beaufort-Hyde (CDBH). With firm roots in local churches, CDBH has made phenomenal progress toward improving poor housing conditions and addressing the needs of the rural elderly. Its members have also demonstrated the exceptional problem-solving potential that can be realized when bridges are built between a rural area's black and white communities.[7]

The school boycott leaders followed many different paths after 1969, but most kept an abiding commitment to racial justice and the Hyde County schools. Golden Frinks remained the North Carolina field director for the SCLC until 1977. Though later enmeshed in a number of controversies, he figured prominently in the most important civil rights campaigns and racial protests in coastal North Carolina during the 1970s.[8] Retired and still living in Edenton, Frinks has not been forgotten in that part of the state. One still encounters his portrait displayed with honor in many homes and businesses. Milton Fitch also lives in eastern North Carolina, and his son Milton "Toby" Fitch, Jr., now advocates for civil rights and rural economic development as an influential member of the state legislature.

Letha Selby, the revered matriarch who browbeat Golden Frinks into working with local blacks, died in 1973 at the age of eighty-one. Her daughter, Marjorie Selby, recently retired from teaching and is the new president of the school alumni association, a position that Abell Fulford, Jr., held for two decades after the school boycott. Fulford, Etta Mae Greene, and the other Committee of 14 members have devoted their later years largely to school, church, and charitable duties, not to civil rights activism. They tend to the elderly, sick, and infirm. They shore up churches whose congregations continue to grow smaller and older. They make sure that the needy have food and firewood. And, of course, they continue to support the schools. A generation ago a passionate commitment to their children and community led them to fight for the O. A. Peay and Davis schools; afterward they rechanneled that commitment back into the daily devotions and toil necessary to endure in Hyde County. For the young activists, the school boycott was a wondrous coming of age and an awakening of political consciousness. But for the older men and women—the student activists' parents and grandparents—the school boycott was not so much a new awakening as an extraordinary moment in an old struggle to build community institutions of survival and hope under difficult conditions. That struggle went on for them long after 1969. Like so many other rural southerners, black and white, they have held a disintegrating society together with the strength of their own hands.

Likewise, many of the young activists left Hyde County temporarily to seek further education or better employment yet returned to care for elderly parents or, as O. A. Peay had admonished an earlier generation, "to make a contribution" to the community in another way. Alice Spencer, now Alice Mackey, teaches mentally handicapped children in Fairfield. Ida Murray, the young cafeteria worker fired for attending a protest rally, returned to school herself and eventually received her college degree in the same year that her daughter graduated from high school. Ms. Murray later taught in the local schools and directed an important community-based day care center. Henry Johnson, Jr., the young maverick most often arrested during the school boycott, became an outstanding English teacher and later the educational supervisor for the school district. Thomas Whitaker and several other ex–school boycotters organized against various economic injustices in the early 1980s, when unemployment often extended to a quarter of Hyde County people, and former student activists have also led the local NAACP chapter over the past decade. Working through their schools and churches, or on their own, many other school boycotters have expressed an equally strong devotion to the community.

The fierce commitment and community activism displayed by those men and women, as by their elders, remains essential to the survival of Hyde County. Poverty is still widespread and unemployment very high, and human welfare needs grow without the public funds to meet them. Under those conditions, black and white citizens rely more than ever on their schools as the catalysts of economic advancement and community growth. The strength of the schools and the persistence of community activists offer momentary relief from what often seems like a cascade into oblivion for rural people. They also reveal a resiliency and resourcefulness that may yet transcend that fate.

How did the Hyde County protests relate to school desegregation elsewhere in the South? The school boycott was perhaps the most sustained civil rights protest in North Carolina history. It was the first to bring national attention to strong undercurrents of black ambivalence toward school desegregation and to patterns of racial discrimination in the merging of black and white schools throughout the South. The boycott also asserted forcefully that the much-maligned black schools had both good qualities and a proud heritage. Though rarely expressed so powerfully, the same pride, misgivings, and concerns existed throughout the region. The Hyde County school boycott was only the crest of a large wave of protests, and one cannot possibly isolate its influence on the hundreds of local black protests that later challenged racial discrimination in school desegregation.

After 1969, black North Carolinians more often challenged school closings and more forcibly advocated racial justice in school desegregation. Having seen what happened in Hyde County, local school leaders elsewhere worked arduously to avoid similar crises. They struggled to balance longstanding white resistance to school desegregation with rising black expectations for racial equality in its implementation.[9] The school boycott also worried state educational leaders, who responded by developing more sophisticated methods both for satisfying the higher black expectations and for directing them into channels of compromise and reform.[10] Many black protests still escalated into open revolts against school closings. The conflict over East Arcadia High School in Bladen County was probably the most serious in North Carolina. During the 1970–71 school year, Bladen County blacks protested a desegregation plan that required closing their school and transporting its students to a white school forty miles away. Their protests elicited bitter white reprisals that transformed the county's usually placid swamps into a race war battleground.[11]

Civil rights activists observed similar unrest throughout the South. The SCLC, for its part, increasingly fought black school closings and other racist practices in school desegregation. SCLC organizers spearheaded especially strong movements against school closings and teacher firings in Perry County, Georgia, in 1970 and Butler, Alabama, in 1971.[12] The more SCLC organizers renewed their work in the South, the more the depth of black anxiety over school closings impressed them.[13] The potential to bring about significant national reforms did not seem to exist, however. Not only had the SCLC lost much of its organizational strength by 1970, but it also could not rely on the broad public support for challenging school desegregation's flaws that it had attracted during earlier campaigns against segregation. The SCLC never developed a major campaign to press for fundamental reforms in the school desegregation process.

By 1970, other civil rights groups were no more capable of influencing national policy. Though many local NAACP chapters defended historically black schools, national NAACP leaders frankly chastised "small extremist groups of Negroes" that made the retention of a school the litmus test for an acceptable desegregation plan.[14] Other civil rights leaders criticized the NAACP for this stand. They believed NAACP leaders did not recognize that their school heritage offered something important for black children, and they charged the NAACP with encouraging black students to settle for cultural assimilation and second-class status within white-controlled institutions. However, the critics of the national NAACP no longer had the power to influence the course of school desegregation. The Congress of Racial Equality (CORE), the Student Nonviolent Coordinating Committee (SNCC), and more nationalist groups like the Black Panthers may have been more philosophically disposed to fight for black schools, but they had lost their grassroots base in the South. Battered by internal divisions and government attacks, they were unable to unite as a single voice decrying the fate of black schooling.

The federal courts offered limited relief to some black communities, at least curbing the firing of black teachers. The NEA and the NAACP Legal Defense and Educational Fund had filed more than a hundred legal challenges to teacher firings before the Hyde County school boycott, but no civil rights group established a broad precedent until 1969.[15] Endeavoring to distribute the burdens of school desegregation more equitably, the United States Fifth Circuit Court of Appeals ruled that year, in what was called the "Singleton decree," that a Mississippi school district must apply "reasonable, objective, and nondiscriminatory criteria" when school desegregation required staff layoffs.[16] The Singleton decree covered only faculty, though, and school districts applied it very unevenly. Local school leaders often subverted the ruling, which dealt only with continuing employment, by not hiring new black teachers.[17] Later, in the early 1970s, federal courts ordered educational leaders to keep some black schools open and integrate them, but again those rulings had narrow parameters and applied only to specific school districts in Georgia, Louisiana, and Alabama.[18] Local black activists gained important concessions and some victories, but school desegregation overall continued to close black schools and eliminate black educational leadership, and the numbers of black teachers, guidance counselors, and coaches declined further as all but a few public school systems desegregated from 1969 to 1973. A leading civil rights attorney concluded, "It was one issue that simply got away."[19]

The consequences of losing black schools and educational leadership proved far-reaching. Though many white educators taught black students with dedication and without prejudice, southern school leaders in general acted determined to fetter black talents and aspirations within the desegregated institutions. They tracked black children into lower-ability, vocational, and special education classes at disproportionate rates, leading to virtual segregation within many schools.[20] Many school districts even designed segregated bus routes and excluded black students from certain extracurricular activities. Black students also encountered other classroom problems, including hostile attitudes, high rates of suspensions and expulsions, low academic expectations, and little encouragement to prevent them from dropping out.[21]

Leon Hall watched all of this happen. In the 1970s, Hall worked on school desegregation for the Southern Regional Council, a venerable champion of racial justice based in Atlanta. The young black man traveled extensively, interviewed hundreds of students, and assisted many students and teachers in improving the racial atmosphere in public schools. In a path-breaking article, Hall later expressed one of the best-informed judgments on school desegregation to that point and on the actions of white school leaders in the South. "I am convinced," he wrote in *Southern Exposure*, "that they have chosen the most disruptive, discouraging and damaging means to incorporate black children and black educators." Though deeply committed to school desegregation himself, he assessed the situation with candid frustration:

> They have decided to handle desegregation in a way that makes the price black communities must pay so high that black citizens themselves will stop pushing for desegregation and ask: is it worth it? Many black parents are forced to raise this question when they look into the eyes of their children, eyes that once held gaiety, spontaneity and joy and that now show sadness, frustration and anger. Is it worth sending children to encounter teachers who don't respect their personhood? Is it worth having children tested in a way that labels them slow learners or educable mentally retarded or uneducable?[22]

The closer scholars and educational activists looked to the grassroots level, the better they discerned what Leon Hall described so well.[23] Estranged so abruptly from black schooling and its attentiveness to their special needs, cultural values, family backgrounds, and learning styles, the black students often performed worse academically, and many began a crippling slide in self-esteem and motivation.

Within the new biracial schools, black students did not quietly succumb to disillusionment or passively accept racist treatment. Especially from 1969 to 1973, they organized school boycotts and other protests across the South. The spark might be a racial slur, an expulsion, a teacher firing, or one of a hundred other incidents, but the underlying issues were always the deep strains of racial prejudice and white cultural arrogance that had infected school desegregation. Even in Hyde County, where black protests had caused the schools to desegregate on unusually democratic terms, racial tensions almost overwhelmed the Mattamus-keet School. In 1972, racial unrest sparked by the failure of an honor society to admit black students led the Hyde County Board of Education to end classes two weeks early and to hold separate graduation cere-monies for black and white seniors.[24] Only the hiring of a black principal at Mattamuskeet finally put the school on track. It was an extraordinary gesture of reconciliation at a time when black principals had nearly been eliminated from high schools. Elsewhere, desegregated schools that did not respect black educational traditions or the needs of black students suffered much worse.

Student protests reached into every corner of North Carolina. Deeply shaken by both racist educational climates and their own sense of dislocation, black students staged large demonstrations in almost every eastern county and in Piedmont cities with large black populations, in-cluding Durham, Greensboro, Winston-Salem, Charlotte, and States-ville.[25] Black students boycotted classes, white hate groups lashed out against them, students and police clashed, political leaders enacted curfews, and sometimes schools shut down entirely. The worst con-flagration occurred in early 1971 in the coastal town of Wilmington, where student protests led to a four-day riot and a murderous siege. Echoing the Hyde County protests, Wilmington students had called for the reopening of the Williston High School, which had been closed by desegregation, as a black school. Violence broke out in many other places as well.[26] State troopers and National Guardsmen repeatedly entered high schools and junior high schools.[27] While many educa-tional leaders responded with meaningful reforms, others only cracked down harder on the black students, punishing protesters and insisting that they conform to white expectations or leave school. Similar sce-narios played out with tragic frequency throughout the South. The public schools would not soon recover from those ordeals.

Black schools have not been forgotten in the South. A rapidly growing number of parents, students, and educators are working to rekindle the spirited flame that illuminated education in these schools. Their efforts are taking many different forms. One has been to reclaim those symbols of racial pride from the past. The schools closed during desegregation languished unused for decades in city neighborhoods and rural communities, but they have been undergoing a recent renaissance. Several groups have purchased and restored as historical landmarks the buildings that recognize black educational accomplishments in the segregated South. More often, black citizens have renovated the old schools to serve modern community needs for assembly halls, Head Start programs, senior centers, adult classrooms, after-school tutoring sites, libraries, and health-care clinics.[28] The renovations necessary to revive the older buildings are usually costly, necessitating long fund-raising campaigns and community labor, but few people would fail to see an element of justice in such rebirths.

Black school alumni associations have also flourished. These groups continue not only to honor the struggle for good schools in the segregated past but also to improve schooling for black children today. The O. A. Peay–Hyde County Alumni Association is a preeminent case, but others abound. A promising and fairly typical example can be found in New Bern, about a hundred miles southwest of Swan Quarter in Craven County, where the West Street/J. T. Barber Alumni Association has long reunited the alumni of two former black schools. Two years ago, inspired by former teachers who belong to the alumni association, several younger members—mostly single mothers—founded Concerned Parents of Craven County to address educational issues affecting poor and minority students.[29] They have worked successfully to increase parent involvement in their children's educations, and they have challenged tracking, unfair disciplining, and other forms of racial bias in the local schools. Compelled by the persistent racism in schools, similar groups of black parents are organizing throughout North Carolina and the South.[30]

What most truly seek, however, is more complex even than achieving racial justice. They hope also to recover and adapt for the 1990s something of the lost soul of black schooling—the spirit of commitment, community, and social mission that educators like O. A. Peay and Letha Selby relied on to uplift poor, rural people. Today a talented group of young scholars, many of whom studied under such educators, share that concern, and they have begun to explore and articulate the "good qualities" of black schools in the segregated South.[31] None of those scholars or community people miss the age of segregation, but they recognize that something valuable was lost in the process of the great civil rights victory that integrated the public schools. Now they are searching for it, and they do so with the strong conviction that what they find will offer important lessons for educating children of all races today. They appreciate more than ever what W. E. B. Du Bois wrote soon after the Supreme Court's decision in *Brown*: that "great as is this victory, many and long steps along Freedom Road lie ahead."[32]

Introduction

1. See Stephan, "A Brief Historical Overview of School Desegregation," p. 18; Sinowitz, "School Integration and the Teacher"; and Lottman, "Many Negro Schools are Closing."

2. Even the best historical accounts of the civil rights movement and the post–World War II era have not treated school desegregation's negative impact on black communities. See Franklin and Moss, *From Slavery to Freedom*; Powledge, *Free at Last?*; Goldfield, *Black, White, and Southern*; Chafe, *Unfinished Journey*; Blumberg, *Civil Rights*; Ashmore, *Hearts and Minds*; Eagles, *Civil Rights Movement in America*; and Weisbrot, *Freedom Bound*.

3. See especially Ethridge, "Integration and Employment"; Allen, "Effects of School Desegregation"; Coffin, "Black Administrator," p. 159; Abney, "Status of Florida's Black School Principals," pp. 3–8; and U.S. Congress, Senate, Committee on Equal Opportunity, *Displaced and Present Status of Black School Principals*, especially p. 4943. See also Cruse, *Plural But Equal*, p. 249, and Egerton, "When Desegregation Comes."

4. John Smith and Betty Smith, "For Black Educators," p. 7, and the Raleigh *News and Observer* (hereafter cited N&O), Dec. 13, 1970.

5. Hardy, "Making the Extra Effort," p. 94. Statistics are based on a statewide survey conducted by the North Carolina Human Relations Council. In 1974, only 13 school districts in 11 southern states had black superintendents. See Leon Hall, "Implementor's Revenge," p. 122.

6. N&O, May 20, 1972. This estimate was based on an NEA report that drew on raw statistics from HEW.

7. N&O, Feb. 16, 1973.

8. See Coffin, "Black Administrator," p. 159.

9. John Smith and Betty Smith, "For Black Educators," p. 7. See also Ethridge, "Integration and Employment."

10. Sinowitz, "School Integration and the Teacher," p. 32; Stephan, "A Brief Historical Overview of School Desegregation," p. 18; and John Smith and Betty Smith, "For Black Educators," p. 7.

11. See Butler, "Black Educators in Louisiana"; Hooker, "Blacks Losing Teaching Jobs," pp. 165–80; Griggs, "Displacement Still Faces Black Teachers"; Cooper, "The Effects of Desegregation"; and Glass, "Numbers of Alabama Black Educators." In addition, see NEA Task Force III, *School Desegregation: Louisiana and*

Mississippi. Nancy Arnez, whose articles in the *Journal of Afro-American Issues* and *Journal of Negro Education* remain the best overviews of the negative impact of school desegregation on black students, has argued convincingly that the wholesale dismissal of black educators did not slow significantly until the mid-1970s. By 1976, she argues, new federal requirements regarding minority education placed greater constraints on school districts that had discriminated against black educators. See Arnez, "Desegregation of Public Schools," and "Implementation of Desegregation," p. 41.

12. Based on data from the Office of Civil Rights, blacks represented only 325 of the approximately 17,500 southern school board members in 1974; see Leon Hall, "The Implementor's Revenge," p. 122. For general background on patterns of race-oriented voting in North Carolina, see Bass and DeVries, *Transformation of Southern Politics,* pp. 245–47, 441–45.

13. *Carolina Times,* Aug. 27, 1966.

14. See Arnez, "Implementation of Desegregation."

15. V. P. Franklin, "American Values, Social Goals, and the Desegregated School," p. 205.

16. Later chapters will document more fully the treatment of black students in desegregated schools, but for a good overview and further references see Arnez, "Implementation of Desegregation."

17. Adam Fairclough is one of the few historians to discuss this period, however briefly. See *To Redeem the Soul of America,* pp. 394–95.

18. Quoted in *Washington Post,* Nov. 25, 1968.

19. See especially Huckaby, *Crisis at Central High;* Spitzberg, *Racial Politics in Little Rock;* Mayfield, "'Middle Ground Turns to Quicksand'"; Muse, *Virginia's Massive Resistance;* Braden, "The History That We Made"; Coles, *Children of Crisis;* and Bob Smith, *They Closed Their Schools.*

20. For background and further references, see Rassell and Hawley, *Consequences of School Desegregation;* Rist, *Desegregated Schools;* and United States Commission on Civil Rights, *Racial Isolation in the Public Schools,* vol. 1.

21. See especially Kluger, *Simple Justice;* Orfield, *Reconstruction of Southern Education;* Crain, *Politics of School Desegregation;* Wilkinson, *From Brown to Bakke;* Wolters, *Burden of Brown;* Graglia, *Disaster by Decree;* and Schwartz, *Swann's Way.*

22. Chafe, *Civilities and Civil Rights,* p. 3. Chafe's pioneering study of the civil rights movement in Greensboro, North Carolina, is one of the few works that examines black ambivalence toward school desegregation even briefly (see pp. 229–32). The large national civil rights groups have sometimes been referred to as the "Big 5." They included the National Association for the Advancement of Colored People (NAACP), the Southern Christian Leadership Conference (SCLC), the Student Nonviolent Coordinating Committee (SNCC), the Congress of Racial Equality (CORE), and the National Urban League. Several first-rate books on those organizations have been published, including Branch, *Parting the Waters;* Fairclough, *To Redeem the Soul of America;* David Garrow, *Bearing the Cross;* Meier

and Rudwick, *CORE: A Study of the Civil Rights Movement*; Wilkins, *Standing Fast*; Carson, *In Struggle*; Forman, *Making of Black Revolutionaries*; Peake, *Keeping the Dream Alive*; Weiss, *Whitney M. Young, Jr.*; Farmer, *Lay Bare the Heart*; and Oates, *Let the Trumpet Sound*.

23. While historians have yet to publish works on this aspect of the school desegregation era, a number of ethnographers and other scholars have begun to reexamine black schooling and its fate under school desegregation. In the last few years, they have written several important articles and unpublished works. See especially Siddle Walker, "Interpersonal Caring" and "Caswell County Training School"; Foster, "The Politics of Race"; Dempsey and Noblit, "The Demise of Caring"; and Lowe, "Ravenswood High School and the Struggle for Racial Justice."

24. The complex school desegregation conflicts in western and northern cities have inspired a number of important works, especially Lukas, *Common Ground*; Bonacich, *Deadlock in School Desegregation*; Fine, *When Leadership Fails*; Landis, "Crawford Desegregation Suit"; Monti, *Semblance of Justice*; and Wolf, *Trial and Error*.

25. Important exceptions to this absence of school desegregation studies on the rural South include Hanks, *Struggle for Black Political Empowerment*, and McPhail, *History of Desegregation Developments in Certain Mississippi School Districts*. Fine studies of school desegregation in the urban South after 1968 include Gaillard, *Dream Long Deferred*; Chafe, *Civilities and Civil Rights*; Pride, *Burden of Busing*; and Woodard, "Busing Plans, Media Agendas, and Patterns of White Flight" (on Nashville and Louisville).

26. Regarding the history of black schools in the segregated South, see James D. Anderson's path-breaking book *Education of Blacks in the South*.

27. Several recent works that raise local or personal history to a more universal level have been especially interesting, including Greene, *Praying for Sheetrock*; Lukas, *Common Ground*; King, *Freedom Story*; Youth of the Rural Organizing and Cultural Center, *Minds Stayed on Freedom*; Crawford, "Grassroots Activists"; Beifuss, *Memphis, the 1968 Strike, and Martin Luther King*; and David Garrow, ed., *We Shall Overcome*, vols. 1–3.

28. "Black Belt" generally refers to the swath of counties running between Tidewater Virginia and the Mississippi Delta where blacks comprised 50 percent or more of the total population. They are predominantly rural, agricultural counties that were dominated by plantation slavery before the Civil War.

29. Those interested in studying the civil rights movement in eastern North Carolina must begin by reading Raymond Gavins's work. In his trailblazing essays on black survival strategies and local NAACP organizing in the Jim Crow era, Gavins has hewn out a firm path for understanding the modern civil rights movement in the region. See his "NAACP in North Carolina" and "North Carolina Black Folklore." In addition, Waynick et al., *North Carolina and the Negro*, and Crow et al., *History of African Americans in North Carolina*, pp. 177–207, both include brief but useful discussions of civil rights activism in the region. While Michael Myerson's work is largely polemical, his *Nothing Could Be Finer* does review briefly

some labor and civil rights activism in Ayden, Roanoke Rapids, and a few other towns. Godwin's "Taming a Whirlwind" has begun to open up the history of the civil rights movement in Wilmington.

Several unpublished works also provide important background on the civil rights movement in eastern North Carolina. See Thomas, "True Story Behind the Wilmington 10"; Barksdale, "Indigenous Civil Rights Movement"; Irons and Unruhe, "Black Wilson"; Windham, "Green Hands"; and especially Tyson, "Kissing Case."

30. Bass and DeVries, *Transformation of Southern Politics*, p. 242.

31. Du Bois's article was part of a pivotal edition of the *Journal of Negro Education* that reviewed the goal of school integration from moral, legal, strategic, political, and philosophic points of view. Du Bois, however, was the only author who did not assume that school integration ought to be a main goal of black struggle or, specifically, of the NAACP's efforts for racial equality. Though he clearly opposed inferior schools for blacks, Du Bois worried that white educators would not be free enough of racism to educate black children properly. See W. E. B. Du Bois, "Does the Negro Need Separate Schools?"

32. See, for example, Cruse, *Plural But Equal*; V. P. Franklin, "American Values, Social Goals, and the Desegregated School"; Bell, *And We Are Not Saved*; and Adair, *Desegregation*.

33. For the most far-reaching work of this kind and further references, see the two articles by Emilie V. Siddle Walker.

34. *Sojourners* 19, no. 7 (August/September 1990) includes articles by Harold Cruse, Anthony Parker, Manning Marable, Delores Williams, Eugene Rivers, and Danny Collum.

Prologue, 1954–1964

1. For background on the timber boom and Hyde County's economic failures since the Civil War, see Ward, "Lake Mattamuskeet"; Fortescue, "History of Hyde County"; Wager, "County Government and County Affairs in Hyde County, N.C."; Chambliss, "Development in Hyde County"; and "Scranton's Lumbermen," especially pp. 65–66.

2. For background on the natural history and ecology of Hyde County, see Lukin and Mauger, *Environmental Geologic Atlas*, and Lynch and Peacock, *Natural Areas Inventory*.

3. North Carolina Department of Conservation and Development and North Carolina Department of Labor, *Industrial Directory and Reference Book*, pp. 414–15. Depressed farm prices, mechanization, federal price support policies, agricultural monopoly, and rising labor costs have all spurred a steady migration away from eastern North Carolina farm communities that has lasted throughout the twentieth century. Tobacco is one of the few crops that has consistently brought relatively high prices and required intensive labor. See Flowers, *Throwed Away*, especially chaps. 1–4.

4. For two remarkable studies on the industrial transformation of the North

Carolina Piedmont, see Jacquelyn Dowd Hall et al., *Like a Family*, especially pp. 3–113, and Tullos, *Habits of Industry*, especially pp. 86–171.

5. See Selby et al., *Hyde County History*, especially sect. 1, pp. 6–9, 32–40; sect. 2, pp. 15–20; sect. 3, pp. 14–15, 24–26, 30; and sect. 5, pp. 61, 70–75. In 1976 Hyde County citizens compiled one of the best books in a statewide bicentennial project to document local history from the perspective of the residents. Editors Marjorie Selby, R. S. Spencer, Jr., and Rebecca Swindell accumulated and published a treasure trove of oral histories, folklore, photographs, family albums, genealogies, and primary documents. Their book provides a collage of local life in the twentieth century, useful to amateur and professional historians alike, and represents one of the few local bicentennial projects in North Carolina that included meaningful participation from both the white and black communities. It is a remarkable and useful publication.

6. The white Baptist churches published the monthly *Hyde County Messenger* in Fairfield from 1926 to 1941.

7. Ocracoke Island, one of the Outer Banks, has long been within Hyde County's territorial limits; but because their island is separated from the mainland by half a day's travel, Ocracokers have had little interaction with the rest of Hyde County and were not involved in the civil rights or school issues discussed in this book. For a discussion of the island's history, see Stick, *Outer Banks*, especially pp. 72–73, 298–301.

8. United States Bureau of the Census, *1950 Census of the Population*.

9. United States Bureau of the Census, *1950 Census of Housing*.

10. For discussions on the "Red Shirt" backlash against black economic advancement and political participation in the late 1890s, see Eric Anderson, *Race and Politics in North Carolina*; Evans, *Ballots and Fence Rails*; Edmonds, *The Negro and Fusion Politics*; Prather, *Resurgent Politics and Educational Progressivism*; and Kousser, *Shaping of Southern Politics*.

11. Interviews with Vanderbilt Johnson, James "Little Brother" Topping.

12. Though a federal agency owned and managed the wildlife refuge, this policy did not change until 1961. See *Hickory Daily Record*, Sept. 6, 1961, North Carolina Advisory Committee on Civil Rights (NCACCR) clipfile.

13. Greg Zeph, personal communication (Winter 1983). Zeph was then a community organizer in Hyde County. His observation was confirmed by interviews with local citizens.

14. Interview with Vanderbilt Johnson.

15. Interview with Albert Whitaker.

16. A Beaufort County newspaper reported on one incident; see *Washington Daily News*, Mar. 25, 1956. For a broader examination of miscegenation and Jim Crow in North Carolina, see Tyson, "Kissing Case." Focusing thus far on Monroe, Oxford, and Wilmington, North Carolina, Tyson's work breaks an important new path in civil rights history by chronicling the pivotal role that sexual domination played in maintaining the Jim Crow social order well into the 1950s and 1960s.

17. Interview with James "Little Brother" Topping.

18. Interview with Ida Murray.

19. The best history of the NAACP's campaign to end racial segregation in public schools remains Kluger's *Simple Justice*.

20. Interviews with Johnnie Midgette, Doris Weston. See Gavins, "NAACP in North Carolina," for a broad review of the NAACP's early growth and organizing in the state.

21. Minutes, Hyde County Board of Education, 1954 to 1965.

22. Quoted in Chafe, *Civilities and Civil Rights*, p. 49.

23. Chafe, *Civilities and Civil Rights*, pp. 48–60. Chafe's study of the civil rights movement in Greensboro, North Carolina, includes undoubtedly the best review of the State of North Carolina's strategy for avoiding school desegregation. I have drawn principally from his analysis in my own discussion.

24. Ibid.

25. See Luebke, *Tar Heel Politics*, pp. 109–10.

26. Chafe, *Civilities and Civil Rights*, pp. 53–54. Governor Hodges managed to equate the NAACP and the Ku Klux Klan as "extremist groups," between which a "moderate route" was desirable. On the almost unanimously favorable state and national press response to the Pearsall Plan, see p. 56 of Chafe's study.

27. Ibid., p. 60.

28. Minutes, Hyde County Board of Education, 1955–59.

29. See Wilkinson, *From Brown to Bakke*, p. 110.

30. In his autobiography, Dr. Hubert Eaton provides a good description of the legal battle to equalize school facilities in New Hanover County, North Carolina. Led by two black physicians, Eaton and D. C. Roane, the Wilmington Committee on Negro Affairs filed suit on March 12, 1951, to force the county board of education to eliminate the large disparity in black and white school facilities. The suit was successful and led to enormous improvements in the black schools. See Eaton, *Every Man Should Try*, pp. 41–52. Prompted by black demands for school integration, white school leaders organized campaigns to improve black schools in most eastern North Carolina counties in the 1950s. For Carteret County, see *Wilmington Star-News*, Feb. 27, 1955; Halifax County, *Scotland Neck Commonwealth*, June 23, 1950; and *N&O*, Feb. 7, 1957; Johnston County, *N&O*, May 24, 1953; Pamlico County, *N&O*, Nov. 18, 1951, and Sept. 23, 1956; Pitt County, *N&O*, Apr. 7, 1950; Sampson County, *Sampson News*, June 14, 1951.

31. See *N&O*, Feb. 11, 1959, and Sept. 2, 1961, and *Carolina Times*, Sept. 9, 1961; May 4, 1963; and Sept. 14, 1963.

32. *Carolina Times*, Aug. 6, 1960.

33. See *N&O*, July 22, 1951; Nov. 18, 1951; Nov. 8, 1953; and Sept. 23, 1956.

34. *N&O*, Sept. 23, 1956.

35. See *N&O*, Aug. 19, 1951.

36. Gray, "History of the Hyde County Training School," pp. 30–31. To be precise, the O. A. Peay School was still called the Hyde County Training School until 1961. The name had not changed when the school closed in Sladesville and relocated to Swan Quarter in 1953.

37. Selby et al., *Hyde County History*, sect. 1, pp. 30–33; sect. 3, pp. 53–54; sect. 5, pp. 36, 118–19.

38. Ibid., sect. 5, pp. 118–19.

39. United States Bureau of the Census, *1970 Census of Population* and *1970 Census of Housing*.

40. Military towns were the most striking exceptions. In the late 1950s, when the Army and Marine Corps asserted their influence to bring local schools in alignment with federal desegregation policy, several towns near military bases had integrated their classrooms. Black soldiers often had a strong role in pressuring the military camps to abide by the federal policy. In Havelock, next to the Cherry Point Marine Corps Air Station in Craven County, both the Catholic parochial school and the public elementary schools had been integrated by 1959. *N&O*, July 14 and Aug. 26, 1959.

41. While white editors often deliberately chose not to report on civil rights activities in eastern North Carolina, the black-owned *Carolina Times*, based in Durham, frequently covered them. Regarding the reaction in eastern North Carolina to the 1960 Greensboro sit-ins against segregation in public accommodations, see *Carolina Times*, Feb. 13, July 23, July 30, and Oct. 22, 1960. The last two of these editions describe pickets and sit-ins against segregation in public accommodations organized by the NAACP Youth Council in New Bern. In 1962 the newspaper also covered protests to desegregate public accommodations in Edenton and Elizabeth City. See *Carolina Times*, Feb. 10, Feb. 17, Mar. 3, Oct. 27, Nov. 3, Nov. 23, and Dec. 22, 1962. Concerning NAACP and CORE protests in Dunn in 1963, see *Carolina Times*, Aug. 17, Sept. 14, and Dec. 12, 1963. Regarding Cherry Point Marines who protested segregation in Havelock businesses, see *Carolina Times*, July 27, 1963. About CORE protests in Wilmington and other North Carolina towns against segregated businesses in 1963, see *Carolina Times*, May 18 and June 1, 1963. For coverage and a summary of the "Williamston Freedom Movement," see *Carolina Times*, Jan. 11, 1964, and *Chapel Hill Weekly*, July 26, Aug. 26, and Aug. 16, 1964.

42. *Carolina Times*, May 21 and May 28, 1960, and Apr. 18, May 9, and Dec. 19, 1964. In addition, see NCACCR clipfile, "Employment file," 1960–63, for a good review of black activism for fair employment opportunity.

Chapter 1

1. Interview with Vanderbilt Johnson.

2. Letter from Lloyd Henderson to Rosa O'Neal, Aug. 30, 1968, National Education Association Papers (hereafter cited as NEA Papers).

3. For a good review of the impact of Title VI of the Civil Rights Act of 1964 on school desegregation in the South, see Orfield, *Reconstruction of Southern Education*, chaps. 2–8.

4. Transcript of A. J. Howell testimony, May 2, 1969, NEA Papers.

5. Ibid.

6. HEW internal memorandum from W. Kenneth Haddock and Anne Lassiter to

agency files, Sept. 16, 1966, United States Department of Health, Education, and Welfare, Office of Civil Rights (hereafter cited as HEW Papers). Also, see transcript of testimony by Dr. Jerome Melton, assistant superintendent of the North Carolina Department of Public Instruction, NEA Papers.

7. Transcript of testimony by Mrs. Doris Weston, NEA Papers.

8. Entry by Dewey Dodds into EEOP File on Hyde County, Oct. 7, 1966, "N.C. Files," HEW Papers.

9. Interviews with Alice Mackey, Phillip Greene, Marjorie Selby.

10. Interview with Morgan Harris.

11. Black educators held an honored status within their community. It is not exaggerating to compare their prestige to that enjoyed by physicians or judges in the wider society today. This high status reflected in part the great value historically placed on education within African American society. Unlike their white counterparts, black educators also had the highest professional ranks and income levels in Hyde County. See James D. Anderson, *Education of Blacks in the South*, especially pp. 4–32, 278–85.

12. For path-breaking research and further references on the positive educational qualities of black schools in the age of segregation, including this element of caring, see two recent articles by Emilie V. Siddle Walker, "Interpersonal Caring" and "Caswell County Training School." I have borrowed heavily from Professor Siddle Walker's work to understand this aspect of school character, which was repeatedly described by black residents in Hyde County.

13. Siddle Walker, "Interpersonal Caring," pp. 72–74.

14. Transcript of Albert Whitaker testimony, NEA Papers.

15. Entry by Dodds, Oct. 7, 1966, HEW Papers.

16. Memorandum from W. Kenneth Haddock to Hyde County Files regarding community attitude toward desegregation, Apr. 12, 1967, HEW Papers.

17. Interview with Johnnie Midgette.

18. Memorandum from W. Kenneth Haddock to Hyde County Files regarding community attitude toward desegregation, Apr. 12, 1967, HEW Papers.

19. Ibid.

20. Transcripts of James Barrow testimony, NEA Papers.

21. Though Reverend Boomer was a strikingly mild-mannered and modest man, the Klan's night riders had many reasons for lashing out against him. In addition to supporting the NAACP's efforts in Hyde County, he had been a leader in a campaign to desegregate public schools in northeastern Beaufort County, where he lived. He was also the chief plaintiff in a pivotal legal suit, *Boomer v. Beaufort County Board of Education*, challenging the racist treatment of black children in desegregated schools. Boomer later became a prominent bishop in the Disciples of Christ church. Personal communication with Bishop Booker Boomer, Pantego, N.C., July 22, 1984.

22. Interview with Abell Fulford, Jr.

23. Memorandum from W. Kenneth Haddock to Hyde County Files, Apr. 12, 1967, HEW Papers.

24. Interview with Johnnie Midgette.

25. Interview with James "Little Brother" Topping.

26. For general background on the Ku Klux Klan and its history in North Carolina since 1900, see Sims, *The Klan*; Haas, *KKK*; Wheaton, *Codename GREENKIL*; and especially Bryant, ed., *Mark of the Beast*, a splendid edition of the journal *Southern Exposure*.

27. Within one four-month period in 1966, Klansmen organized public rallies in these Province 1 locales: Moyock, Ayden (twice), Murfreesboro, Ahoskie, Windsor, Pantego, Greenville, Jones County, Ernul, New Bern, Dover, Lewiston, Grifton, Columbia, Williamston, Plymouth, and Jasper. Location of Klan rallies is listed in a series of monthly SHP memoranda entitled "Expenditures of Patrol Time . . . on Ku Klux Klan Activities, Civil Rights Activities and Labor Disturbances," from the SHP to Gov. Dan K. Moore, dated Aug. 16, Sept. 19, Oct. 10, and Nov. 10, 1966, North Carolina Division of Motor Vehicles, State Highway Patrol, Commander's Correspondence File and Report of Investigations File, 1959–1970 (hereafter cited as SHP Papers). More astounding yet, these were not the only sites in Province 1 where Klaverns were located. Between 1964 and 1967, other Klaverns existed in Sunbury, Elizabeth City, Hertford, Weeksville, Washington, and Pineville, at the least. See "Report No. 7 from SBI Director Walter F. Anderson to Governor's Law and Order Committee," Oct. 31, 1966, SHP Papers.

28. Statewide, the Klan had approximately 7,000 members in 1965 and 1966. This sizeable number still did not reflect the KKK's reach or popularity. According to SBI and SHP records, only a tiny fraction of the people who attended rallies belonged to the Klan. For example, at a Sept. 8, 1966 rally in Ernul, in Craven County, state troopers counted only 11 Klansmen, 3 Klanswomen, and 10 Klan "security guards" among a crowd of 500 to 600 people. See memorandum from Col. Charles A. Speed, SHP, to Gov. Dan K. Moore, Sept. 8, 1966, SHP Papers.

29. For good estimates of attendance at Klan rallies, along with their sites and activities, see SBI and SHP field memoranda and daily monitoring reports, 1964–69, SHP Papers.

30. The stereotypical image of the marginalized "redneck" Klansmen, if it was ever accurate at all, has not been accurate in eastern North Carolina since World War II. See "Field Reports," Troop A, State Highway Patrol, 1964–69, and "Intelligence Bulletins" (weekly), N.C. State Bureau of Investigation, 1961–69, SHP Papers.

31. *Chapel Hill Weekly*, Aug. 26, 1964. Detailed SBI documents on Klan activity in Craven County support this generalized view. See SBI Field Reports on New Bern rally (Sept. 15, 1966) and on the Ernul rally (Sept. 9, 1966), file M-24-361-25, SHP Papers.

32. Memorandum from SBI director Charles Dunn to Gov. Dan Moore, Apr. 25, 1966, SHP Papers.

33. SBI intrabureau correspondence from agent Willie V. O'Donnell to the director, Nov. 9, 1966, file M-24-361-48, SHP Papers.

34. Dodds memorandum, Oct. 7, 1966, HEW Papers.

35. Interviews with Walter Lee Gibbs and Margaret Gibbs.

36. Interview with Doris Weston.

37. ESEA is the acronym for Elementary and Secondary Education Act, which created a number of important federally supported programs for poor children in local schools in the mid-1960s.

38. Minutes, meeting between Hyde County Board of Education and team from Office of Education of HEW, Aug. 19, 1966, NEA Papers.

39. HEW internal memorandum from W. Kenneth Haddock and Anne Lassiter to agency files, Sept. 16, 1966, HEW Papers.

40. Minutes, meeting between Hyde County Board of Education and team from Office of Education of HEW, Aug. 19, 1966, NEA Papers.

41. Ibid.

42. Ibid. Federal circuit courts and the U.S. Supreme Court would later overrule virtually all of those lower court decisions. But for several years, especially between 1964 and 1968, local school boards and southern states closely based their progress toward school desegregation on the vicissitudes of state and lower federal court rulings that interpreted the Civil Rights Act and *Brown*. See especially Orfield, *Reconstruction of Southern Education*, pp. 312–41.

43. Minutes, meeting between Hyde County Board of Education and team from Office of Education of HEW, Aug. 19, 1966, NEA Papers.

44. Ibid.

45. Ibid.

46. On the social role of southern black schools, see James D. Anderson, *Education of Blacks in the South*, especially pp. 33–78, 186–237. In this landmark study, Anderson argues that northern philanthropists and liberal southern educators who advocated public education for blacks had a vision of education that would socialize black children to their traditional underclass status. Many local white leaders, on the other hand, opposed all public education for blacks. What the all-black schools actually did, however, is an open question. While Anderson makes a convincing argument with respect to the intent of southern progressives and northern philanthropists, his study stops in 1935 and pays little attention to the kind of education and the philosophy of education actually employed by black educators and students in all-black schools.

47. Quoted in Gatewood, "Eugene Clyde Brooks and Negro Education," p. 365.

48. Minutes, meeting between Hyde County Board of Education and team from Office of Education of HEW, Aug. 19, 1966, NEA Papers.

49. Ibid.

50. Ibid.

51. Ibid.

52. Transcript of telephone call between W. Kenneth Haddock, Anne Lassiter, and Supt. Allen Bucklew, Sept. 16, 1966, HEW Internal files, NEA Papers.

53. Ibid.

54. Memorandum from Dewey Dodds to HEW Hyde County files regarding board meeting and on-site visit of Oct. 3, 1966; Oct. 7, 1966, NEA Papers.

55. Ibid.

56. Ibid.

57. Ibid.

58. Letter from Allen Bucklew to Dewey Dodds, Oct. 7, 1966, NEA Papers.

59. Memorandum from Dewey Dodds to HEW Hyde County files regarding board meeting and on-site visit of Oct. 3, 1966; Oct. 7, 1966, NEA Papers.

60. Letter from EEOP director John Hope to Allen Bucklew, Oct. 25, 1966, NEA Papers.

61. Letter from U.S. Commissioner of Education Harold Howe II to Bucklew, Oct. 27, 1966, NEA Papers.

62. Letter from Bucklew to HEW secretary John W. Gardner, Dec. 1, 1966, NEA Papers.

63. Minutes, Mar. 10, 1967, Hyde County Board of Education.

64. Letter from Stephen J. Pollack, assistant attorney general, Civil Rights Division of the U.S. Justice Dept., to Mr. and Mrs. James Topping, New Holland, N.C., Nov. 19, 1968, NEA Papers.

65. Letter from J. D. Williams to George Davis, July 4, 1967. Copy in the minutes, Hyde County Board of Education meeting, July 12, 1967.

66. See Orfield, *Reconstruction of Southern Education*, chaps. 6 and 7.

67. Letter from J. D. Williams to George Davis, July 4, 1967. Copy in the minutes, Hyde County Board of Education meeting, July 12, 1967.

68. Minutes, July 12, 1967, Hyde County Board of Education.

69. See Orfield, *Reconstruction of Southern Education*, chaps. 6 and 7.

70. In Beaufort County, the NAACP Legal Defense and Educational Fund filed suit in 1966 alleging that intimidation of black students who transferred to white schools the previous year had made school desegregation impossible without federal intervention. See *Carolina Times*, Mar. 5, 1966.

71. Minutes, Oct. 25, 1967, Hyde County Board of Education.

72. Minutes, Oct. 6, 1967, and Oct. 25, 1967, Hyde County Board of Education.

73. Minutes, Oct. 25, 1967, Hyde County Board of Education.

74. Pupil enrollment and overcrowding information are from transcript of testimony by Dr. Jerome Melton, NEA Papers, and "School District Assessment Reports," 1966–69, North Carolina Department of Public Instruction Papers (hereafter cited as NCDPI Papers).

75. Letter from J. D. Williams to George Davis and Allen Bucklew, May 17, 1968, NEA Papers.

76. Ibid.

77. Letter from Lloyd R. Henderson to Rosa O'Neal, Aug. 30, 1968, NEA Papers.

78. Letter from Williams to Davis and Bucklew, May 17, 1968.

79. The U.S. Supreme Court upheld the Fifth Circuit Court in *Green v. New Kent County*. See Orfield, *Reconstruction of Southern Education*, p. 341. For background on the internal discussions within the U.S. Department of Justice about

the import of *Green,* refer to the documents collected in Belknap, *Administrative History of the Civil Rights Division,* vol. 17, part 2, pp. 5–20.

80. Chafe, *Civilities and Civil Rights,* pp. 166–70.

81. Memorandum from the N.C. Dept. of Public Instruction to County School Superintendents, Apr. 16, 1968, NCDPI Papers.

82. Memorandum from J. D. Williams to Walter S. Warfield, June 24, 1968, NEA Papers.

83. Minutes, May 24, 1968, Hyde County Board of Education (includes text of resolution).

84. Letter from Ruby Martin, director, Office of Civil Rights, HEW, to Bucklew, July 3, 1968, NEA Papers.

85. Minutes, July 12 and July 19, 1968, Hyde County Board of Education.

86. Minutes, Aug. 5, Aug. 20, and Aug. 29, 1968, Hyde County Board of Education.

Chapter 2

1. Transcript of Golden Mackey testimony, NEA Papers.

2. Quoted in *Washington Post,* Nov. 25, 1968.

3. Selby et al., *Hyde County History,* sect. 3, pp. 48–49.

4. Interview with Phillip Greene.

5. *Handbook of North Carolina,* pp. 74–77, and *North Carolina Business Directory, 1896,* p. 111.

6. Selby et al., *Hyde County History,* sect. 3, pp. 54–55.

7. Ibid., sect. 2, pp. 32–33, and sect. 5, pp. 55, 76.

8. See *North Carolina Year Book and Business Directory,* Hyde County chapters, 1901–39 editions; see especially the 1915 edition, pp. 266–67.

9. The history of the Hyde County Training School and the O. A. Peay School, except where otherwise cited, is drawn from interviews with alumni and educators and from Selby et al., *Hyde County History.*

10. The situation in Hyde County was not unusual. Statewide, until 1960 the median amount of schooling for rural blacks was no more than six years. See Flowers, *Throwed Away,* p. 80.

11. James D. Anderson, *Education of Blacks in the South,* pp. 196–97.

12. For a succinct overview of black/white disparities in North Carolina schools during the Jim Crow era, see a guest column by McNeill Smith, "School Desegregation Discussed," in *N&O,* Oct. 26, 1960. In 1884, black teachers in North Carolina earned on average 94 percent of white teachers' salaries. In Hyde County in that era, the pay was often equal. By 1915 black salaries averaged only 52 percent of white salaries statewide; in 1925, 54 percent.

13. James D. Anderson, *Education of Blacks in the South,* p. 156.

14. Interview with Marjorie Selby.

15. Interviews with Alice Mackey; Thomas Whitaker; James "Little Brother" Topping; Henry Johnson, Jr.; Ida Murray; and Doris Blount.

16. Interview with Phillip Greene.

17. Gray, "History of the Hyde County Training School," p. 32.

18. Interview with Phillip Greene.

19. "Memories of the Hyde County Training School Banner." The Hyde County Training School was a "Rosenwald School," one of hundreds of black high schools in the South built partially with donations from the Sears & Roebuck heirs. For background information about the history of the Rosenwald schools, see Lance Jones, *Negro Schools in the Southern States*, pp. 102–20, and Redcay, *County Training Schools and Public Secondary Education*. For a good discussion of the pedagogical philosophy encouraged by the Rosenwald Fund and other northern philanthropists, see James D. Anderson, *Education of Blacks in the South*, pp. 152–83 and 206–37.

20. Gray, "History of the Hyde County Training School," pp. 30–31.

21. The concern over segregation within the Mattamuskeet School later came to the attention of SCLC organizers and law enforcement personnel. See transcripts of James Barrow testimony, NEA Papers, and memorandum from Capt. R. F. Williamson to Maj. John Laws, Sept. 17, 1968, North Carolina Division of Motor Vehicles, State Highway Patrol, Troop A (hereafter cited as SHP Troop A Papers).

22. For an excellent study of the importance of community involvement in historically black schools, see Siddle Walker, "Caswell County Training School."

23. This incident was mentioned in several interviews and statements to NEA investigators. For example, see transcript of James Barrows testimony, NEA Papers.

24. N&O, Nov. 14, 1968.

25. Transcripts of Johnnie Midgette testimony and Early Bryant testimony, NEA Papers.

26. Chafe, *Civilities and Civil Rights*, p. 166.

27. For background on the political backlash against the civil rights movement and school integration, see especially Orfield, *Reconstruction of Southern Education*, pp. 341–48, and Rubin, "Politics of Rage."

28. By 1968, several important civil rights groups, including SNCC, CORE, and the Black Panthers, no longer favored biracial schools, at least not under the existing circumstances. However, their position had the effect of removing them from the policy discussion over the character of school integration and from the concerns of southern blacks confronted by unfair school desegregation plans. See especially Carson, *In Struggle*; Weisbent, *Freedom Bound*; Haines, *Black Radicals and the Civil Rights Mainstream*; and Cruse, *Plural But Equal*, pp. 222–23.

29. Interview with Johnnie Midgette. Also, transcripts of Johnnie Midgette and Early Bryant testimony, NEA Papers.

30. The Hyde County Board of Education regularly appointed three-person advisory boards at all three schools to serve as liaisons between the school board and parents. Black teachers belonged to the North Carolina Teachers Association (NCTA), the black state affiliate of the National Education Association. The NEA's North Carolina chapters remained segregated by race until 1971. For background on the NCTA, see Murray, *History of the North Carolina Teachers Association*.

31. Interview with Phillip Greene.

32. Interview with Abell Fulford, Jr., and Selby et al., *Hyde County History*, pp. 44, 101.

33. For good background on Mutual, see Weares, *Black Business in the South*.

34. Interview with Abell Fulford, Jr.

35. Ibid.

36. Ibid.

37. Interview with Albert Whitaker.

38. Interview with Abell Fulford, Jr.

39. See National Education Association Commission on Professional Rights and Responsibilities (hereafter cited NEACPRR), *Hyde County, North Carolina*, pp. 5–10, for a good discussion of these early interactions between black leaders and the school board.

40. *Carolina Times*, Feb. 20, 1965.

41. Interview with James Ferguson II; transcript of Early Bryant testimony, NEA Papers.

42. Minutes, Aug. 5, 1968, Hyde County Board of Education.

43. Transcript of Albert Whitaker testimony, NEA Papers; interview with Albert Whitaker.

44. Minutes, Aug. 5, 1968, Hyde County Board of Education.

45. Copy of letter and petition in NEACPRR, *Hyde County, North Carolina*, p. 29.

46. Letter from Rosa O'Neal et al. to Walter S. Warfield, chief district director, Civil Rights Compliance Office, HEW, Aug. 5, 1968, NEA Papers.

47. Letter from Lloyd Henderson, education branch chief, Office of Civil Rights, HEW, to Rosa O'Neal, Aug. 7, 1968, NEA Papers.

48. Transcript of Albert Whitaker testimony, NEA Papers.

49. Minutes, Aug. 5, 1968, Hyde County Board of Education; minutes, undated, Hyde County Board of Commissioners (filed with school board minutes).

50. Letter from Supt. Allen Bucklew to Dr. Charles Carroll, Aug. 7, 1968, NCDPI Papers.

51. Interview with Dudley Flood; telephone conversation with Andrew Vanore, N.C. Attorney General's Office, Feb. 3, 1993.

52. Letter from Lloyd R. Henderson, education branch chief, Office of Civil Rights, HEW, to Rosa O'Neal, Aug. 30, 1968, NEA Papers.

53. Ibid.

54. Ibid.

55. Interviews with James Ferguson II, Golden Frinks.

56. Transcript of Early Bryant testimony, NEA Papers; interview with Golden Frinks.

57. Interview with Abell Fulford, Jr.

58. Ibid.

59. Interviews with Golden Frinks, Phillip Greene, Abell Fulford, Jr.

60. Interviews with Milton Fitch, Golden Frinks.

61. The remainder of the chapter is drawn largely from the interview with Golden Frinks.

62. Ibid.

63. Interview with Marjorie Selby; Selby et al., *Hyde County History*, sect. 5, p. 105.

64. Interview with Golden Frinks.

Chapter 3

1. Interview with Golden Frinks. After growing up in Siler City, North Carolina, Frinks moved to Washington, D.C., and operated a small photo developing service. He joined an NAACP picket line when he encountered a client's shop refusing to serve blacks, and he often participated in similar protests against racial discrimination in public accommodations thereafter. Though never a civil rights leader in Washington, the young Frinks sought to learn more about black activism there and would occasionally visit the Inspiration House to listen to civil rights speakers such as Paul Robeson and Thurgood Marshall. Frinks relocated to Edenton and started a small nightclub in the old Oddfellows Hall in 1956.

2. For newspaper coverage of the Edenton movement, see *Carolina Times*, Feb. 10, Feb. 17, Mar. 3, Oct. 27, Nov. 3, and Nov. 23, 1962, as well as a long feature story on Jan. 26, 1963.

3. See, for instance, *Carolina Times*, Dec. 22, 1962, regarding the economic boycott aimed at unfair employment practices in the Elizabeth City area organized by the Albemarle Improvement Association, the Pasquotank NAACP, and the SCLC.

4. *Carolina Times*, Jan. 26, 1963.

5. Interview with Golden Frinks.

6. The civil rights movement in Plymouth, in Washington County, is covered in passing in N&O, Sept. 2, 1965, and the civil rights movements in Bertie and Halifax counties are discussed very briefly in *Carolina Times*, July 30, 1966.

7. *Carolina Times*, Jan. 26, 1963.

8. The Williamston Freedom Movement started in June 1963 and included thirty-two straight days of demonstrations and sit-ins, as well as an economic boycott of downtown businesses and several attempts to enroll black students at the local white high school. Black activists eventually won a number of important concessions: integrated hospitals, creation of a public library open to blacks and whites, the use of courtesy titles, integrated tax books, school desegregation, and the removal of "colored/white" signs from public places. The Ku Klux Klan repeatedly threatened black residents in Williamston and other Martin County communities, and Frinks was in such danger that he rarely spent more than two or three days at a time in the county. See *Carolina Times*, Jan. 11, 1964, and especially a long series in *Chapel Hill Weekly*, July 26, Aug. 16, and Aug. 26, 1964.

9. See Fairclough, *To Redeem the Soul of America*, p. 478, regarding SCLC plans for the national voting rights campaign. The Williamston Freedom Movement has

yet to attract mention in the literature on the civil rights movement, even in the scholarly studies on the SCLC.

10. The SCLC's troubles between 1965 and 1968 are well-chronicled in David Garrow, *Bearing the Cross*, pp. 431–624; Oates, *Let the Trumpet Sound*, pp. 387–498; and Fairclough, *To Redeem the Soul of America*, pp. 254–383.

11. Interview with Golden Frinks.

12. Ibid.

13. Ibid.; *N&O*, Sept. 4, 1968.

14. Letter from Charles Carroll to Gov. Dan K. Moore (Sept. 4, 1968). Governors Papers: Daniel K. Moore, 1965–1969.

15. "Petition from Concerned, Distressed, and Rejected Parents of Communities in Hyde County, North Carolina to Commissioner, HEW, Office of Education," Sept. 5, 1968, HEW Papers.

16. Transcript of A. J. Howell testimony, NEA Papers.

17. Interdepartmental memorandum from A. J. Howell to Walter S. Warfield, Office of Civil Rights, HEW, Sept. 9, 1968, HEW Papers.

18. Minutes, Sept. 3, 1968, Hyde County Board of Education.

19. Minutes, Sept. 6, 1968, Hyde County Board of Education.

20. Memorandum from A. J. Howell to Walter S. Warfield, HEW, Sept. 9, 1968, HEW Papers.

21. Ibid.

22. Interview with Dudley Flood.

23. Ibid.

24. This average is based on SHP daily estimates. See SHP daily memoranda for all of September 1968, SHP Papers. For daily reports, see also memoranda and intrabureau correspondence, files HQ-173-5889, sects. 1 and 2, Hyde County File, United States Department of Justice, Federal Bureau of Investigation (hereafter cited as FBI).

25. Memorandum, State Highway Patrol (Troop A, Greenville), Maj. John Laws to Capt. R. F. Williamson, Re: Civil Rights Marches—Hyde County, Sept. 17, 1968, SHP Troop A Papers.

26. See Goodwyn, *The Populist Moment*, especially pp. vii–xxiv and 20–54, for the source of the term "movement culture," as well as for a seminal discussion of democratic activism that sheds as much light on the civil rights movement as on the nineteenth-century agrarian revolt that is the subject of his book.

27. Interviews with Golden Frinks, Milton Fitch, Phillip Greene, Marjorie Selby, and Ida Murray.

28. Interviews with Thomas Whitaker and Alice Spencer Mackey.

29. *N&O*, Sept. 4, 1968.

30. SHP memorandum from Capt. R. F. Williamston to Maj. John Laws, Sept. 17, 1968, SHP Papers.

31. Ibid. Concerning the KKK meeting, see SHP memorandum from Maj. John Laws to Capts. R. F. Williamson, J. B. Kuykendall, and W. S. McKinney, Re: Ku Klux Klan Activity, Sept. 11, 1968, SHP Papers.

32. N&O, Sept. 20, 1968.

33. SHP memorandum from Lt. L. J. Lance to Maj. John Laws, Re: Incident which occurred during civil disturbance at Swan Quarter, N.C., 19 Sept. 1968. Sept. 20, 1968, SHP Papers.

34. Ibid.

35. N&O, Sept. 23, 1968.

36. Ibid.

37. Ibid.

38. SHP memorandum from Lt. Col. Edwin C. Guy to Col. Charles A. Speed, Re: Incident in Swan Quarter, N.C. Sept. 25, 1968, SHP Papers.

39. N&O, Sept. 26, 1968.

40. SHP memorandum from Lt. Col. Edwin C. Guy to Col. Charles Speed, Sept. 25, 1968, SHP Papers.

41. N&O, Sept. 27, 1968.

42. Letter from Charles Carroll to Gov. Dan K. Moore, Sept. 4, 1968, Governors Papers: Daniel K. Moore, 1965–1969.

43. Carroll deemed many of the more isolated incidents as beneath the governor's attentions. He did not tell the governor, for example, about the bomb threat at a Maysville elementary school, or about a Harnett County farmer who withdrew his teenage girl from school when teachers seated her between two black boys. N&O, Sept. 3 and Sept. 4, 1968.

44. Operating the O. A. Peay and Davis schools during the boycott required normal staffing and maintenance costs, but neither the State of North Carolina nor the Hyde County Board of Education received federal matching funds for unregistered students. Carroll was also reluctant to invest state matching funds in the two schools when they served so few students. See memorandum from Superintendent Carroll to Gov. Dan K. Moore, Sept. 4, 1968, Governors Papers: Daniel K. Moore, 1965–1969.

45. In June 1966, blacks in Roanoke Rapids organized mass pickets against local school officials who closed a historically black school. See SBI memorandum from Sgt. J. P. Thomas to the director, June 29, 1966, file M-2122, SHP Papers.

46. Telephone and Conference Record of call from David Coltrane to William Mammarella, Sept. 9, 1968, EEOP Official File, HEW Papers.

47. Letter from Ruby G. Martin, OCR director, to the Rev. Ralph Abernathy, Nov. 11, 1968, SCLC Papers.

48. Letter from Ruby G. Martin, OCR director, to the Rev. Ralph Abernathy, Nov. 20, 1968, SCLC Papers.

49. Minutes, Sept. 18, 1968, Hyde County Board of Education.

50. Minutes, Oct. 4, 1968, Hyde County Board of Education.

51. Minutes, Sept. 13, 1968, Hyde County Board of Education.

52. Interviews with Golden Frinks, James "Little Brother" Topping.

53. Interview with Dudley Flood.

54. Memorandum from D. S. Coltrane to Gov. Dan K. Moore, Oct. 2, 1968,

Governors Papers: Daniel K. Moore, 1965–1969, North Carolina Good Neighbor Council Papers (hereafter cited as NCGNC Papers).

55. Ibid.

56. Oct. 4, 1968 minutes, Hyde County Board of Education.

57. Memorandum from D. S. Coltrane to Gov. Dan K. Moore, Oct. 9, 1968, NCGNC Papers. It is unclear whether the school board chose to act unilaterally because of a misunderstanding with Coltrane at the October 1 meeting, or because the petition did not have enough signatures, or for some other reason.

58. Letter from Hyde County Board of Education to Dr. Lloyd Henderson, OCR, Oct. 4, 1968, HEW Papers.

59. Memorandum from D. S. Coltrane to Gov. Dan K. Moore, Oct. 9, 1968, NCGNC Papers.

60. Ibid.

61. D. S. Coltrane to Governor Moore, Oct. 2, 1968, NCGNC Papers.

62. Undated letter from Lloyd Henderson, education branch chief, Office of Civil Rights, to Superintendent Bucklew, NEA Papers. According to a copy of an undated letter from Ruby G. Martin, OCR director, to Rev. Ralph Abernathy, the request was rejected on Oct. 18, 1968. NEA Papers.

63. Minutes, Oct. 24, 1968, Hyde County Board of Education.

64. Interview with Golden Frinks.

65. Interview with James "Little Brother" Topping.

66. Interview with Ida Murray.

67. Black citizens operated the "movement schools" at the following churches: Job's Chapel, Old Richmond, St. Mary's, Snow Hill, Slocumb, Mt. Pilgrim, and Pleasant Grove.

68. Niles Hunt, director of general education in the state Department of Public Instruction, to Supt. Allen Bucklew, Oct. 11, 1968, NCDPI Papers.

69. State Supt. Charles Carroll to Supt. Allen Bucklew, Oct. 15, 1968, NCDPI Papers.

70. Interview with James "Little Brother" Topping.

71. Interview with Dudley Flood.

72. Interview with Alice Spencer Mackey.

73. Interview with Thomas Whitaker.

74. Interview with Phillip Greene.

Chapter 4

1. The school board's actions seemed wholly defensive at this point. The board tightened security around school buildings, and it resolved in early November to require students to attend at least 150 days of school in order to receive credit for a full year of study. See minutes, Nov. 4, 1968, Hyde County Board of Education.

2. In interviews, many black citizens recalled that poor whites had better access to welfare programs. They remembered, for example, that the welfare agency often allowed white clients to request services by telephoning or by sending word of their

needs, while it always required blacks to visit the agency's offices in Swan Quarter. Also, when federal surplus food was given away, the agency allegedly required even elderly black men and women to wait outside in long lines, rain or shine, while other accommodations were made for white recipients.

3. Interview with Golden Frinks.

4. SHP memorandum from Lt. Col. Edwin C. Guy to Charles Dunn, Re: Incident in Swan Quarter, Nov. 8, 1968, SHP Papers.

5. N&O, Nov. 9, 1968.

6. N&O, Nov. 12, 1968.

7. State troopers later claimed that they held the doors shut because the children were tossing the smoke and tear gas bombs back out the door. See N&O, Nov. 13, 1968.

8. Interview with James "Little Brother" Topping.

9. Charlotte Observer, Nov. 12, 1968.

10. Interview with Golden Frinks.

11. Charlotte Observer, Nov. 12, 1968.

12. N&O, Nov. 12, 1968. The six arrested teenagers included twins Alvin and Allen Spencer of Fairfield; Henry Johnson, Jr., Benjamin Phelps, and Samuel Bryant of Engelhard; and Preston Simons of Swan Quarter.

13. New York Times, Nov. 14, 1968.

14. N&O, Nov. 13, 1968; SHP memorandum from Capt. R. F. Williamson to Maj. John Laws, Re: civil disorders—Hyde County, Nov. 12, 1968, SHP Papers.

15. Charlotte Observer, Nov. 13, 1968.

16. SHP memorandum from Capt. R. F. Williamson to Maj. John Laws, Re: civil disorders—Hyde County, Nov. 12, 1968, SHP Troop A Papers.

17. Charlotte Observer, Nov. 14, 1968.

18. Interview with James "Little Brother" Topping.

19. N&O, Nov. 14, 1968.

20. New York Times, Nov. 14, 1968.

21. SHP memorandum from Capt. R. F. Williamson and Lt. L. J. Vance to Maj. John Laws, Re: civil disorders, Hyde County—supplemental, Nov. 18, 1968, SHP Papers.

22. N&O, Nov. 15, 1968.

23. Charlotte Observer, Nov. 16, 1968.

24. SHP memorandum from Captain Williamson and Lieutenant Vance to Major Laws, Nov. 18, 1968, SHP Troop A Papers.

25. According to internal SHP reports, at least two sheriffs in closer municipalities, Greenville and Washington, no longer accepted Hyde County protesters because business leaders feared demonstrations by local civil rights groups. Those sheriffs, in fact, wanted the protesters out of their jails. Sheriff Jack Harris in Washington requested that all six demonstrators be removed from his jail, and a professional bondsman mysteriously posted bail for the young prisoners in the Pitt County jail without the authority of their parents or the SCLC. See SHP memorandum from Captain Williamson to Major Laws, Nov. 20, 1968, SHP Troop A Papers.

26. *N&O*, Nov. 17, 1968, and "Statement of Hyde County Blacks," Nov. 16, 1968, copy in Hyde County file, HQ-173-5889, sect. 3, FBI.

27. SHP memorandum from Captain Williamson and Lieutenant Vance to Major Laws, Nov. 18, 1968, SHP Troop A Papers.

28. SHP memorandum from Capt. R. F. Williamson to Maj. John Laws, Re: civil disorders, Hyde County, Nov. 20, 1968, SHP Troop A Papers.

29. Ibid., and SHP memorandum from Williamson to Laws, Nov. 22, 1968, SHP Troop A Papers.

30. The nine boys were sent to jail in Greene County; the one girl was probably kept at the Hyde County Jail. The next day, a hundred adults and young people marched through Swan Quarter but without any acts of civil disobedience. See SHP memorandum from Lt. L. J. Lance to Maj. John Laws, Re: civil disorders, Hyde County, Nov. 25, 1968, SHP Troop A Papers. See also *N&O*, Nov. 23, 1968.

31. SHP memorandum from Captain Williamson and Lieutenant Lance to Major Laws, Nov. 18, 1968, SHP Troop A Papers.

32. Quoted in *N&O*, Nov. 14, 1968.

33. Ibid.

34. Transcripts of Daniel Williams testimony, NEA Papers; interview with Dudley Flood.

35. SHP memorandum from Captain Williamson and Lieutenant Lance to Major Laws, Nov. 18, 1968, SHP Troop A Papers.

36. Interview with Albert Whitaker.

37. Interviews with Ida Murray, Erskine Mackey, Doris Weston.

38. Transcript of Sheriff Charles Cahoon testimony, NEA Papers.

39. *Southern Patriot* 27, no. 1 (January 1969).

40. *N&O*, Nov. 14, 1968.

41. *Charlotte Observer*, Nov. 28, 1968.

42. *Charlotte Observer*, Nov. 15, 1968.

43. *N&O*, Nov. 13, 1968.

44. Taylor had been a psychology professor from 1929 to 1959. As president of the N.C. Teachers Association, he had also played a leading role in the struggle to obtain equal salaries for black public school teachers in North Carolina. He served as vice-chairman of the N.C. Good Neighbor Council from its founding in 1963. His appointment followed by a few hours a resolution from the N.C. Baptist State Convention that urged the governor to fill the position immediately. See *N&O*, Nov. 14, 1968.

45. Interview with Charles Dunn.

46. *Charlotte Observer*, Nov. 18, 1968.

47. In 1960, Dr. Hawkins, who was also a Presbyterian minister, had filed suit to desegregate the N.C. Dental Society and later challenged segregation at the state Board of Dental Examiners. Both groups fiercely fought the entrance of black dentists. Dr. Hawkins also led efforts to give medical aid recipients the freedom to choose their own doctors and hospitals. Especially between 1960 and 1964, his challenge of segregation in the dental profession spurred a wider campaign to

desegregate the N.C. Medical Society, state hospitals, mental institutions, nursing homes, and ambulance services. In retaliation for his civil rights activism, white extremists repeatedly targeted his home and family. He was also a gubernatorial candidate in the 1968 Democratic primary. See *Charlotte Observer*, Mar. 31, 1960; *Southern Patriot* 26, no. 10 (December 1968); and the "Medical Care file, 1960–1963," North Carolina Advisory Committee on Civil Rights (NCACCR) clipfile.

48. SHP memoranda (especially for Nov. 20, 1968) and news reports suggest Hawkins's intentions. He also tried to persuade James Ferguson to visit Hyde County again in late November to discuss legal strategies that might satisfy local blacks enough that the children could return to school during litigation.

49. Memoranda from Charlotte FBI office to the director for Nov. 25 (HQ-173-5889-81) and Nov. 20, 1968 (HQ-173-5889-87), Hyde County file, FBI.

50. See especially Berube and Gittell, eds., *Confrontation at Ocean Hill-Brownsville*.

51. *N&O*, Nov. 21, 1968.

52. The SHP estimated that approximately four hundred blacks participated in the protest. SCLC leaders put the number closer to one thousand. See SHP memorandum from Lieutenant Lance to Major Laws, Nov. 25, 1968, SHP Troop A Papers; *Charlotte Observer*, Nov. 25, 1968.

53. SHP memorandum from Lieutenant Lance to Major Laws, Nov. 27, 1968, SHP Troop A Papers.

54. *N&O*, Nov. 27, 1968, and *Charlotte Observer*, Nov. 28, 1968.

55. *N&O*, Nov. 27 and Nov. 28, 1968.

56. *N&O*, Nov. 28, 1968.

57. Ibid.

58. This period is discussed in four SHP memoranda from Captain Williamson to Major Laws, Re: civil disorders, Hyde County, dated Nov. 29, Dec. 2, Dec. 3, and Dec. 4, SHP Troop A Papers. See also *N&O*, Nov. 29 and Dec. 2, 1968.

59. *N&O*, Dec. 6, 1968, does not include Simons among the participants, but SHP memorandum from Lieutenant Lance to Major Laws, Dec. 6, 1968, does.

60. See SHP memorandum from Lieutenant Lance to Major Laws, Dec. 6, 1968, SHP Troop A Papers. According to the *Charlotte Observer*, six black parents had met with the school board on Nov. 16. A meeting between the Committee of 14 and the school board had been scheduled for Nov. 12, but apparently the committee failed to show.

61. Ibid.

62. *N&O*, Dec. 6, 1968, and NEA memorandum from Boyd Bosma to Samuel Ethridge, Jan. 15, 1969, NEA Papers. The police officers would have arrested more demonstrators if they had had more agents on duty. SHP memorandum from Lieutenant Lance to Major Laws, Dec. 6, 1968, SHP Troop A Papers.

63. Principal Simons taught these few students in one classroom. School officials reported that the threats did not affect attendance at the other two schools, though they noted that many students and teachers seemed "fearful." *N&O*, Dec. 7, 1968.

64. Regarding this week of protests, see *N&O*, Dec. 7, 1968; and SHP memo-

randa from Lieutenant Lance to Major Laws, Dec. 9, 1968; from First Sgt. M. S. Parvin to Major Laws, Dec. 10, 1968; and from First Sgt. M. S. Parvin to Major Laws, Dec. 11, 1968, all in SHP Troop A Papers. As throughout rural North Carolina, district court judges visited Hyde County intermittently, usually two or three times a year. Sessions usually lasted about a week.

65. Dec. 11, 1968 minutes, Hyde County District Court.

66. Most of those arrested had been charged with blocking traffic, a misdemeanor. In addition, though, the thirteen boys who were sixteen or older who had occupied Principal Simons's office on December 5 had been charged with disrupting school. Allen Long and A. T. Johnson had been charged with contributing to the delinquency of minors for encouraging children under the age of sixteen to participate in civil disobedience. And Henry Johnson, Jr., a fifteen-year-old whose family lived in Engelhard, had been charged with vandalism for breaking a courthouse window during a protest. See minutes, December 1968 sessions, Hyde County District Court.

67. N&O, Dec. 12, 1968; minutes, Dec. 11, 1968, Hyde County District Court.

68. Concerning protests during the week of December 12, see SHP memorandum from Captain Williamson and First Sergeant Parvin to Major Laws, Dec. 16, 1968, SHP Troop A Papers; N&O, Dec. 14, 1968; SHP memoranda from Line Sgt. Charles Smith to Major Laws, Dec. 17 and Dec. 19, 1968, SHP Troop A Papers.

69. The convicted twenty-nine were again given suspended sentences except for Henry Johnson, Jr., who received an active thirty-day sentence for vandalizing the courthouse. N&O, Dec. 19, 1968.

70. N&O, Dec. 19, 1968.

71. Interview with James "Little Brother" Topping; SHP memorandum from Line Sergeant Smith to Major Laws, Dec. 19, 1968, SHP Troop A Papers.

72. Late that night Sheriff Cahoon released to their parents the thirty-one juveniles charged with contempt.

73. N&O, Dec. 19, 1968.

74. N&O, Dec. 19, 1968, and SHP memorandum, Dec. 16, 1968. The latter document refers to confidential information concerning the internal tensions within the SCLC that evidently was obtained through FBI or SBI monitoring via either wiretaps or an informer.

75. The guilty verdicts were all appealed to superior court by James Ferguson and James Frazier, a black attorney in New Bern. See minutes, Dec. 19, 1968, Hyde County District Court.

76. NEACPRR, Hyde County, North Carolina, p. 35.

77. Interview with Phillip Greene.

78. Transcript of Daniel Williams testimony, NEA Papers.

79. Washington Post, Nov. 25, 1968.

80. Transcript of Jonathan Weston testimony, NEA Papers.

81. Interview with Marjorie Selby.

82. Interview with Morgan Harris.

83. NEACPRR, Hyde County, North Carolina, p. 32.

84. N&O, Nov. 14, 1968.

85. Ibid.

86. Interview with Dudley Flood.

87. N&O, Nov. 14, 1968.

88. Hyde County Schools memorandum from Principal Simons to all staff members, undated, NEA Papers.

89. Ibid.

90. Hyde County Schools memorandum from Principal Simons to all staff members at the O. A. Peay School, Oct. 1, 1968, NEA Papers.

91. Transcript of Etta Mae Greene testimony, NEA Papers.

92. Hyde County Schools memorandum from Superintendent Bucklew to principals and teachers, Oct. 24, 1968, NEA Papers.

93. Transcript of James Barrow testimony, NEA Papers; NEACPRR, *Hyde County, North Carolina*, p. 36.

94. Transcript of James Barrow testimony, NEA Papers. This date may be imprecise, given that his statement was taken six months after Etta Mae Greene's dismissal.

95. Interview with Ida Murray.

96. Ibid.

97. Especially interviews with Phillip Greene, Abell Fulford, Jr., Marjorie Selby, and Alice Spencer Mackey.

98. *Washington Post*, Nov. 25, 1968.

99. Transcript of Daniel Williams testimony, NEA Papers.

100. NEA memorandum from Boyd Bosma and Samuel Ethridge, Jan. 15, 1969, NEA Papers.

101. Ibid.

102. Letter from the Hyde County Unit of the NCTA to the Hyde County Board of Education, Nov. 25, 1968, NEA Papers.

103. Ibid.

104. Teletype from Charlotte FBI office to the director and Atlanta, HQ-173-5889-93, Nov. 29, 1968, Hyde County file, FBI.

105. Minutes, Dec. 2, 1968, Hyde County Board of Education.

106. In private meetings with NEA staff from Washington, D.C., a month later, the black teachers discussed several complaints having to do with the administration of the Elementary and Secondary Education Act (ESEA) programs in the school district. This federal program was designed to provide supplemental educational programs for children from poor families, but roughly 25 percent of the $129,741 in ESEA funds allotted to Hyde County had been diverted to constructing additional classrooms to accommodate black students at the Mattamuskeet School. The teachers believed this diversion deprived black children of important educational benefits. In addition, they complained that few black educators were employed within ESEA programs and that the black community had not participated in writing proposals or in planning those programs, as required by federal statute. Finally, the teachers also believed that black children were not benefiting proportionally from ESEA pro-

grams. They cited a reduction in ESEA lunches and the assignment of reading teachers hired with ESEA funds to Mattamuskeet instead of Peay or Davis. See HEW memorandum from Genevieve O. Dane, chief of the operations branch, DCE, to Boyd Bosma, NEA, Re: Title I, ESEA Allocations—Hyde County, N.C., Apr. 10, 1969; and NEA memorandum from Boyd Bosma to Samuel B. Ethridge, Re: Visit to Hyde County, N.C., Jan. 15, 1969, NEA Papers. Regarding the community participation requirements of ESEA, see HEW, *Policies on Elementary and Secondary School Compliance with Title VI of the Civil Rights Act of 1964.*

107. *N&O*, Dec. 2, 1968, and SHP memorandum, Nov. 27, 1968.

108. NEA memorandum from Boyd Bosma to Samuel Ethridge, Jan. 15, 1969.

109. Ibid. See also NEACPRR, *Hyde County, North Carolina*, p. 8.

110. *N&O*, Dec. 25, 1968.

111. *N&O*, Dec. 21, 1968.

Chapter 5

1. Concerning how white citizens perceived Bucklew's racial attitudes, see especially transcript of testimony by Sheriff Charles Cahoon, NEA Papers.

2. Moreover, state and federal agencies were ill prepared to mediate a settlement during the gubernatorial and presidential transitions. The gubernatorial succession involved two politically aligned Democrats, Dan K. Moore and Robert Scott, but civil rights leaders expected major changes in school desegregation policy when Republican president Richard Nixon inherited Lyndon Johnson's HEW.

3. According to SHP records, Hyde County blacks held protests and/or mass meetings on Dec. 28, 29, 30, and 31, 1968, and Jan. 1, 6, 7, 9, 12, 16, and 18, 1969. The number of protesters ranged from a few dozen to more than a hundred, but averaged less than fifty in January. See the series of SHP memoranda from Line Sergeant Smith to Major Laws dated Dec. 30 and Dec. 31, 1968, and Jan. 2, Jan. 6, Jan. 8, Jan. 13, Jan. 14, Jan. 17, and Jan. 20, 1969, SHP Troop A Papers. The school boycott activists did not conduct protests during the court sessions that tried the last 93 demonstrators arrested for blocking traffic. Thirty-four protesters were tried in district court in Swan Quarter on Jan. 3, 1969, approximately 25 more on Jan. 15, and 13 more on Jan. 21. In addition, 21 juveniles were tried on Jan. 10. Of all those cases, all but one defendant was found guilty and given a suspended sentence. All appealed to superior court. See minutes, January 1969, Hyde County District Court.

4. SHP memorandum from Line Sergeant Smith to Major Laws, Jan. 2, 1969.

5. SHP memoranda for Dec. 30, 1968, and Jan. 10, 1969. Sara Small had been one of the most important leaders in the Williamston Freedom Movement; in 1966, she was the state's first black candidate for the U.S. Congress since Reconstruction. Reverend Nixon led the civil rights movement in New Bern. In North Carolina, black activists rarely met more widespread Klan resistance, including several murder attempts and a church bombing, than in New Bern. The very important civil rights movement in that Craven County town still awaits the attention of historians. SHP

and SBI documents cover the New Bern movement extensively, however. See especially SBI intrabureau correspondence and director's reports for 1965–67, files M-24-361-25, M-24-361-61, and M-24-361-67, SHP Papers. See also *Carolina Times*, July 30 and Oct. 22, 1960; Feb. 20, 1965; Mar. 12, 1966; and Aug. 20, 1966.

6. A total of forty-two other young people arrested for contempt of court had been released from the Women's Prison in Raleigh on January 3 and from the jail in Warrenton on January 10 after they apologized to Judge Ward for disrupting his court. See *N&O*, Jan. 4, 1969, and SHP memorandum from Line Sergeant Rogers to Major Laws, Jan. 13, 1969, SHP Papers. Frinks had acknowledged from the first that the protest that provoked the contempt-of-court conviction was unwise and a mistake. Undoubtedly this fact contributed to the desire of the demonstrators to be released from prison. More important, though, Women's Prison was the maximum security prison for women in North Carolina, and the penal atmosphere was consequently much harsher than that in even the worst county jails in eastern North Carolina. Many of the incarcerated young women from Hyde County were frankly intimidated; hence they wrote an almost obsequious letter apologizing to Judge Ward. When the *News and Observer* printed it, this letter appeared to be something of a black mark to the school boycott.

7. SHP memorandum from Line Sergeant Smith to Major Laws, Jan. 17, 1969, SHP Papers.

8. See SHP memorandum from Line Sergeant Smith to Major Laws, Jan. 20, 1969, SHP Papers.

9. Nixon had apparently also implied that Frinks might be guilty of financial improprieties in handling SCLC funds. Sources do not indicate the basis of this allegation, however, nor how the participants in the meeting reacted. The only evidence regarding what was discussed at this pivotal gathering, unfortunately, are SHP documents almost certainly informed by FBI surveillance records that may not be reliable and certainly are not close to complete. See SHP memorandum from Line Sergeant Smith to Major Laws, Jan. 20, 1969, SHP Papers.

10. See especially Fairclough, *To Redeem the Soul of America*, chaps. 14 and 15.

11. SHP memorandum from Capt. R. F. Williamson to Major Laws, Re: Swan Quarter situation, Jan. 22, 1969, SHP Papers.

12. See SHP memorandum, Jan. 10, 1969, SHP Papers.

13. Transcript of Sheriff Charles Cahoon testimony, NEA Papers.

14. Interview with Golden Frinks. Flowers had long been a principal crop in the rural community of Terra Ceia, just across the northwest boundary of Hyde County. This rural community was settled by Dutch immigrants in the 1930s.

15. Interviews with Alice Spencer Mackey and Thomas Whitaker.

16. This idea remained a low priority, but it made an important point. Land reform was one of the few economic development strategies viable in an agrarian economy where blacks—half the population on Hyde County's mainland—owned far less than 5 percent of the land.

17. Interview with Golden Frinks.

18. Ibid.

19. Interview with Abell Fulford, Jr.

20. The history of labor activism in eastern North Carolina remains at least as undocumented and unknown as the region's rich civil rights history. Scholars interested in the subject must begin with primary sources, especially the CIO Organizing Committee Papers titled "Operation Dixie," Series 1, subtitled "CIO Organizing Committee, North Carolina, 1932–1958," which cover worker organizing in the textile, tobacco, slaughterhouse, and logging and sawmill industries. Series 7 and 8 will also be relevant to historians interested in the larger CIO organizing campaign in North Carolina. In addition, the first—and a very useful— study of tobacco worker organizing in the region has recently been completed. See Windham, "Green Hands: A History of the Food, Tobacco, and Agricultural Workers of America in Greenville, N.C., 1946." Other published studies of labor activism in eastern North Carolina include Adams, *Unearthing Seeds of Fire*, pp. 54–71; Finger, "Stevens vs. Justice," pp. 38–44; and Bob Hall, "Bucking the System," pp. 66–73.

21. Regarding the eighteen-month strike by black workers at Rose Hill Poultry, a slaughterhouse in Duplin County long notorious for dangerous conditions, see N&O, Nov. 8, 1968. For background on several important union campaigns in 1970 by slaughterhouse and tobacco workers in Wilson, see the National Labor Relations Board's monthly election reports (hereafter cited as NLRB Reports) for 1970, as well as Windham, "Green Hands," pp. 58–59. Knowledge of the Washington strike at Scoville Manufacturing is based on the author's conversations (both in May 1984) with former union president Allen Robertson and with Father Charles Mulholland, a Catholic priest who organized community support for the workers. Civil rights activism also contributed to the success of textile workers who organized unions at J. P. Stevens plants in Halifax and Duplin counties. See Finger and Krivosh, "Stevens vs. Justice," pp. 38–44. Major union organizing campaigns dovetailed with the civil rights movement in other rural locales, including Smithfield, Whiteville, Lumberton, and Rich Square; NLRB Reports, 1967–73. Even more common, though, were wildcat strikes and other less formal labor actions that did not involve national unions. The 1970 strike by seasonal blueberry pickers in Bridgeton, a small town in Craven County, is a good example. See "Racial Incidents in North Carolina, 1970," Governors Papers: Robert W. Scott, 1969–1973, NCGNC Papers.

22. Interview with Alice Spencer Mackey.

23. Interview with Vanderbilt Johnson.

24. On February 2, for instance, a sixty-car caravan had passed between Sladesville and Scranton urging black families to continue the school boycott during the March on Raleigh. Memorandum HQ-173-5889-172, Hyde County file, FBI.

25. N&O, Feb. 10, 1969, and memorandum HQ-173-5889-174, Hyde County file, FBI.

26. *Washington Daily News*, Feb. 10 and 11; *Daily Reflector*, Feb. 12 and 13; N&O, Feb. 10–15, 1969.

27. The marchers encountered several obstacles along the route, especially in

Greenville. They staged sit-ins there on Wednesday afternoon after local police prevented them from entering certain neighborhoods specified by the city council. The police took the protesters under custody and escorted them out of the town limits. In addition, a church that allowed the school boycotters to hold a rally on Tuesday night was burned the next day. See *N&O*, Feb. 12, 1969.

28. Irons and Unruhe, "Black Wilson," pp. 33–37; memorandum HQ-173-5889-196, Hyde County file, FBI.

29. *N&O*, Feb. 15, 1969.

30. The Shaw students later prepared dinner for the marchers and gave them accommodations for the night. Memorandum HQ-173-5889-200, Hyde County file, FBI.

31. Ibid.

32. Quoted in *N&O*, Jan. 29, 1969.

33. Ibid.

34. *N&O*, Feb. 15, 1969.

35. *N&O*, Feb. 21, 1969.

36. *N&O*, Feb. 18, 1969; minutes, Feb. 17, 1969, Hyde County Board of Education.

37. Minutes, Feb. 17 and Feb. 19, 1969, Hyde County Board of Education.

38. Interview with Albert Whitaker. A few students apparently accepted those conditions. On February 19, a date on which reliable numbers can be obtained from state school officials, 74 black students were enrolled at the O. A. Peay School, 70 at the Davis School, and 22 at the Mattamuskeet School.

39. Transcripts of Sheriff Charles Cahoon testimony and Early Bryant testimony, NEA Papers.

40. Transcript of Sheriff Charles Cahoon testimony, NEA Papers.

41. The goals of the march are described in a three-page petition to the governor titled "Mountain Top to Valley March on Raleigh," Governors Papers: Robert W. Scott, 1969–1973.

42. *N&O*, Mar. 25, 1969.

43. Interview with Milton Fitch.

44. Interview with Golden Frinks.

45. Interviews with Milton Fitch and Golden Frinks.

46. *N&O*, Apr. 17, 1968.

47. This case involved a Mrs. Sarah Davis, who was allegedly brutalized by a white police officer during her arrest for larceny.

48. *N&O*, May 8, 1969.

49. *N&O*, Apr. 30 and May 8, 1969.

50. *N&O*, Apr. 30, 1969.

51. *N&O*, May 8, 1969.

52. Letter from Lloyd R. Henderson, Office of Civil Rights, HEW, to Mr. Cecil Silverthorne, chairman, Hyde County Board of Education, Apr. 28, 1969, HEW Papers. HEW was evidently not aware that Silverthorne no longer served on the school board.

53. Minutes, May 5, 1969, Hyde County Board of Education.

54. N&O, May 25, 1969.

Chapter 6

1. While such a meeting would have attracted three hundred or more white citizens in 1965 or 1966, attendance at Klan gatherings had by this time declined considerably in Hyde County and elsewhere in eastern North Carolina. Less than eighty Klansmen attended this night, and a large proportion of that number came from outside the county. See SHP memorandum from Lt. L. J. Vance to Col. Charles Speed, July 7, 1969, SHP Papers.

2. Interviews with Erskine Mackey and Vanderbilt Johnson.

3. SHP memorandum, July 7, 1969, SHP Papers.

4. Ibid.

5. N&O, July 6, 1969.

6. Interview with Dudley Flood.

7. Ibid.

8. Flood had already encountered Golden Frinks several times in eastern North Carolina. Frinks had even led a one-day school boycott at Flood's school in Pitt County to mark the assassination of Martin Luther King, Jr., in April 1968. Interview with Dudley Flood.

9. Ibid.

10. Ibid.

11. Ibid.

12. Minutes, June 30, 1969, Hyde County Board of Education.

13. Ibid.

14. Ibid.

15. Minutes, July 7, 1969, Hyde County Board of Education.

16. Minutes, July 10, 1969, Hyde County Board of Education; interview with Dudley Flood.

17. Minutes, July 16, 1969, Hyde County Board of Education.

18. Minutes, July 15, 1969, Hyde County Board of County Commissioners.

19. Minutes, July 16, 1969, Hyde County Board of Education.

20. Ibid.

21. "Voting rolls," 1968–1970, Hyde County Board of Elections.

22. Quoted in Charlotte Observer, Sept. 1, 1969.

23. For example, see minutes, July 15, 1969, Hyde County Board of Education.

24. Minutes, Aug. 19, 1969, meeting between Hyde County Board of Education and team from HEW's Office of Education, NEA Papers.

25. Charlotte Observer, Sept. 1, 1969.

26. Letter from the "Undersigned black people of Hyde County" to the Hon. Robert Scott, Aug. 8, 1969, Governors Papers: Robert W. Scott, 1969–1973.

27. Interviews with Johnnie Midgette, Mary Gibbs.

28. Many Hyde County blacks who remember the incident still wonder if Bryant

was "put up to" writing the letter by law enforcement agents or local white leaders. Even some people who knew him well do not believe that Bryant actually wrote the letter, though they acknowledge it expressed his opinions accurately. Evidence is inconclusive, however.

29. Letter from SBI director Charles Dunn to Gov. Robert Scott, including preliminary SBI report on activities of Golden Frinks, Oct. 31, 1969, SBI file CI-48, SHP Papers.

30. Ibid.

31. The SBI completed its investigation without finding any evidence of criminal activity, but the agency never publicized its findings.

32. N&O, Sept. 2, 1969.

33. N&O, Sept. 3, 1969.

34. *Charlotte Observer*, Sept. 3, 1969.

35. Memorandum from FBI Director to SAC, Charlotte, Re: public school opening, Fall 1969; Aug. 14, 1969, HQ-173-5889-NR, Hyde County file, FBI.

36. Untitled memorandum related to "Investigation of Committee of 14 and Golden Frinks and his associates," undated, Governors Papers: Robert W. Scott, 1969–1973.

37. Ibid. There is more than a reasonable likelihood that this investigation was carried out, but there is no firm evidence other than this rather mysterious document.

38. Hyde County Superior Court records, Sept. 1969. See also N&O, Sept. 3, 1969.

39. See Hyde County Superior Court records, Sept. 10, 1969, and N&O, Sept. 11, 1969.

40. "November 1969 election records," Hyde County Board of Elections.

41. Interview with R. S. Spencer, Jr.

42. James D. Anderson, *Education of Blacks in the South*, p. 278.

Epilogue

1. Cecelski, "'Missing our Grandmothers,'" p. 2.

2. Cecelski, "Crab Processing and Mexican H2-B Workers," pp. 1–3.

3. *Statistical Abstract of North Carolina Counties, 1991*, pp. P-2 and P-3.

4. Cecelski, "'Missing our Grandmothers,'" pp. 3–7.

5. John Hope Franklin, *Color Line*, p. 72.

6. Cecelski, "'Missing our Grandmothers,'" p. 28. Based on data in the *North Carolina Rural Profile* and the *Local School Finance Study*.

7. In rural North Carolina, the potential for interracial cooperation has been demonstrated most forcefully in several recent environmental conflicts. See especially the essays in Bob Hall, *Environmental Politics*; Cecelski and Kerr, "Hog Wild"; Cecelski, "Endangered Species, Endangered Communities," pp. 10–25; and Kerr, "Toxic Race."

8. For a discussion of Frinks's involvement in one famous civil rights trial, the

murder case against a Washington, North Carolina woman named Joan Little, see Reston, *Innocence of Joan Little*. Any reader interested in the Joan Little case, however, would benefit by also referring to two articles in *Southern Exposure* 6, no. 1 (Spring 1978): Pinsky, "The Innocence of James Reston," pp. 39–41, and Joan Little with Rebecca Ransom, "'I am Joan,'" pp. 42–47.

9. Daunted by rising black dissent, many school leaders paused to find ways to merge the black and white schools more equitably. For example, in Washington County, just northwest of Hyde, white school leaders and fourteen hundred black residents jointly petitioned HEW in 1969 not to force them to desegregate schools that year. Citizens of both races had agreed that they required more time to negotiate a plan respectful of both communities. *New York Times*, Apr. 27, 1969.

10. Interview with Dudley Flood.

11. *Southern Patriot*, February 1971 and June 1971. Also, interview with James Ferguson II.

12. Fairclough, *To Redeem the Soul of America*, pp. 394–96.

13. Even the SCLC's Andrew Young, who had wholeheartedly supported school desegregation, was by 1972 expressing new concerns about the reality of its implementation. In a speech that year, Young articulated a new, broader outlook on desegregation:

> An integrated education requires a great deal more than simply integrating pupils. We must see to it that there is a continually integrated school board, that there [is] an integrated administration, that integrated school planning and construction take place. We must make sure that integrated curriculum and textbooks are part of the educational system, that we have integrated supervisors and training personnel, integrated faculty, integrated custodial staff, and finally integrated classrooms. (Quoted in Cruse, *Plural But Equal*, pp. 248–49)

14. See Morsell, "Racial Desegregation and Integration in Public Education," p. 282. Morsell was then a national vice-president of the NAACP.

15. For a good overview of legal challenges to black teacher firings prior to 1970, see NAACP Legal Defense and Educational Fund, "A Report to the People of the United States."

16. Sinowitz, "School Integration and the Teacher," p. 32.

17. Even when federal courts challenged the firing of black teachers, school districts frequently found subtle ways of evading the law to demote, fire, or fail to hire blacks. See Hooker, "Displacement of Black Teachers"; John Smith and Betty Smith, "For Black Educators," p. 7; and Sinowitz, "School Integration and the Teacher," p. 32. The concurrent rise in the use of entrance and exit tests, such as the National Teachers Examination, to license teachers dovetailed with this trend. Today scholars dispute whether educational policymakers in the South intended those exams to limit black access to the teaching profession, but it is widely recognized that they had little validity in measuring teacher performance and disproportionately prevented black aspirants from becoming teachers. See George,

"Competency Controversy"; Butler, "Black Educators in Louisiana"; and Hoover-Rhodes, "Teacher Competency Tests as Educational Genocide."

18. Sinowitz, "School Integration and the Teacher," p. 31.

19. Interview with James Ferguson II.

20. Arnez, "Implementation of Desegregation," pp. 37–39, and Mills and Bryan, *Testing-Grouping: the New Segregation in Southern Schools?*

21. In a study of 2,862 school districts in nine states, the Children's Defense Fund showed that administrators suspended black children at twice the rate of any other ethnic group. See Children's Defense Fund, *Children Out of School in America* and *School Suspensions: Are They Helping Children?* See also Southern Regional Council and the Robert F. Kennedy Memorial, *Student Pushout.*

22. Leon Hall, "Implementor's Revenge," pp. 122–23.

23. See especially Arnez, "Implementation of Desegregation."

24. Interview with Walter Lee Gibbs.

25. Civil rights activist Jim Grant, then moonlighting as a correspondent for the *Southern Patriot*, provided by far the most in-depth coverage of the black student protests in North and South Carolina. See *Southern Patriot* for September 1969 through December 1971. See also N&O, Apr. 10, 1969, and May 22, 1969.

26. N&O, Nov. 12, 1970, and Jan. 13, 1971; Thomas, "True Story Behind the Wilmington 10"; and *Southern Patriot*, March 1971 and July 1971. The situation was almost as bad in Elizabethtown, not far from Wilmington, where black student protests led to a number of burnings and shootings. *Southern Patriot*, June 1971.

27. By the end of 1971, the student protests had also spread into the segregated public colleges as their students and alumni fought off plans to desegregate the state college system by closing those historic institutions. *Southern Patriot*, December 1971.

28. Interviews with Stephanie Allen, Willis Williams, and Edward Brown.

29. Interview with Stephanie Allen.

30. While the Craven County parents group has not done so yet, many others have also advocated for local schools to employ reasonable proportions of black teachers and other staff. At least one such group in eastern North Carolina has mounted a strong legal challenge to the tracking of black children into remedial and lower-level classes. See Cecelski, "'Missing Our Grandmothers,'" pp. 40–41.

31. See especially two recent articles by Emilie V. Siddle Walker, "Interpersonal Caring" and "Caswell County Training School."

32. *National Guardian*, May 31, 1954.

Manuscripts and Archival Collections

Governors Papers: Daniel K. Moore, 1965–1969. State Archives, North Carolina
Division of Archives and History, Raleigh, N.C.

Governors Papers: Robert W. Scott, 1969–1973. State Archives, North Carolina
Division of Archives and History, Raleigh, N.C. The documents collected in
the Governors Papers for Governor Scott and Governor Moore include correspondence, interoffice memoranda, field reports, and a wide assortment of
other papers from the Governor's Office but also from the Councils of State,
including detailed records related to the Hyde County school boycott from the
State Highway Patrol, the State Bureau of Investigation, the Department of
Public Instruction, the Attorney General's Office, the North Carolina Good
Neighbor Council, and other parts of the state government.

Hyde County Board of Commissioners. Minutes, 1967–1973. Hyde County
Courthouse, Swan Quarter, N.C.

Hyde County Board of Education. Minutes, 1954–1973, especially Books IV and
V (1967–1970). Offices of the Board of Education, Swan Quarter, N.C.

Hyde County Board of Elections. "Voting Rolls," 1968–1970. Offices of the
Hyde County Board of Elections, Swan Quarter, N.C.

Hyde County District Court. "Index to Criminal Actions." Hyde County Clerk of
Court, Swan Quarter, N.C.

Hyde County District Court. Minutes. Court sessions for December 2 and 18,
1968; January 2, 15, and 21, 1969; March 12, 1969; May 26, 1969; July 18,
1969; and September 2, 1969. Hyde County Clerk of Court, Swan Quarter,
N.C.

Hyde County Superior Court. Minutes. Court sessions for May, June, and September 1969. Hyde County Clerk of Court, Swan Quarter, N.C.

National Association for the Advancement of Colored People Papers. Library of
Congress. Washington, D.C.

National Education Association Papers. Reports, interview transcripts, memoranda, and other papers related to the NEA's investigation of the Hyde County
school boycott. Housed at the internal archives at NEA national headquarters,
Washington, D.C.

North Carolina Advisory Committee on Civil Rights. Newspaper clipfile on civil
rights activism, 1960–1963. North Carolina Collection, University of North
Carolina, Chapel Hill, N.C.

North Carolina Department of Administration. Human Relations Council Papers. Director's Correspondence, 1968–1969. In Human Relations Files, State Archives Annex, North Carolina Division of Archives and History, Raleigh, N.C. Includes general records, correspondence, interoffice memoranda, assistants' files, consultants' files, various reports, and other documents in addition to reports from State Bureau of Investigation and Council of State departments.

North Carolina Department of Public Instruction. County, Subject, and Memorandums files (State Superintendent's Office), 1966–1970; Principals' High School and Elementary Annual Reports File, 1967–1970; Administrative Units Correspondence File, 1966–1970; General Correspondence File, 1968–1970. State Archives and Archives Annex, North Carolina Division of Archives and History, Raleigh, N.C.

North Carolina Division of Motor Vehicles. State Highway Patrol. Commander's Correspondence File and Report of Investigations File, 1959–1970. Includes field reports from State Highway Patrol and State Bureau of Investigation related to racial violence, the Ku Klux Klan, and intelligence monitoring of the civil rights movement. State Records Center, North Carolina Division of Archives and History, Raleigh, N.C.

North Carolina Division of Motor Vehicles. State Highway Patrol, Troop A. Field reports and daily monitoring reports on events in Hyde County. Filed at Troop A Headquarters, Greenville, N.C.

Operation Dixie: The CIO Organizing Committee Papers. Series I, subtitled "CIO Organizing Committee, North Carolina, 1932–1958." Series I, VII, and VIII. Perkins Library, Duke University, Durham, N.C.

Southern Christian Leadership Conference Papers. Martin Luther King, Jr. Center for Non-Violent Social Change, Atlanta, Ga.

United States Department of Health, Education, and Welfare. Office of Civil Rights. Assorted correspondence, interoffice memoranda, and policy statements related to the Hyde County school boycott. National Education Association internal archives, Washington, D.C.

United States Department of Justice. Federal Bureau of Investigation. General case file on the Southern Christian Leadership Conference, 1963–1971. Freedom of Information Act release no. 100-438794. Housed at the archives of the Martin Luther King, Jr. Center for the Study of Non-Violent Social Change, Atlanta, Ga.

United States Department of Justice. Federal Bureau of Investigation. Field reports, intelligence monitoring, and intrabureau correspondence on the Hyde County school boycott. Files HQ-173-5889 and CE-157-177, sub. B. Freedom of Information Act release no. 315,680.

Newspapers and Journals

Asheville Citizen-Times
Atlanta Constitution

Carolina Times
Chapel Hill Weekly
Charlotte Observer
Durham *Morning Herald*
Good Neighbors at Work in North Carolina
Greenville *Daily Reflector*
Hyde County Messenger
Integrated Education: A Report on Race and Schools
New Bern *Sun Journal*
New York Times
North Carolina Public Schools
Raleigh *News and Observer (N&O)*
Sampson News
Scotland Neck Commonwealth
Southern Courier
Southern Education Report
Southern Patriot
Today's Education
Tri-County News
Virginian-Pilot
Washington Daily News
Washington Post
Wilmington Star-News

Government Documents

Mitchell, Memory F., ed. *Addresses and Public Papers of Robert Walter Scott, Governor of North Carolina 1969–1973.* Raleigh: Division of Archives and History, 1974.
———, ed. *Messages, Addresses, and Public Papers of Daniel Kilian Moore, Governor of North Carolina 1965–1969.* Raleigh: State Department of Archives and History for the Council of State, 1971.
National Labor Relations Board. Monthly Election Reports, 1967–1976.
North Carolina Department of Conservation and Development and North Carolina Department of Labor. *Industrial Directory and Reference Book of the State of North Carolina.* Raleigh, 1938.
North Carolina Manual 1969. Raleigh: Office of the Secretary of State, 1970.
North Carolina Superintendent of Public Instruction. *School Absenteeism: NC Laws, Regulations, and Policies.* Publication no. 412. Raleigh, 1969.
North Carolina Superintendent of Public Instruction, Division of School Planning. *Hyde County 1974–75 Survey.* Raleigh, 1975.
Statistical Abstract of North Carolina Counties, 1991. State Data Center, Management and Information Services, Office of State Budget and Management. Raleigh, 1991.

United States Bureau of the Census. *1950 Census of Housing. Vol. 1: General Characteristics, Part 5: North Carolina.* Washington, D.C.: Government Printing Office, 1953.

———. *1950 Census of the Population. Vol. 2: Characteristics of the Population, Part 33: North Carolina.* Washington, D.C.: Government Printing Office, 1952.

———. *1970 Census of Housing. Vol. 1: Housing Characteristics for States, Cities, and Counties, Part 35: North Carolina.* Washington, D.C.: Government Printing Office, 1972.

———. *1970 Census of Population. Vol. 1: Characteristics of the Population, Part 35: North Carolina.* Washington, D.C.: Government Printing Office, 1973.

United States Commission on Civil Rights. *Desegregation in the Nation's Schools: A Status Report.* Washington, D.C.: Government Printing Office, 1979.

———. *Racial Isolation in the Public Schools.* 2 vols. Washington, D.C.: Government Printing Office, 1967.

———. *Reviewing a Decade of School Desegregation: 1968–1976.* Washington, D.C.: Government Printing Office, 1977.

———. *School Desegregation in Communities.* Washington, D.C.: Clearinghouse Publications, 1973.

———. *Twenty Years After Brown: A Report.* Washington, D.C.: Government Printing Office, 1975.

United States Congress. Senate. Committee on Equal Opportunity. *Hearing on Displaced and Present Status of Black School Principals in Desegregated School Districts.* 92d Cong., 1st sess., June 1971.

United States Department of Health, Education, and Welfare. *Policies on Elementary and Secondary School Compliance with Title VI of the Civil Rights Act of 1964.* Washington, D.C.: Government Printing Office, 1968.

———. *Status Report on School Desegregation.* Washington, D.C.: Government Printing Office, 1968.

Interviews by the Author

Allen, Stephanie. New Bern, N.C., March 22, 1992.
Blount, Doris. Fairfield, N.C., February 13, 1989.
Brothers, Muriel. Washington, N.C., May 23, 1991.
Brown, Edward. Vanceboro, N.C., December 11, 1991.
Dunn, Charles. Raleigh, N.C., March 9, 1989.
Ferguson, James, II. By telephone, January 25, 1993.
Fitch, Milton, Sr. Wilson, N.C., February 14, 1993.
Flood, Dr. Dudley. Raleigh, N.C., March 9, 1989.
Frinks, Golden. Edenton, N.C., February 23, 1989.
Frost, William. Maysville, N.C., March 20, 1992.
Fulford, Abell, Jr. Swan Quarter, N.C., February 13, 1989.
Gibbs, Annette. Engelhard, N.C., March 3, 1993.
Gibbs, Margaret. Engelhard, N.C., March 3, 1993.

Gibbs, Mary. New Holland, N.C., March 7, 1989.
Gibbs, Walter Lee. Engelhard, N.C., March 3, 1993.
Grant, Jim. Wilson, N.C., March 18, 1992.
Greene, Phillip. Swan Quarter, N.C., March 7, 1989.
Harris, Morgan. Swan Quarter, N.C., March 7, 1989.
Howe, Harold, II. By telephone, February 18, 1993.
Johnson, Henry, Jr. Swan Quarter, N.C., January 20, 1989.
Johnson, Henry Vanderbilt. Engelhard, N.C., February 27, 1989.
Mackey, Alice Spencer. Engelhard, N.C., February 13, 1989.
Mackey, Erskine. Engelhard, N.C., March 3, 1993.
Midgette, Johnnie. Engelhard, N.C., March 2, 1993.
Moore, Reverend David. Washington, N.C., May 23, 1991.
Murray, Ida. Fairfield, N.C., February 13, 1989.
Selby, Marjorie. Swan Quarter, N.C., March 7, 1989.
Spencer, R. S., Jr. By telephone, April 16, 1993.
Topping, James "Little Brother." New Holland, N.C., March 7, 1989.
Weston, Doris. Engelhard, N.C., February 22, 1993.
Whitaker, Albert. Fairfield, N.C., March 8, 1989.
Whitaker, Thomas. Engelhard, N.C., February 13, 1989.
Williams, Willis. Jamesville, N.C., March 21, 1992.

Papers, Reports, and Miscellaneous Documents

Alabama League for the Advancement of Education. "The Slow Death of the Black Educator in Alabama." A special report. Montgomery, Ala. 1971.
Belknap, Michael R., ed. *Civil Rights, the White House, and the Justice Department, 1945–1968.* 18 vols. Vol. 17, *Administrative History of the Civil Rights Division of the Department of Justice During the Johnson Administration.* New York: Garland, 1991.
Cecelski, David S. "Crab Processing and Mexican H2-B Workers on the North Carolina Coast." Research report. Durham, N.C.: Institute for Southern Studies, 1991.
———. "Endangered Species, Endangered Communities: A Working Paper on Poverty, Race, and the Environment in Eastern North Carolina." Research report. Wilson, N.C.: Legal Services of Eastern Carolina, 1992.
———. "'Missing Our Grandmothers': Poverty and Rural Upheaval in the Pamlico Sound Vicinity." Research report. Raleigh: Legal Services of North Carolina/Pamlico Sound Legal Services, 1992.
Children's Defense Fund. *Children Out of School in America.* Washington, D.C.: Washington Research Projects, Inc., 1974.
———. *School Suspensions: Are They Helping Children?* Washington, D.C.: Washington Research Projects, Inc., 1975.
Congressional Black Caucus. *Proceedings of the National Policy Conference on Education for Blacks.* Washington, D.C., March 29–April 1, 1972.

Egerton, John. *School Desegregation: A Report Card from the South.* Atlanta: Southern Regional Council, 1976.

Ethridge, Samuel F. "Integration and the Employment of the Black School Principal/Teacher." Paper presented at the convention of the Association for the Study of Afro-American Life and History, New York, October 18, 1973.

Fortescue, Z. T., Jr. "History of Hyde County." 1923. Unpublished typescript. North Carolina Collection, University of North Carolina, Chapel Hill, N.C.

"The Hyde County Movement." Scrapbook of newspaper articles, movement literature, and photographs. Compiled by Alice Spencer Mackey and in possession of Thomas Whitaker, Columbia, N.C.

Irons, Janet, and Steven Unruhe. "Black Wilson: The Second City, 1930–1980." Paper prepared for the NAACP Legal Defense and Educational Fund. Durham, 1983.

Local School Finance Study. Raleigh: Rural Initiative Forum, 1990.

"Memories of the Hyde County Training School Banner." Scranton, N.C.: n.p., 1940.

Mills, Roger, and Miriam Bryan. *Testing-Grouping: The New Segregation in Southern Schools?* Atlanta: Southern Regional Council, 1976.

NAACP Legal Defense and Educational Fund. "A Report to the People of the United States by the Legal Defense Fund, 1940–1970." New York, 1970.

National Education Association Commission on Professional Rights and Responsibilities. *Beyond Desegregation: The Problem of Power.* Washington, D.C.: National Education Association, 1970.

—————. *Hyde County, North Carolina: School Boycott and the Roots of Conflict.* Washington, D.C.: National Education Association, 1969.

National Education Association Task Force III. *School Desegregation: Louisiana and Mississippi.* Washington, D.C.: National Education Association, 1970.

Southern Regional Council. "The Federal Retreat in School Desegregation." Atlanta: Southern Regional Council, 1969.

Southern Regional Council and the Robert F. Kennedy Memorial. *The Student Pushout—Victims of Continued Resistance to Desegregation.* Atlanta: Southern Regional Council, 1974.

Tyson, Tim. "The Kissing Case." Draft of unpublished article. Feb. 1993.

Ward, Mary P. "Lake Mattamuskeet and the Failure of the Effort to Drain It." 1948. Unpublished typescript. North Carolina Collection, University of North Carolina, Chapel Hill, N.C.

Wager, Paul W. "County Government and County Affairs in Hyde County, N.C." 1926. Unpublished typescript. North Carolina Collection, University of North Carolina, Chapel Hill, N.C.

Books, Articles, and Dissertations

Abney, Everett E. "The Status of Florida's Black School Principals." *Journal of Negro Education* 43 (Winter 1974): 3–8.

Adair, Alvis. *Desegregation: The Illusion of Black Progress*. Lanham, Md.: University Press of America, 1984.

Adams, Frank. *Unearthing Seeds of Fire: The Idea of Highlander*. Winston-Salem: John F. Blair, 1975.

Adams, Frank, and Bob Hall, eds. *Just Schools*. Special edition of *Southern Exposure*. Durham, N.C.: Institute for Southern Studies, 1979.

Allen, Jesse Lee. "The Effects of School Desegregation on the Employment Status of Negro Principals in North Carolina." Ed.D. diss., Duke University, 1969.

Anderson, Eric. *Race and Politics in North Carolina, 1872–1901: The Black Second*. Baton Rouge: Louisiana State University Press, 1981.

Anderson, James D. *The Education of Blacks in the South, 1860–1935*. Chapel Hill: University of North Carolina Press, 1988.

Arnez, Nancy. "Desegregation of Public Schools: A Discriminatory Process." *Journal of Afro-American Issues* 4 (Spring 1976): 274–82.

———. "Implementation of Desegregation as a Discriminatory Process." *Journal of Negro Education* 47 (Winter 1978): 28–45.

Ashmore, Harry. *Hearts and Minds: The Anatomy of Racism from Roosevelt to Reagan*. New York: McGraw-Hill, 1982.

———. *The Negro and the Schools*. Chapel Hill: University of North Carolina Press, 1954.

Bagwell, William. *Desegregation in the Carolinas: Two Case Studies*. Columbia: University of South Carolina Press, 1972.

Barksdale, Marcellus C. "Civil Rights Organization and the Indigenous Movement in Chapel Hill, N.C., 1960–1965." *Phylon* 47 (1986): 29–42.

———. "The Indigenous Civil Rights Movement and Cultural Change in North Carolina: Weldon, Chapel Hill, and Monroe, 1946–1965." Ph.D. diss., Duke University, 1977.

Bass, Jack, and Walter DeVries. *The Transformation of Southern Politics*. New York: Basic Books, 1976.

Beifuss, Joan Turner. *Memphis, the 1968 Strike, and Martin Luther King*. New York: Carlson, 1989.

Bell, Derrick. *And We Are Not Saved: The Elusive Quest for Racial Justice*. New York: Basic Books, 1987.

———. "School Desegregation: Seeking New Victories among the Ashes." *Freedomways* 17 (1977): 35–38.

Berube, Maurice R., and Marilyn Gittell, eds. *Confrontation at Ocean Hill–Brownsville: The New York School Strikes of 1968*. New York: Praeger, 1969.

Blumberg, Rhoda Lois. *Civil Rights: The 1960s Freedom Struggle*. Boston: Twayne, 1984.

Boggs, Wade Hamilton, III. "The Final Steps for the First State Supported Negro Normal School in North Carolina, 1877." M.A. thesis, Duke University, 1969.

Bolner, James, and Arnold Vedlitz. "The Affinity of Negro Pupils for Segregated

Schools: Obstacle to Desegregation." *Journal of Negro Education* 40 (Fall 1971): 313–21.

Bonacich, Edna. *Deadlock in School Desegregation: A Case Study of Inglewood, California.* New York: Praeger, 1972.

Bond, Horace Mann. *The Education of the Negro in the American Social Order.* New York: Prentice Hall, 1934.

Braden, Anne. "The History That We Made: Birmingham, 1956–1979." *Southern Exposure* 7 (Summer 1979): 48–53.

Branch, Taylor. *Parting the Waters: America in the King Years, 1954–63.* New York: Simon and Schuster, 1988.

Brown, Hugh. *A History of the Education of Negroes in North Carolina.* Goldsboro, N.C.: Irving Swain Press, 1964.

———. *Equality Education in North Carolina among Negroes.* Goldsboro, N.C.: Irving Swain Press, 1961.

Bryant, Pat, ed. *Stayed on Freedom.* Special edition of *Southern Exposure.* Durham, N.C.: Institute for Southern Studies, 1981.

———, ed. *Mark of the Beast.* Special edition of *Southern Exposure.* Durham, N.C.: Institute for Southern Studies, 1980.

Bullock, Henry Allen. *A History of Negro Education in the South from 1619 to the Present.* Cambridge: Harvard University Press, 1967.

Butler, Johnny S. "Black Educators in Louisiana—A Question of Survival." *Journal of Negro Education* 43 (Winter 1974): 9–24.

Button, James W. *Blacks and Social Change: Impact of the Civil Rights Movement in Southern Communities.* Princeton, N.J.: Princeton University Press, 1989.

Carson, Clayborne. *In Struggle: SNCC and the Black Awakening of the 1960s.* Cambridge: Harvard University Press, 1981.

Cashman, Sean Dennis. *African-Americans and the Quest for Civil Rights, 1900–1990.* New York: New York University Press, 1991.

Cecelski, David S., and Mary Lee Kerr. "Hog Wild: How Corporate Hog Operations are Slaughtering Family Farms and Poisoning the Rural South." *Southern Exposure* 20 (Fall 1992): 8–15.

Chafe, William. *Civilities and Civil Rights: Greensboro, North Carolina and the Black Struggle for Freedom.* New York: Oxford University Press, 1980.

———. *The Unfinished Journey: America Since WWII.* New York: Oxford University Press, 1986.

Chambliss, Thomas W. "Development in Hyde County." *Sky-Land Magazine* 1 (July 1913): 28–30.

Chujo, Ken. "The Black Struggle for Education in North Carolina, 1877–1900." Ph.D. diss., Duke University, 1988.

Coffin, Gregory C. "The Black Administrator and How He's Being Pushed to Extinction." *The American School Board Journal* 5 (May 1972): 159.

Colburn, David. *Racial Change and Community Crisis, St. Augustine, Florida, 1877–1980.* New York: Columbia University Press, 1985.

Coleman, James, Sara Kelley, and John A. Moore. *Trends in School Segregation, 1968–73*. Washington, D.C.: Urban Institute, 1975.

Coles, Robert. *Children of Crisis*. Boston: Little, Brown, and Co., 1967.

Cooper, Bobby G. "The Effects of Desegregation on Black Elementary and Secondary School Teachers in Mississippi, 1970–1973." Ph.D. diss., University of Colorado at Boulder, 1977.

Couto, Richard A. *Ain't Gonna Let Nobody Turn Me Round: The Pursuit of Racial Justice in the Rural South*. Philadelphia: Temple University Press, 1991.

Crain, Robert. *The Politics of School Desegregation*. Chicago: Aldine, 1968.

Crawford, Vicki Lynn. "Grassroots Activists in the Mississippi Civil Rights Movement." *Sage: A Scholarly Journal on Black Women* 5 (1988): 24–29.

Cross, Theodore. *The Black Power Imperative: Racial Inequality and the Politics of Non-violence*. New York: Faulkner, 1984.

Crow, Jeffrey J., Paul D. Escott, and Flora J. Hatley. *A History of African Americans in North Carolina*. Raleigh: Division of Archives and History, N.C. Department of Cultural Resources, 1992.

Crow, Jeffrey J., and Flora J. Hatley, eds. *Black Americans in North Carolina and the South*. Chapel Hill: University of North Carolina Press, 1984.

Cruse, Harold. *The Crisis of the Negro Intellectual*. New York: William Morrow and Co., 1967.

———. *Plural But Equal: A Critical Study of Blacks and Minorities and America's Plural Society*. New York: William Morrow and Co., 1987.

Current, Gloster B. "The Significance of the N.A.A.C.P. and Its Impact in the 1960s." *Black Scholar* 19 (1988): 9–18.

Dempsey, Van, and George Noblit. "The Demise of Caring in an African-American Community: One Consequence of School Desegregation." *The Urban Review* 25 (March 1993): 47–61.

Dent, Harry. *The Prodigal South Returns to Power*. New York: Wiley-Interscience, 1978.

Doddy, Hurley H., and G. Franklin Edwards. "Apprehensions of Negro Teachers Concerning Desegregation in South Carolina." *Journal of Negro Education* 24 (Winter 1955): 26–43.

Du Bois, W. E. B. "Does the Negro Need Separate Schools?" *Journal of Negro Education* 4 (July 1935): 328–35.

———. *The Education of Black People: Ten Critiques, 1906–1960*. Edited by Herbert Aptheker. Amherst: University of Massachusetts Press, 1973.

Eagles, Charles, ed. *The Civil Rights Movement in America*. Jackson: University Press of Mississippi, 1986.

Eaton, Hubert. *Every Man Should Try*. Wilmington, N.C.: Bonaparte Press, 1984.

Edmonds, Helen G. *The Negro and Fusion Politics in North Carolina, 1894–1901*. Chapel Hill: University of North Carolina Press, 1951.

Egerton, John. "When Desegregation Comes, the Negro Principal Goes." *Southern Education Report* 3 (December 1967): 8–12.

Ehle, John. *The Free Men*. New York: Harper and Row, 1965.

Evans, W. McKee. *Ballots and Fence Rails: Reconstruction on the Lower Cape Fear*. Chapel Hill: University of North Carolina Press, 1966.

Fairclough, Adam. *To Redeem the Soul of America: The Southern Christian Leadership Conference and Martin Luther King, Jr.* Athens: University of Georgia Press, 1987.

———. "The SCLC and the Second Reconstruction, 1957–1973." *South Atlantic Quarterly* 80 (Spring 1981): 177–94.

Fancher, Betsy. *Voices from the South: Black Students Talk About Their Experiences in Desegregated Schools*. Atlanta: Southern Regional Council, 1970.

Farmer, James. *Lay Bare the Heart: An Autobiography of the Civil Rights Movement*. New York: Arbor House, 1985.

Federal Writers' Project. *A Guide to the Old North State*. Chapel Hill: University of North Carolina Press, 1939.

Fine, Doris. *When Leadership Fails: Desegregation and Demoralization in the San Francisco Schools*. New Brunswick, N.J.: Transaction Books, 1986.

Finger, Bill, and Mike Krivosh. "Stevens vs. Justice." *Southern Exposure* 4 (Spring/Summer 1976): 38–44.

Flowers, Linda. *Throwed Away: Failures of Progress in Eastern North Carolina*. Knoxville: University of Tennessee, 1990.

Forbes, Jack D. "Segregation and Integration: The Multi-Ethnic or Uni-Ethnic School." *Phylon* 30 (Spring 1969): 34–41.

Forman, James. *The Making of Black Revolutionaries*. Washington, D.C.: Open Hand, 1985.

Foster, Michèle. "The Politics of Race: Through the Eyes of African-American Teachers." *Journal of Education* 172 (November 1990): 123–41.

Franklin, John Hope. *The Color Line: Legacy for the Twenty-First Century*. Columbia: University of Missouri Press, 1993.

Franklin, John Hope, and Alfred A. Moss, Jr. *From Slavery to Freedom: A History of Negro Americans*. 6th ed. New York: Knopf, 1988.

Franklin, V. P. "American Values, Social Goals, and the Desegregated School: A Historical Perspective." In *New Perspectives on Black Educational History*, edited by Vincent Franklin and James D. Anderson, pp. 193–211. Boston: G. K. Hall, 1978.

———. *Black Self-Determination: A Cultural History of the Faith of Our Fathers*. Westport, Conn.: Lawrence Hill and Co., 1984.

———. " 'They Rose and Fell Together': African American Educators and Community Leadership, 1795–1954." *Journal of Education* 172 (November 1990): 39–64.

Gaillard, Frye. *The Dream Long Deferred*. Chapel Hill: University of North Carolina Press, 1988.

Garrow, David. *Bearing the Cross: Martin Luther King, Jr. and the Southern Christian Leadership Conference*. New York: William Morrow and Co., 1986.

———, ed. *St. Augustine, Florida, 1963–1964: Mass Protest and Racial Violence*. New York: Carlson, 1989.

———, ed. *We Shall Overcome: The Civil Rights Movement in the United States in the 1950s and 1960s.* 3 vols. New York: Carlson, 1989.

Garrow, Patrick H. *The Mattamuskeet Documents: A Study in Social History.* Raleigh: Division of Archives and History, N.C. Department of Cultural Resources, 1975.

Gatewood, Willard B., Jr. "Eugene Clyde Brooks and Negro Education in North Carolina, 1919–1923." *North Carolina Historical Review* 38 (July 1961): 362–79.

Gavins, Raymond. "The NAACP in North Carolina During the Age of Segregation." In *New Directions in Civil Rights Studies,* edited by Armstead L. Robinson and Patricia Sullivan, pp. 105–25. Charlottesville: University Press of Virginia, 1991.

———. "North Carolina Black Folklore and Song in the Age of Segregation: Toward Another Meaning of Survival." *North Carolina Historical Review* 66 (October 1989): 412–42.

George, Pam. "The Competency Controversy." *Southern Exposure* 7 (Summer 1979): 114–18.

———. "Teacher Testing and the Historically Black College." *Journal of Teacher Education* 36 (November-December 1985): 54–57.

Glass, Mary. "Numbers of Alabama Black Educators Continue to Suffer Slow Death." *Alabama Journal of Education.* August 30, 1971.

Godwin, John L. "Taming a Whirlwind: Black Civil Rights Leadership in the Community Setting, Wilmington, North Carolina, 1950–1972." In *Proceedings of the South Carolina Historical Association: 1992,* pp. 67–75. Columbia: South Carolina Historical Association, 1992.

Goldfield, David. *Black, White, and Southern: Race Relations and Southern Culture, 1940 to the Present.* Baton Rouge: Louisiana State University Press, 1990.

Goodwyn, Lawrence. *The Populist Moment: A Short History of the Agrarian Revolt in America.* New York: Oxford University Press, 1978.

Graglia, Lino. *Disaster by Decree: the Supreme Court Decisions on Race and the Schools.* Ithaca: Cornell University Press, 1976.

Gray, Hester Slade. "A History of the Hyde County Training School." In *Hyde County History: A Hyde County Bicentennial Project,* edited by Marjorie T. Selby, R. S. Spencer, Jr., and Rebecca Swindell, section 1, pp. 30–32. Hyde County Historical Society, 1976.

Greene, Melissa Fay. *Praying for Sheetrock.* Reading, Mass.: Addison-Wesley, 1991.

Griggs, Anthony. "Displacement Still Faces Black Teachers." *Race Relations Reporter* 4 (August 6, 1973): 5.

Gutman, Herbert. "Schools for Freedom: The Post-Emancipation Origins of African-American Education." In *Power and Culture: Essays on the American Working Class,* edited by Ira Berlin, pp. 260–97. New York: Pantheon, 1987.

Haas, Ben. *KKK.* New York: Tower Publications, 1963.

Haines, Herbert. *Black Radicals and the Civil Rights Mainstream, 1954–1970.* Knoxville: University of Tennessee, 1988.

Hall, Bob, ed. *Environmental Politics: Grassroots Strategies for Change.* Durham, N.C.: Institute for Southern Studies, 1988.

———. "Bucking the System: The Success and Survival of Organized Workers in Rural, Anti-union North Carolina." *Southern Exposure* 10 (September/October 1982): 66–73.

———. *Who Owns North Carolina?* Durham, N.C.: Institute for Southern Studies, 1986.

Hall, Jacquelyn Dowd, James Leloudis, Robert Korstad, Mary Murphy, Lu Ann Jones, and Christopher B. Daly. *Like a Family: The Making of a Southern Cotton Mill World.* Chapel Hill: University of North Carolina Press, 1987.

Hall, Leon. "The Implementor's Revenge." *Southern Exposure* 7 (Summer 1979): 122–24.

Hall, Morrill M., and Harold W. Gentry. "Isolation of Negro Students in Integrated Public Schools." *Journal of Negro Education* 38 (Spring 1969): 156–61.

Handbook of North Carolina. Raleigh: P. M. Hale, 1886.

Hanks, Lawrence. *The Struggle for Black Political Empowerment in Three Georgia Counties.* Knoxville: University of Tennessee Press, 1987.

Harding, Vincent. *There Is a River: The Black Struggle for Freedom in America.* New York: Harcourt Brace Jovanovich, 1981.

Hardy, Charles. "Making the Extra Effort . . . Again." *Southern Exposure* 7 (Summer 1979): 94–97.

Harlan, Louis. *Separate and Unequal: Public School Campaigns and Racism in the Southern Seaboard States, 1901–1915.* Chapel Hill: University of North Carolina Press, 1958.

Hickerson, Nathaniel. "Physical Integration Alone Is Not Enough." *Journal of Negro Education* 38 (Spring 1966): 110–16.

Hobbs, Samuel Huntington, Jr. *North Carolina: Economic and Social.* Chapel Hill: University of North Carolina Press, 1930.

Hooker, Robert. "Blacks Losing Teaching Jobs." *Race Relations Reporter* 1 (December 9, 1970).

———. "Displacement of Black Teachers in the Eleven Southern States." *Afro-American Studies* 2 (December 1971): 165–80.

Hoover-Rhodes, Mary E. "Teacher Competency Tests as Educational Genocide for Blacks: the Florida Teacher Certification Examination." *Negro Educational Review* 35 (April 1984): 70–77.

Huckaby, Elizabeth. *Crisis at Central High, Little Rock, 1957–1958.* Baton Rouge: Louisiana State University Press, 1980.

Johnson, Evelyn A. *A History of Elizabeth City State University: A Story of Survival.* New York: Vantage Press, 1979.

Jones, Lance. *Negro Schools in the Southern States.* Oxford: Clarendon Press, 1928.

Jones, Leon. *From Brown to Boston: Desegregation in Education, 1954–1974.* Metuchen, N.J.: Scarecrow Press, 1979.

Kauchak, Donald. "Testing Teachers in Louisiana: A Closer Look." *Phi Delta Kappan* 65 (May 1984): 626–28.

Kerr, Mary Lee. "Toxic Race." *Southern Exposure* 19 (Fall 1991): 59–63.

Kilbian, Lewis. *The Impossible Revolution, Phase 2: Black Power and the American Dream.* Lanham, Md.: Random House, 1968.

King, Mary. *Freedom Story: A Personal Story of the 1960s Civil Rights Movement.* New York: William Morrow and Co., 1987.

Kirby, Jack Temple. *Rural Worlds Lost: The American South, 1920–1960.* Baton Rouge: Louisiana State University Press, 1987.

Klibaner, Irwin. *Conscience of a Troubled South: The Southern Conference Educational Fund, 1946–1966.* Brooklyn, N.Y.: Carlson, 1989.

Kluger, Richard. *Simple Justice.* New York: Knopf, 1976.

Knight, Edgar. *Public School Education in North Carolina.* Boston: Houghton Mifflin, 1916.

Kousser, J. Morgan. *The Shaping of Southern Politics: Suffrage Restriction and the Establishment of the One-Party South, 1880–1910.* New Haven: Yale University Press, 1974.

Landis, Jeane T. "The Crawford Desegregation Suit in Los Angeles, 1977–1981: The Multi-ethnic Community Versus BUSTOP." Ph.D. diss., University of California at Los Angeles, 1984.

Levy, Peter B., ed. *Documentary History of the Modern Civil Rights Movement.* New York: Greenwood Press, 1992.

Lightfoot, Sara Lawrence. *Balm in Gilead: Journey of a Healer.* Reading, Mass.: Addison-Wesley, 1988.

———. *The Good High School: Portraits of Character and Culture.* New York: Basic Books, 1983.

Lincoln, C. Eric. *The Avenue, Clayton City.* New York: William Morrow and Co., 1988.

Lincoln, C. Eric, and Lawrence H. Mamiya. *The Black Church in the African-American Experience.* Durham, N.C.: Duke University Press, 1990.

Little, Joan, with Rebecca Ransom. " 'I am Joan.' " *Southern Exposure* 6 (Spring 1978): 42–47.

Locke, Mamie E. "The Role of African-American Women in the Civil Rights and Women's Movements in Hinds County and Sunflower County, Mississippi." *Journal of Mississippi History* 53 (Fall 1991): 229–39.

Logan, Frenise A. "Legal Status of Public School Education for Negroes in North Carolina, 1877–1894." *North Carolina Historical Review* 32 (Fall 1955): 346–57.

Long, Hollis Moody. *Public Secondary Education for Negroes in North Carolina.* Contributions to Education, no. 529. New York: Teachers College, 1932.

Lottman, Michael. "Many Negro Schools are Closing." *Southern Courier* (September 7, 1968).

Lowe, Robert. "Ravenswood High School and the Struggle for Racial Justice in the Sequoia Union High School District." Ph.D. diss., Stanford University, 1989.

Luebke, Paul. *North Carolina Politics: Myths and Realities*. Chapel Hill: University of North Carolina Press, 1990.

Lukas, J. Anthony. *Common Ground: A Turbulent Decade in the Lives of Three American Families*. New York: Knopf, 1985.

Lukin, Craig G., and Lucy L. Mauger. *Environmental Geologic Atlas of the North Carolina Coastal Zone: Dare, Hyde, Tyrrell, and Washington Counties*. Greenville, N.C.: Institute for Coastal and Marine Resources and the Department of Geology, East Carolina University, 1983.

Lynch, J. Merrill, and S. Lance Peacock. *Natural Areas Inventory of Hyde County, North Carolina*. Raleigh: North Carolina Coastal Energy Impact Program, 1982.

McElroy-Johnson, Beverly. "Giving Voice to the Voiceless." *Harvard Educational Review* 63 (Spring 1993): 85–104.

McMillen, Neil. *Dark Journey: Black Mississippians in the Age of Jim Crow*. Urbana: University of Illinois Press, 1989.

McPhail, James. *A History of Desegregation Developments in Certain Mississippi School Districts*. Hattiesburg: University of Southern Mississippi, 1971.

Mayfield, Chris. "'The Middle Ground Turns to Quicksand': Little Rock, 1957–1960." *Southern Exposure* 7 (Summer 1979): 40–44.

Meier, August. "The Dilemma of Negro Protest Strategy." *New South* 21 (Spring 1966): 1–18.

Meier, August, and Elliot Rudwick. *Along the Color Line: Explorations in the Black Experience*. Urbana: University of Illinois Press, 1976.

———. *CORE: A Study of the Civil Rights Movement, 1942–1968*. Urbana: University of Illinois Press, 1975.

Mercer, Walter. "The Gathering Storm: Teacher Testing and Black Teachers." *Educational Leadership* 41 (October 1983): 70–71.

Montgomery, William E. "Negro Churches in the South, 1865–1915." Ph.D. diss., University of Texas at Austin, 1975.

Monti, David. *A Semblance of Justice: St. Louis School Desegregation and Order in Urban America*. Columbia: University of Missouri Press, 1985.

Moreland, Laurence W., Robert P. Steed, and Tod A. Baker, eds. *Blacks in Southern Politics*. New York: Praeger, 1987.

Morris, Allen D. *The Origins of the Civil Rights Movement: Black Communities Organizing for Change*. New York: Free Press, 1984.

Morris, Willie. *Yazoo: Integration in a Deep-Southern Town*. New York: Harper and Row, 1971.

Morsell, John. "Racial Desegregation and Integration in Public Education." *Journal of Negro Education* 38 (Summer 1969): 276–84.

Murray, Percy. *History of the North Carolina Teachers Association*. Washington, D.C.: National Education Association, 1984.

Muse, Benjamin. *Virginia's Massive Resistance*. Bloomington: Indiana University Press, 1961.

Myers, John. "The Negro Common School in North Carolina." *Crisis* 34 (June 1927): 117–18.

Myerson, Michael. *Nothing Could Be Finer.* New York: International Publishers, 1978.

North Carolina Business Directory for 1866–1906. Published annually. Raleigh: Branson and Farrar, 1866–1906.

North Carolina Rural Profile. Raleigh: North Carolina Rural Development Center and North Carolina A&T University, 1988.

North Carolina Year Book. Raleigh: The *News and Observer.* Published annually from 1901 to 1939 under this title or *The North Carolina Year Book and Business Directory.*

Oates, Stephen. *Let the Trumpet Sound: The Life of Martin Luther King, Jr.* New York: Harper and Row, 1982.

Oppenheimer, Martin. *The Sit-in Movement of the 1960s.* New York: Carlson, 1989.

O'Reilly, Kenneth. *"Racial Matters": The FBI's Secret File on Black America, 1960–1972.* New York: Free Press, 1989.

Orfield, Gary. *The Reconstruction of Southern Education: The Schools and the 1964 Civil Rights Act.* New York: Wiley-Interscience, 1969.

Peake, Thomas. *Keeping the Dream Alive: A History of the SCLC from King to the 1980s.* New York: Peter Lang, 1987.

Peebles, Wilma. "School Desegregation in Raleigh, North Carolina, 1954–1964." Ph.D. diss., University of North Carolina at Chapel Hill, 1984.

Peeks, Edward. *The Long Struggle for Black Power.* New York: Charles Scribners' Sons, 1971.

Pentecoste, Joseph. "Black Psychology." *The Black Liberator* 5 (June 1969): 4–6.

Pierce, J. M., et al. *White and Negro Schools in the South.* Englewood, N.J.: Prentice-Hall, 1955.

Pinkney, Alphonso. *The Myth of Black Progress.* Cambridge: Cambridge University Press, 1984.

———. *Red, Black, and Green: Black Nationalism in the United States.* Cambridge: Cambridge University Press, 1982.

Pinsky, Mark. "The Innocence of James Reston." *Southern Exposure* 6 (Spring 1978): 39–41.

Poinsett, Alex. "Battle to Control Black Schools." *Ebony* 24 (May 1969): 44–46.

Powledge, Fred. *Free at Last?: The Civil Rights Movement and the People Who Made It.* Boston: Little, Brown, 1991.

Prather, H. Leon, Sr. *Resurgent Politics and Educational Progressivism in the New South: North Carolina, 1890–1913.* Rutherford, N.J.: Fairleigh Dickinson University Press, 1979.

Pride, Richard. *The Burden of Busing: The Politics of Desegregation in Nashville, Tennessee.* Knoxville: University of Tennessee Press, 1985.

Radin, Beryl A. *Implementation, Change, and the Federal Bureaucracy: School Desegregation Policy in HEW, 1964–1968.* New York: Teachers College Press, 1977.

Raines, Howell. *My Soul Is Rested: Movement Days in the Deep South Remembered.* New York: G. P. Putnam's Sons, 1977.

Raper, Arthur F. *Preface to Peasantry: A Tale of Two Black Belt Counties.* Chapel Hill: University of North Carolina Press, 1936.

Rassell, Christine, and Willis Hawley. *The Consequences of School Desegregation.* Philadelphia: Temple University Press, 1983.

Redcay, Edward. *County Training Schools and Public Secondary Education for Negroes in the South.* Washington, D.C.: John F. Slater Fund, 1935.

Reed, Linda. *Simple Decency and Common Sense: The Southern Conference Movement, 1938–1963.* Bloomington: Indiana University Press, 1991.

Reston, James, Jr. *The Innocence of Joan Little: A Southern Odyssey.* New York: Times Books, 1977.

Rist, Ray. *Desegregated Schools: Appraisals of an American Experiment.* New York: Academic Press, 1979.

Robinson, Dorothy R. *The Bell Rings at Four: A Black Teacher's Chronicle of Change.* Austin, Tex.: Madrona Press, 1979.

Rosenthal, Jonas O. "Negro Teachers' Attitudes Toward Desegregation." *Journal of Negro Education* 26 (Winter 1957): 63–71.

Rubin, Lillian. "The Politics of Rage: School Desegregation and the Revolt of Middle America." Ph.D. diss., University of California at Berkeley, 1971.

Schwartz, Bernard. *Swann's Way: The School Busing Case and the Supreme Court.* New York: Oxford University Press, 1986.

"Scranton's Lumbermen: A Brief History of Companies and Corporations." *The Racket* 3 (April 1891): 64–66.

Selby, Marjorie T., R. S. Spencer, Jr., and Rebecca Swindell, eds. *Hyde County History: A Hyde County Bicentennial Project.* Hyde County Historical Society, 1976.

Sharpe, Bill, ed. *North Carolina: A Description by Counties.* Raleigh: Warren Publishing Co., 1948.

Sherer, Robert. *Subordination or Liberation?: The Development and Conflicting Theories of Black Education in Nineteenth-Century Alabama.* University, Ala.: University of Alabama Press, 1977.

Siddle Walker, Emilie V. "Caswell County Training School, 1933–1969: Relationships between Community and School." *Harvard Educational Review* 63 (Summer 1993): 161–82.

———. "Interpersonal Caring in the 'Good' Segregated Schooling of African-American Children: Evidence from the Case of the Caswell County Training School." *The Urban Review* 25 (March 1993): 63–77.

———. "Relations Between Community and School: Learning from the 'Good' Segregated Schooling of African-American Children." Paper presented at the American Educational Research Association meeting (April 1992).

Silberman, Charles E. *Crisis in Black and White.* New York: Vantage Books, 1964.

Sims, Patsy. *The Klan.* New York: Stein and Day, 1978.

Sinowitz, Betty E. "School Integration and the Teacher." *Today's Education* 62 (May 1973): 31–33.

Smith, Bob. *They Closed Their Schools: Prince Edward County, Virginia, 1951–1964.* Chapel Hill: University of North Carolina Press, 1965.

Smith, John W., and Betty M. Smith. "For Black Educators: Integration Brings the Axe." *The Urban Review* 6 (May 1973): 7–12.

Smith, McNeill. "School Desegregation Discussed." Guest commentary in the Raleigh *News and Observer*, October 25, 1960, p. A9.

Spitzberg, Irving. *Racial Politics in Little Rock, 1954–1964.* New York: Garland, 1987.

Spruill, Albert W. "The Negro Teacher in the Process of Desegregation of Schools." *Journal of Negro Education* 29 (Winter 1960): 80–84.

Stephan, Walter. "A Brief Historical Overview of School Desegregation." In *School Desegregation: Past, Present, and Future,* edited by Walter Stephan and Joe Feagin, pp. 3–23. New York: Plenum, 1980.

Stick, David. *The Outer Banks of North Carolina, 1584–1958.* Chapel Hill: University of North Carolina Press, 1958.

Thomas, Larry Reni. "The True Story Behind the Wilmington 10." M.A. thesis, University of North Carolina at Chapel Hill, 1980.

Tindall, George. *The Emergence of the New South, 1913–1945.* Baton Rouge: Louisiana State University Press, 1967.

Tullos, Allen. *Habits of Industry: White Culture and the Transformation of the Carolina Piedmont.* Chapel Hill: University of North Carolina Press, 1989.

"Vanishing Black Principals and Teachers in the South." *School and Society* 97 (December 1969): 470–72.

Viorst, Milton. *Fire in the Streets: America in the 1960s.* New York: Simon and Schuster, 1979.

Wade, Wyn Craig. *The Fiery Cross: The KKK in America.* New York: Simon and Schuster, 1987.

Walker, Eugene. "A History of SCLC, 1955–1965: The Evolution of a Southern Strategy for Change." Ph.D. diss., Duke University, 1978.

Watters, Pat, and Reese Cleghorn. *Climbing Jacob's Ladder.* New York: Harcourt Brace Jovanovich, 1967.

Waynick, Capus M., John C. Brooks, and Elsie W. Pitts, eds. *North Carolina and the Negro.* Raleigh: North Carolina Mayors' Co-operating Committee, 1964.

Weares, Walter B. *Black Business in the South: A Social History of the North Carolina Mutual Life Insurance Company.* Urbana: University of Illinois Press, 1973.

Weinberg, Meyer. *A Chance to Learn: A History of Race and Education in the United States.* Cambridge: Cambridge University Press, 1977.

Weisbrot, Robert. *Freedom Bound: A History of America's Civil Rights Movement.* New York: W. W. Norton and Co., 1990.

Weiss, Nancy. *Whitney M. Young, Jr., and the Struggle for Civil Rights.* Princeton: Princeton University Press, 1989.

Westin, Richard. "The State and Segregated Schools: Negro Public Education in North Carolina, 1863–1923." Ph.D. diss., Duke University, 1966.

"What's Wrong with Integration." Special edition. *Sojourners* 19 (August/ September 1990).

Wheaton, Elizabeth. *Codename GREENKIL: The 1979 Greensboro Killings.* Athens: University of Georgia Press, 1987.

Wilkins, Roy. *Standing Fast: The Autobiography of Roy Wilkins.* New York: Viking, 1982.

Wilkinson, J. Harvie, III. *From Brown to Bakke: The Supreme Court and School Integration, 1954–1978.* New York: Oxford University Press, 1979.

Williams, Juan. *Eyes on the Prize: America's Civil Rights Years, 1954–1965.* New York: Viking, 1987.

Williamson, Joel. *The Crucible of Race: Black-White Relations in the American South since Emancipation.* New York: Oxford University Press, 1984.

Wilson, Franklin. *Trends in Segregation of Minorities in Public Schools, 1968–1976.* Madison, Wis.: Institute for Research on Poverty, 1982.

Windham, Lane. "Green Hands: A History of the Food, Tobacco, and Agricultural Workers of America in Greenville, N.C., 1946." Senior honors thesis, Duke University, 1991.

Wolf, Eleanor. *Trial and Error: The Detroit School Desegregation Case.* Detroit: Wayne State University Press, 1981.

Wolters, Raymond. *The Burden of Brown: 30 Years of School Desegregation.* Knoxville: University of Tennessee Press, 1984.

Woodard, J. David. "Busing Plans, Media Agendas, and Patterns of White Flight: Nashville, Tennessee, and Louisville, Kentucky." Ph.D. diss., Vanderbilt University, 1978.

Woodson, Carter G. *The Mis-Education of the Negro.* New York: AMS Press, 1977.

Woodward, C. Vann. *The Strange Career of Jim Crow.* 2d rev. ed. New York: Oxford University Press, 1966.

Wright, Nathan. *What Black Educators are Saying.* New York: Hawthorn, 1970.
———. *What Black Revolutionaries are Saying.* New York: Hawthorn, 1970.

Yonker, Thomas W. "The Negro Church in North Carolina, 1700–1900." M.A. thesis, Duke University, 1955.

Young, Whitney, Jr. "Minorities and Community Control of the Schools." *Journal of Negro Education* 38 (Summer 1969): 285–90.

Youth of the Rural Organizing and Cultural Center. *Minds Stayed on Freedom: The Civil Rights Struggle in the Rural South, an Oral History.* Boulder, Colo.: Westview, 1991.